The Modern Political Campaign

Mudslinging, Bombast, and the Vitality of American Politics

Richard K. Scher

M.E. Sharpe
Armonk, New York
London, England

Library of Congress Cataloging-in-Publication Data

Scher, Richard K.
The modern political campaign : mudslinging, bombast, and
the vitality of American politics / by Richard K. Scher.
p. cm.
Includes biographical references and index.
ISBN 1-56324-860-3 (cloth : alk. paper). —
ISBN 1-56324-861-1 (pbk. : alk. paper)
1. Electioneering—United States.
2. Electioneering—United States—History.
I. Title.
JK2281.S34 1997
324.7′0973—dc21   97-5896
CIP
Printed in the United States of America

The paper used in this publication meets the minimum requirements of
American National Standard for Information Sciences—
Permanence of Paper for Printed Library Materials,
ANSI Z 39.48-1984.

EB (c) 10   9   8   7   6   5   4   3   2   1
EB (p) 10   9   8   7   6   5   4   3   2   1

Contents

Preface

My interest in political campaigns is long-standing. I have early memories, still vivid, of my parents' talking about candidates, campaigns, and elections; that their views differed sharply from my maternal grandfather's was confusing to a small boy, but the discussions (never arguments) they had about them remain fixed in bold relief in memory. I recall walking with my mother to the polling station at the elementary school up the street, waiting outside the booth while she cast her ballot, and listening to her talk about her choices. I recall further my father trying hard to explain to a child why following campaigns was important, because voting was not just a right but an obligation, and therefore a voter had to make informed choices. I understood almost none of what they said, but somehow I got the feeling that what they were trying to tell me was important stuff.

My first real campaign experience came in high school. I was a sophomore, and was accosted one day by the chair of the Social Sciences Department. A tall, imposing man, he was not only known for the rigor of his classes, the demands he made on students, and his capacity to terrify them; he was (gasp!) a known, card-carrying Republican in a predominantly Democratic state. He took one look at my campaign button, and loudly sneered. I knew then that politics was hardball business. I successfully avoided his classes like the plague for the next two years.

I was a little more active in college. The congressman representing the district there was an attractive fellow named William Fitz Ryan, a great name for a New York politician. He won every election with no trouble, and it was fun to stand out on street corners on a nice fall afternoon passing out literature for him. There was always plenty of food and other refreshments for volunteers at his headquarters. Since my college was all male, it was also a good way to meet girls.

The high point of my college campaign experience came in 1964, when Robert Kennedy came to my school in the midst of his Senate campaign. He gave a talk in the auditorium of the student center. The place was packed, and the air crackled with excitement. Kennedy was electric; he literally set the place on fire, as a television light exploded and ignited during the speech. No one even moved. Then he went outside and stood on top of a car to talk to the even larger crowd who could not get inside. There was bedlam. As he climbed down into the car and it began to move away, someone shoved me hard from behind. My glasses, always ill fitting, fell under the car and were crushed by a tire. I didn't care—I was hooked. Nor did I ever send the campaign a bill for a new pair.

Fast forward to January 1987. I was attending a posh cocktail party in Coral Gables, Florida, hosted by my wife's law firm. It was, as might be expected, a staid affair, but I was enjoying myself because the senior partner was a well-educated, erudite man who much preferred to talk history and politics than law business, and we had become good friends. After several glasses of excellent wine, he remembered that there was to be a meeting the following Monday (which happened to be Martin Luther King's birthday) concerning the candidacy of a friend of his for mayor of Coral Gables; as it was a legal holiday, the meeting had been scheduled in the offices of the campaign advertising firm, and would I like to attend? I demurred at first, claiming little local political knowledge, but a refilled glass gave me the courage to say yes.

The meeting bowled me over. I was stunned at the level of discussion. The people present, including my friend and the candidate, were very bright and sophisticated, but they knew next to nothing about campaigns. There were too many unanswered questions, and too many unquestioned answers. But I was terribly impressed with everyone present and their desire to pull this campaign off successfully. After the meeting, I wrote a lengthy memo outlining what I thought were the pluses (few) and minuses (many) of the impending candidacy and campaign. A day later I found myself persuaded to serve as campaign consultant and manager. On such small events does a person's professional career take dramatic and irrevocable turns.

In fact, if one is willing to put one's academic knowledge to practical use, I learned, professional political science has a great deal to offer candidates and the conduct of campaigns. My opportunities to serve both have been numerous. I believe the experience has made me a more informed and complete political scientist; the knowledge gained and experiences I have had enrich both my classes and my research and writing. Working as an academic political scientist and political consultant is assuredly the best of all possible worlds for someone interested in politics and public affairs.

As a result of this activity, my intellectual horizons have grown by leaps and bounds. My classes have developed new content; I was even able to establish a new upper-division undergraduate class called "The Modern Political Campaign." It is taught only in the fall semester of election years, and it is always packed. It is not a how-to-do-it course. Rather, it explores the politics of the modern campaign. Why do campaigns in this country take the forms they do? Why are they so often negative? Why are they marked more by their entertainment value than substance? What role do media and money play in campaigns? What is the relationship of political campaigns to other aspects of the American political system? The course, which includes intensive readings and careful analysis of campaigns past and present, provides students with an opportunity to consider campaigns in the light of our political culture, and the way in which we carry out the business of political campaigns in our democratic system.

This book grew out of the course. The classes and readings and students have informed it every bit as much as have my own academic research, practical experience, and relationships with candidates. It struck me that while there are plenty of good books available on campaigns—Hess's *The Presidential Campaign;* Salmore and Salmore's *Candidates, Parties, and Campaigns*; Thurber and Nelson's *Campaigns and Elections, American Style;* Simpson's *Winning Elections;* and Sabato's *Campaigns and Elections* are just a few examples—none spoke exactly to the themes that the course developed, and in which the students were interested.

In particular, two matters needed to be addressed. One has already been mentioned: What are the politics of the modern American campaign? Why do we do things the way we do, and what role do campaigns play in our political system? Very few authors have sought to put the modern campaign into its political context. This book tries to do so.

The other major issue to be confronted is the constant criticism the modern campaign receives. These complaints are detailed in the chapters that follow, but anyone who follows campaigns knows what they are: too long, too negative, too boring, too expensive, and so forth. Are they really all that bad? Are they harmful to us? Do they weaken our democracy? This book tries to address these and related questions. The answers may surprise some people; in many respects, this book defends the campaign as functional, and not necessarily harmful. No doubt there will be controversy over this point, but that's the job of the professor and the consultant: to question the conventional wisdom.

There are too many persons to thank for making this book happen. My students and colleagues in the Department of Political Science have been generous and supportive, and need recognition; special thanks are due my former chair, Professor Ken Wald, for encouraging me to pursue excellence in academia and on the street, and Professor Lynn Leverty, who likes to talk politics and who had vast campaign experiences in Texas. Dean Willard Harrison of the College of Liberal Arts and Sciences and President John Lombardi of the University of Florida have not only been supportive of my work but actually seem to take some pleasure and pride in watching one of the faculty roll around in the grit of the political world. Fellow consultants, such as Bill Hamilton, John Hotaling, and Louis Kalivoda, and other academicians, such as Professor Lance deHaven-Smith of Florida State University and Jon Mills of the College of Law, University of Florida, have been marvelous; so have the candidates themselves, who love to talk and occasionally listen. Journalists have been most helpful when they call me, because they ask stimulating questions and always provide useful insights. Ms. Maureen Tartaglione helped with the research, made excellent comments, and made me work in a timely fashion because she always brought materials to me promptly and accurately. Evelyn Fazio, Patricia Kolb, and Elizabeth Granda of M.E. Sharpe, Inc., continue to be the best possible people to work with in the publishing business; their support and goodwill serve as an inspiration to try to do a good job. It is with regret that I cannot mention each person to whom I have an intellectual debt. The weaknesses of the text, however, are the exclusive property of the author, not those who gave so freely of themselves to him.

Mostly I need to recognize and thank my family: my parents, for making me aware of political campaigns; my brother, who shares an interest in things political; and especially my wife Miriam and children Gregory, Nicholas, and Catherine. These last four deserve a special bow, because politics makes at least some of them nervous. Still, they let me have fun. I could not have written this, or done the things I have done, without the encouragement and support of my wife and children. I thank them profoundly, and the rest of my family, to all of whom I lovingly dedicate this book.

Gainesville, Florida
December 1996

1

Thinking About Political Campaigns in America

Is there any aspect of contemporary American politics more criticized, even reviled, than the modern political campaign? Does anyone have anything good to say about it?

It's hard to find apologists for the modern political campaign. Nobody seems to like it, and the complaints are both broad and deep: It costs too much. It goes on too long. It's negative. It provides little information that voters really need. It doesn't allow for rational, thoughtful discussion of issues. It's too slick. It interrupts regular TV shows. It takes up time on the news when there is usually very little that's news about it. Nobody could really represent the public's interest after going through one of them. What happens in the campaign has nothing to do with serving in office.

The list of complaints is almost endless. They are similar regardless of who voices them. Candidates for office—even those winning election—often find campaigns demeaning. Members of campaign organizations—not just candidates themselves—are exhausted by the physical and mental stress they cause. Lobbyists and PAC representatives tire of the constant appeal for money and other resources. Journalists covering the campaigns may initially be interested in them as candidates take their first steps on the road to office, but not infrequently their attention wanders as the campaigns wear on, especially if the outcome is clear well before election day. Editorialists perhaps have the most fun with campaigns, since they can sit in the comfort of their offices and criticize them, but even the most energetic Jeremiahs realize that they will lose readers and listeners if they don't discuss something else.

Did citizens back in the old days like campaigns? Undoubtedly some did, and some didn't. The point is, they seldom heard the widespread outcries and calumnious attacks on campaigns that we do now. And it was not because campaigns were necessarily "cleaner," more dignified, or more sophisticated than they are at present. In the mid–nineteenth century, campaigns were notorious for personal attacks and scandalous exposures. During the first part of this century, campaigns in state and local elections were often "bought," or stolen, by political bosses. And hokey activities, like the hillbilly bands "Big Jim" Folsom used in his gubernatorial campaigns in Alabama, or Nelson Rockefeller riding the subway in New York City, have been the rule, not the exception.

Perhaps campaigns were seen as a part of the ebb and flow of human life, something akin to the baseball season, or income-tax time, or a flu epidemic. At best, they could be enjoyed. At worst, they had to be endured. Probably most citizens who cared enough to vote simply resigned themselves to their existence. And then when the campaign season ended and the election was held, there was little thought about it until the next cycle began.

There was, to be sure, criticism of campaigns. But it tended to be specific to individual campaigns, rather than systemic in character. That is, the criticism seldom touched the concept of campaigns, or their role in shaping American democracy. These were taken as givens, as though the campaign was a reflection of our democracy, not its molder.

It is not the same now. Something, somewhere, has changed significantly about campaigns. Assuredly part of it is the nature of campaigns and campaigning; the amount of money campaigns cost (including the fact that the public treasury helps pay for them), their negativity, and their slickness undoubtedly have helped alter our perception of them, as well.

The reader at this point should be asked a question: what was he or she taught about political campaigns as a young person? Were we all socialized into the idea that campaigns were free-for-alls, in which anything was possible, anything—no matter how outrageous or scandalous—could be said, huge amounts of money could be spent, and nothing was beneath the dignity of the campaign, or the candidate?

Probably few of us remember hearing anything like this. It would be difficult to find elementary-school teachers who offered civics lessons with this in mind, nor have introductory civics textbooks been written directing children to these ideas. Even basic political science texts used in college—presumably more analytical than civics books found in public schools—do not suggest or imply that these features of the campaign are desirable, even as they recognize that they exist.

Yet more often than not this is the reality, and these are the features, of the modern political campaign. And it is true from our national campaigns, in which candidates for the presidency of the United States offer themselves to the public, through state offices down to the most modest local elections. One of the truly interesting features of the modern political campaign is that its techniques, practices, and styles show remarkable similarities—especially in its use of television— whether it is a national campaign costing scores of millions of dollars, or a local city council race costing a few thousand.

Thus, the modern campaign somehow jars our perception of what political campaigns are supposed to be. Many people have a memory—perhaps distorted—of what campaigns "were," and it doesn't fit with what they observe now. Even as they pay at least some attention to them, they are disheartened, discouraged, and even sickened by what they see. Will young people, growing up politically with the modern campaign, somehow feel better about all this than their parents? We'll have to see, of course, but the outlook is not good. Young people—those under twenty-five—do not participate very much in politics, and seem to have fairly cynical ideas about political behaviors, institutions, organizations, even individuals.[1]

This latter point actually goes to the heart of the matter. Most Americans—whether young or old—do not feel comfortable with politics. The image of political activity conveyed to young Americans is not always a savory one. We seem suspicious of politics, politicians, and political activity, as if somehow it is not something "good" people really like very much, or to which they should devote their time, resources, and energy. If "politics" is cast in terms of "civic duty" or "citizen responsibility," such as voting, about two-thirds of those eligible at least bother to register, and half of that group (on a good day!) show up at the polls. But if it comes to something more active or time consuming—such as running for office, or working with candidates during a campaign—the number of Americans willing to get involved is woefully small.

Interest in politics, then, does not seem to rank high in the pantheon of American values and beliefs. This is in contrast to people in other nations—such as the French, or the Israelis—for whom politics is a kind of national sport. We prefer baseball and football, sex, violence, and scandals.

Yet it is of interest that millions of Americans will watch young men maul one another on the gridiron or ballfield on Saturday and Sunday afternoons, but will feel turned off, irritated, bored, or indifferent when they see political candidates going after one another in a campaign. We shall not pursue the point further, as it requires an exploration into American tastes and preferences that goes beyond our purpose here. Nonetheless, the comparison is useful for underscoring the initial theme of this book: modern campaigns have few defenders, and in recent years seem increasingly to turn Americans off politics, rather than attract them to it as a worthy, even noble, part of public and civic life.

The Purpose of This Book

This book is not intended as another criticism of the modern political campaign. It is, rather, an exploration and explanation of it. It is a premise of this text that political campaigns undoubtedly deserve some of the criticism leveled at them. Our purpose is to explain why campaigns take the form they do in modern American politics. Beyond this, however, is an additional theme to be developed in the book: the modern political campaign is not dysfunctional to American democracy, and while it may often seem expensive and distasteful, it really does not do us any harm, either.

This book is meant to confront these matters. Our goal is to help politically conscious citizens grapple with fundamental issues concerning the modern political campaign. It does so not to try to convince them that it is either good or bad, but to increase their level of insight, and to help them understand the implications of campaigns for democratic politics. But it is also our purpose to speak to those for whom politics, and political campaigns, are a turnoff; if they know more about them, perhaps they will begin to take more of an interest in them.

We will concern ourselves with very basic questions: Why is the modern campaign the way it is? What forces—political and otherwise—shape modern political campaigning? What roles do candidates, issues, campaign advisers such as pollsters and consultants, and orga-nizations like parties and interest groups play in shaping the campaign, and determining its direction? What about money, and political action committees (PACs)? Why is the modern campaign so expensive, and just what does money buy for PACs, fat cats, and other contributors? What is the impact of the media, especially TV? Why is negative campaigning so common? What decisions are made during campaigns that cause the campaign to take the form it does? What are the conse-quences of the modern campaign for American politics, and American democracy? In fact, are they bad for us?

Some might object that the book is therefore a defense of the mod-ern campaign. In a way, it is; as mentioned a moment ago, the author's position is that while campaigns may be unseemly, they don't injure us either—unless they engage in illegal or immoral activity. But the book is also a critique. The warts of political campaigning require illumina-tion. Things happen in campaigns that test the limits of public accept-ability. Money in political campaigns—not so much the amounts as its sources—raise troubling questions for our political system. The author is both conscious and appreciative of the ethical and political issues associated with modern campaigning, and their implications for our political system. The book will deal with them, head on.

The only request the author makes of the reader is a suspension of prior views and opinions of modern political campaigning while we look at the way campaigns unfold. In the end, readers will be in a position to make judgments about what they have read and understood. Indeed, the last chapter will provide them with an opportunity to do just that.

The Purposes of the Modern Political Campaign

At the outset, let us state the major purpose of the modern political campaign in the United States: to get citizens to go to the polls and mark their ballot in support of (or sometimes in opposition to) a partic-ular candidate or issue.[2] That is what all the hoopla is about. Cam-paigns may do other things, but this simple statement is the bottom line. Political campaigns do not exist in the abstract; they cost too much, and are too time, resource, and energy consuming, to constitute purely a hobby, sideshow, form of exercise, or vague happening. They are purposeful, even single-mindedly so—persuading people to vote for (or against) something or someone is their only goal.

In order to make this happen, the campaign must embark on several separate activities. These can loosely be called civic education, marketing a candidate or issue, and public entertainment. They are not equally felt or articulated in each campaign; different campaigns do have different styles, reflecting the nature and level of the office sought, local political customs and rules, wishes of the candidate and advisers. But all three must be included in planning and executing the campaign. Whatever the balance among the three, they still have the same end: election (or defeat) of a candidate or issue. Let us look briefly at each in turn.

Civic Education

Contemporary readers, perhaps jaded by one too many negative TV ads, may find it hard to believe that the modern campaign does attempt to add to their civic education. But it actually tries to do so, for several reasons.

In the first place, many Americans are concerned with politics only because of obligatory feelings about their "civic responsibility" or "duty," not because they love or relish it. They are "supposed" to vote. They are "supposed" to read about or listen to the candidates and the issues, and make up their minds accordingly about how they wish to vote.

Political scientists have long recognized that this model of voting behavior has only limited applicability.[3] Only a relatively few people really make up their minds on how to vote by following such an elaborate, time-consuming cognitive process. Most people use simpler methods for deciding: partisanship ("I vote Republican"); localism and sectionalism ("She's from my home town, of course I'll vote for her"); friendship or business association ("I grew up with his daddy," "She's with the Atlanta office of Bill's firm"); single issues ("I only want to know one thing: what's her position on capital punishment?"); physical appearance (many voters preferred Kennedy over Nixon in 1960 because he looked better on TV, and women voters particularly liked Jackie Kennedy's hats over Pat Nixon's Republican cloth coat). Other powerful affective influences on voting could also be mentioned, including a darker side: prejudices and bigotry can strongly push a person's decision on whether to vote, and how.

Nonetheless, while the "civic responsibility" voter model may explain only a small percentage of voting behavior, many people are under the illusion that it is the process they use for making voting decisions. It fits well, after all, with their sense of civic responsibility and duty, as well as with their suspicion of politics. They feel obliged to carry out their tasks as citizens, but they don't have to lower themselves to "politics"; instead, they can coolly and rationally "decide" how to vote.

Thus it should be clear why, from the standpoint of the campaign, attention has to be paid to "civic education." If at least some voters think the campaign has some substance to offer, or provides materials for their cognitive processes as they make up their minds, so might they pay some attention; so might they be persuaded that the candidate or issue advocated by the campaign is worthy of their attention, and vote accordingly. The campaign has therefore to legitimize the citizen's decision to vote for a candidate or issue, even if it is not the "real" reason. In a sense, then, the campaign tries to reinforce the civics lesson conveyed to the voter so many years ago in elementary school: this is what you are supposed to do, so do it, and while you are at it, vote for this person, or against that idea.

There is another aspect of this as well. The reader should think of the reverse situation. Suppose the campaign offers nothing in the way of civic education. It provides no information about candidates, issues, ideology, partisanship, even the date of the election. It fails to tell voters of the importance of the election. It fails to remind them of the traditional role of voting in the democratic process. And so forth and so on.

From the standpoint of the campaign, failure to provide this information is a mistake. Not to make at least a pretense of civic education undermines, even discredits, the campaign. The campaign cannot afford to have voters say: "They aren't giving me the information I need. They are not helping me understand 'the issues,' or who the candidates are. They are just politicians who want something from me. I want something more."

So the campaign gives more. A little more, but not much more. Enough so that an appeal to "civic responsibility and duty" can be successfully made, but not enough to bore voters. Enough so that the campaign can point to its stand on "the issues." Enough so that it looks like the candidate is truly interested in the quality of government and public life, is sensitive to the public interest, and is above "politics." But not so much that the candidate seems pedantic or sanctimonious instead of a person of action, strength, and vision.

An outraged reader might object at this point that this is pure cynicism. If the candidate and campaign were truly interested in "civic duty," the focus would be on issues and substance, not personalities and antics, as so often seems the case.

We shall deal with the question of issues and substance in a later chapter. For the moment, let us just say that from the standpoint of the modern political campaign, issues and substance are at best a sideshow, and at worst a pain in the *derrière*. Viewed from inside the campaign, issues and substance are only helpful or valuable if they somehow enhance the image and political standing of the candidate, or alternatively make the opponent look bad.

Our exercised reader should relax. Even the modest focus on civic duty and public education is not a mere sham. The point to remember is that in the modern campaign some genuine attention must be paid to "civic education and responsibility." Voters cannot be cheated of the illusion that they think and act rationally; indeed, the campaign must give them the opportunity to think that they are doing so.

The campaign also has other purposes that must be realized: marketing and entertainment. These are not always fully compatible with the loftier purposes of civic education. But from inside the campaign, they may well be much more important.

Marketing the Candidate (or Issue)

We noted a moment ago that noncognitive, emotional influences on voting decisions exist that for many—perhaps most—voters are much more powerful than purely cognitive ones. That is why the marketing and entertainment purposes of campaigns exist. They are separate but complementary. Together they compose what can be called the "second level" of campaigning. This "second level" turns out to be critical to the success or failure of the campaign, since more voters are likely to make up their minds to vote based on this aspect of the campaign than on the "civic education" aspect. Fundamentally, it is an emotional pitch, sometimes blatant, which seeks to attract voters' attention and keep them sufficiently interested (alternatively, amused, amazed, outraged, disgusted—in any case, emotionally charged) so that they will go to the polls and vote as the campaign asks.

Thus the real "message" of the modern campaign, for which American voters (and journalists!) diligently search as though it were the

Holy Grail, only very rarely centers around issues. It is, rather, candidate and image centered.[4] The campaign searches for a "hook" that typifies or enhances some aspect of the candidate, or a substitute reality of the candidate called "image," by which to grab voters, and keep them occupied until it is time to vote.

For most voters, the hook is a purely emotional appeal that is best understood as an exercise in marketing and entertainment. True, for some highly rational voters the hook is primarily a cognitive one. For some others, the hook may be a single issue, although a reasonable argument can be made that single-issue voters (such as pro-lifers, or gun-control opponents) really act on emotion, not cognition. To hook most voters, though, architects of modern campaigns know that victory is more likely attained through an appeal to the heart and emotions than to the brain.

Thus, campaigns have come to focus on individuals, on candidates and their "image," that is, specifically programmed views and words that convey very particular emotional content. The image created may be totally separate from what the candidate "really" is like. It may have little to do with, indeed might mask, the substance of issues. And it may be unlike hooks that were commonly used in the past, such as partisan appeals.

Yet the image, if it is sufficiently slick, appealing, and credible, achieves a life of its own that may be only marginally related to what is "really real." But the voters, of course, will not know the difference during the campaign, and may only find out much later, once the candidate has become officeholder. Sometimes they never find out at all.

From the perspective of the campaign, then, the appeal to voters is primarily viewed as an emotional message. Voters are not really seen as thinking, cognitively driven rational beings. Rather, great pains are taken—and often great expense incurred—to discover what grabs them by their feelings, and motivates them to vote for, or against, someone or something.

This emotional appeal centering on individuals can be used not only to foster a candidate's image, it can also be used to denigrate that of an opponent. Is it any wonder, then, that emotionally evocative symbols are more important in political campaigns than policy positions? Could not Republicans in 1988 convey more about Mike Dukakis, and the kind of image of him they wished people to perceive, by showing voters pictures of a polluted harbor, than by printing "position papers" that virtually no one has time to read, and many wouldn't understand anyway? Was it necessary for Miami's victorious Republican congressional candidate Ileana Ros-Lehtinen to do more than literally wrap herself in an American flag during her 1989 TV commercials while her Democratic opponents bickered among themselves during the primary and runoff? Did not the sometimes contorted faces of Bob Dole shown on Clinton TV ads in 1996 make a more powerful campaign statement, and impression on viewers, than the candidates' seemingly incomprehensible "debate" over Medicare?

The techniques of marketing a candidate are well known, and we shall have occasion to discuss them further in later chapters. For the moment, let us bring to light what some observers have long suspected: marketing candidates is not too much different from marketing any other product, such as beer, deodorant, breakfast cereal, or automobiles.

This is not a happy thought, and it bothers many people. It disturbs and annoys candidates, very much; they do not like to be thought of by their campaign staffs, or the public, as "commodities" such as mouthwash or laundry soap.

But consider the problem from the perspective of the campaign. If the candidate is a fresh face on the political scene, the challenge is similar to introducing a new product into an already crowded market; how does Lever Brothers, for example, seek to persuade consumers into buying another type of soap, when there are already numerous perfectly good kinds on the shelves? If the candidate is an incumbent (that is, the product is an established one), the problem is to increase market share to ensure reelection, and preferably to "scare" new products (that is, potential opponents) from even bothering to compete.

Thus, the whole panoply of marketing devices and techniques can be called into play as the candidate is paraded before the public, depending on the particular electoral problem at hand. True, there are some differences. Candidates have wishes and feelings; bars of soap do not. Candidates do and say things (sometimes helpful and advantageous, sometimes weird or foolish) that influence the course of the campaign; bottles of hair spray or cans of soup just sit on the shelves. And the fantasies created by beer and automobile commercials are perhaps more sensual or erotic than those permissible for candidates for public office.

Yet the overall point is the same. A major thrust of the campaign is to find a hook into the voter by creating an image of the candidate through mass and targeted marketing techniques. It is very similar to ad agencies' efforts to hook consumers into buying their client's beer, and not the one of the other brewery.

Entertaining the Crowd

Marketing of course is more than just creating an image or coming up with a slogan; nowadays it is actually a sophisticated means of identifying and targeting an audience (in this case, voters rather than consumers) to whom this candidate, image, or message is likely to appeal. "The hook," then, is really a multidimensional series of steps involving considerable planning, design, analysis, and testing before the campaign is actually fully launched. In a sense, then, the "marketing" aspect of the campaign constitutes a fundamental aspect of campaign strategy, for it involves identifying the right voter constituency, and determining how to successfully appeal to it.

But what is the "entertainment" purpose of the campaign supposed to do? The answer is that while it is a part of the marketing strategy—that is, it helps keep the hook in—it has an additional purpose: overcoming citizens' negative feelings about politics, candidates, campaigns, even issues in the case of promoting one side, or reinforcing them in the case of the opposition. It is thus a central, tactical part of campaign activity, as it involves implementing the "appeal" the campaign tries to make.

Voters—even sympathetic, interested voters—have to be convinced. To assume that just because the voting population has been carefully scrutinized, identified, analyzed, segmented, and targeted, the campaign will succeed and the candidate will win is foolish. In fact, it is a recipe for disaster.

The campaign has always to assume that voters need enticing and incentive to send money, carry signs, wear buttons, or just vote. Only a relatively few will do the latter just out of a sense of civic duty, and these may not be enough to win the election; indeed, a majority of this group might be in the opposition camp. Rather, most voters must be prodded, cajoled, whatever, even to do the most minimal thing: go to the polls and vote as asked.

There are a variety of ways to do this. In the old days of urban bosses, voters could simply be rounded up and transported to the polls. Perhaps some incentive was available: a little money, some liquor, a holiday from work. Or maybe the stick was applied, in that a public service job or some other benefit provided by the machine would be removed. In the South, where blacks and poor whites were not independent political actors but rather dependent on white organizations that frequently intimidated them, "delivering" the vote was quite common.[5]

Such practices are no longer as widespread, either in the North or South, as they once were. It is easier, and more politically and socially acceptable, to entertain the voters to get them interested and persuade them to vote.

Entertainment takes a variety of forms, and all are used by political campaigns. The reader should remember, however, that entertainment is not just inducing laughter and amazement, or creating fantasies in the voter. It has a dark side, as well. It is possible to grab voters' interest, and hold it, even mesmerize them, by creating anger or appealing to their sense of bigotry and prejudice. Old-time southern demagogues were wizards at this form of entertainment. So are modern campaign strategists, pollsters, and media specialists: it is one of the underpinnings of so-called negative campaigning. A prominent example was the manipulation of the voters, in 1988, in contrasting George Bush's continued emphasis on "positive American values" with the fear, even revulsion, that could be induced in them through pictures of the convicted black rapist-murderer Willie Horton. The technique was effective; it was also entertaining and engrossing, as producers of Hollywood horror movies have long understood.

There is another matter for which the entertainment aspects of campaigns are important. There is a pulse and rhythm to public life in America that the entertainment provided by campaigns underscores. We use these pulses and rhythms to help plan our lives, and to remind ourselves of where we are in our life cycle. Memorial Day, not the calendar, marks the real start of summertime; Labor Day means it is over, and time for school to start. The Christmas season is no longer solely a religious occasion; it is a commercial enterprise of vast importance, and not incidentally a time to reestablish close ties with friends and family. The football season is anchored by the weekend games; but in fact it is a time to relish the glorious outdoors of autumn, just as the baseball season has as much to do with defining spring and summer lifestyles as with which team is in first place.

The entertainment offered by political campaigns underscores this same pulse and rhythm. Indeed, it may be more important than some of

these others. While the baseball season and income-tax day come an-
nually, elections—except for some minor municipal ones—generally
come only every two or four years; indeed, our most important election, that for president, is one of the latter. Thus the "entertainment" of
political campaigns is designed to remind the voting public that it is
time to attend to politics. The cycle has repeated, the pulse and rhythm
are reestablished, and voters need to do what they always do at this
time every couple of years. The fact that the campaign may remind
people in a way that strikes them as noisy, expensive, occasionally
enlightening, sometimes annoying, in no way detracts from this important purpose.

Also important are the rituals in American public life. We expect
things to be done in particular ways. The school day is "supposed to"
start with the Pledge of Allegiance. Sporting events commence with
"The Star-Spangled Banner"—and major ones have bunting and fire-
works for added color and excitement. Between (roughly) Halloween
and New Year's, stores put up Christmas or other holiday displays.
Newscasters on the six o'clock news close by saying something like,
"We will see you at eleven"—even though it is the viewers who do the
seeing, not the broadcasters. There are no laws requiring any of this
(possibly excepting statutes in some states or local board of education
rules concerning the Pledge); rather, they are things we have come to
expect. We notice their absence, and feel cheated without them; woe to
the store that does not recognize the holiday season.

So too does the entertainment aspect of the campaign reinforce the
rituals of public life. Even as we complain about campaigns, we expect
candidates to have them; indeed, our complaint is not so much with the
existence of campaigns as the way they are carried out. Politics, after
all, is a spectator sport in America, complete with the hoopla and
spectacle associated with baseball, football, and basketball. Just as
things have to be done in certain ways during games because the
public expects them (how else to explain the expensive, tedious, over-
blown halftime shows during the Super Bowl?), so too does the public
expect that a candidate must campaign for office. Think of the contrary
situation: what happens to candidates who do not campaign? They
lose. The winner is not always the candidate who campaigns the hard-
est, or puts on the best show; but the one who fails to participate
wholeheartedly in the great American spectacle called the political
campaign is virtually assured of defeat.

Negative Campaigning

An oft-heard criticism of the modern political campaign is that it is "negative." What does this mean? There is no agreed-upon definition. But we can start by talking about what it is not.

In the first place, campaigns that draw attention to an opponent's record or background are not necessarily negative. For example, an officeholder seeking reelection, or running for another office, presumably has some sort of history associated with the previous tenure. There is nothing fundamentally negative about this record being highlighted. Indeed, the very rocks on which our democratic system rests—that public officials are accountable for their actions, and that they must be responsive to public desires and needs—require that their records be brought out in a campaign. Even if the individual's record is belittled and harshly criticized by one or more opponents, the epithet "negative campaign" is probably inappropriate.

But the same standard can and should be applied to private individuals, with no prior record of public service, running for office. Presumably such candidates trumpet their credentials in an effort to establish their qualifications for office. These are legitimate objects of public scrutiny; any deficiencies or inaccuracies are of course fair game for opponents.[6] But even if everything stated is accurate there is every reason why an opponent can raise questions about candidates' appropriateness or suitability for the office sought.

Moreover, campaigns that emphasize personality, and avoid issues, are not necessarily negative. A candidate's personality and style (which, after all, are nothing less than indicators of political identity or persona) may be directly relevant to how that person might behave in office. That issues are downplayed or missing may be more a tribute to inchoate public opinion, the existence of a quiescent or satisfied electorate, or a failure of the candidates to capture the public's imagination during the campaign than anything else. In none of these instances would the term "negative campaign" necessarily apply.

Nor are "hardball" campaigns necessarily negative. They can be vigorous, and sometimes even nasty, without being negative. Indeed the public may well be accepting of hard-fought campaigns; it may even prefer them, and pay more attention to them, just as a close ball game attracts more interest than a rout. The public also believes that campaign "politics as usual" involves behaviors that might not be appropriate in one's home or place of work; the former is a different kettle of fish than either of the latter, and thus what is "normal" in the former would be regarded as out of bounds in the latter two. There are assuredly public standards of acceptability associated with "politics as usual." But the boundaries of these standards are vague, and may vary considerably from one area to the next: candidates in Queens or the Bronx can engage in political activity that would be considered offensive in Scarsdale. To the extent that the public even attends to a political campaign, they want to see candidates competing hard, giving it their all; this is supposed to be an indication of how tough they will be in office, and how hard they will pursue its public purpose. Thus, a tough, hardball, competitive political campaign (as defined by vague, locally determined standards) can actually redound to the benefit of the candidate, and not be regarded as negative.

Negative campaigning, rather, is associated with attacks that are irrelevant or inappropriate to the business at hand, namely, qualifications for running for office and capability of handling it if elected. The line, to be sure, is thin. Calling an opponent a spouse abuser, if true, is not negative campaigning, as it reflects on the worthiness of the person to be given the public trust; but if the charge is not true, it is merely character assassination, and constitutes entirely negative campaigning. Thus, much depends on the veracity and context of the charges brought forward.

The truth, of course, may be difficult to find, or explain. As if this matter doesn't raise sufficient complexity, other factors intrude as well. In a recent campaign for judge in Florida, a male candidate sent out mail severely criticizing the record of his opponent, a sitting judge. It was factually correct. The problem was that the attacker was a male; his opponent, female. The impression conveyed by the mailer was of a man beating up on a woman. Any number of knowledgeable local observers agreed that this may have cost him the race. Thus, differing standards of public acceptability (candidates for judge may not be able to get away with behaviors which those for other offices can), gender issues, local customs and styles—all of these help determine what is regarded as "negative campaigning."

An additional complication of possible negativity results from the motives of the perpetrator. What is the purpose of the mud being thrown? Is it in fact to highlight serious deficiencies—documentable ones—in the opponent? Is it merely to attract attention to an inept or

enfeebled campaign? Is it primarily to mask problems of the perpetrator's own campaign, or deflect attention in the form of negative
press away from himself and onto an opponent? Is the negative campaign merely a result of cruelty or the selection of an inappropriate
target, as for example when Rush Limbaugh was thought to have gone
beyond even his minimal standards of acceptability by attacking Chel-
sea Clinton? These considerations also help define what is, and is not,
negative campaigning.

Why do candidates insist on engaging in negative campaigning? In
part it is because at certain times, and under certain conditions, it
works. Data exist to show that while voters may not like negative
campaigns, they absorb information from them.[7] Candidates who have
an opponent whose "negatives" are high, in terms of how they are
perceived by the public, may find a negative attack successful. If the
charges are true, or regarded as plausible and credible by the voting
public, then negative campaigning may pay off. However, if the
bounds of acceptable public standards are crossed, if the charges are
false, if the candidate has low negative and high positive ratings, if the
motives behind the negative campaign are suspect, if the target chosen
is inappropriate—then negative campaigning can backfire.

In the end, candidates may choose to engage in negative campaigning, in part, because "everyone does it." This somewhat puny excuse
may well simply be a mask for something deeper: better to engage in
negative campaigning first than get hit by it late in the campaign when
it is too late to respond effectively. In a sense, then, the best defense is
a good offense. Better to start lobbing mortar rounds at the opponent
early, and put his campaign off balance, than wait for your own campaign to be hit.

Ethics and the Modern Campaign

The reader might again feel the blood beginning to boil; all this might
seem nothing more than crass, cynical manipulation by the campaign.
Perhaps it is. But the reader must remember two points. The first we
have already discussed: campaigns must, and do, consider the "civic
education" of the voter. If they are to be effective, they must genuinely
appeal to the voter's best, most rational instincts, and provide needed
information to him.

But the reader must also realize that modern political campaigns are a serious, costly business. They are not trifles or hobbies, and while they may be games, they are played by participants—even in campaigns for modest offices in small places—as though the destiny of the human race rode on the result. Those on the inside of the campaign believe that its whole point—indeed, its entire *raison d'être*—is to get voters to vote for its side, or against the other one. The "campaign game" is often played with fanatical zeal by those on the inside; it takes on the aura of a religious crusade, and develops an "us against them" mindset by which the players are ready to undergo the labors of Hercules in order to achieve victory.

Observers and critics may not like this single-mindedness of purpose. They sometimes argue that this distorts judgment in the campaign, creates an inverted sense of priorities, and forces it to engage in practices antithetical to the spirit, and sometimes the laws, of democracy.

True, sometimes candidates will engage in a campaign "to see what happens," or to lay the groundwork for a future campaign. We are not talking about these campaigns here, as they are less and less common. We are talking about campaigns designed, however hopefully or misguidedly, to win. And while this does not mean "anything goes," or "the end justifies any means," or "win at all costs," it does say that campaigns will use virtually any and all methods and techniques—and often skirt the borders of legality, legitimacy, ethics, and decency—in order to capture enough votes to win.

Internal debates take place in campaigns about the kind of strategy and tactics that should be used. Candidates, and their advisers, consider such matters as how negative to go on an opponent, and whether a "slash and burn" campaign makes more sense than a "rose garden" strategy. Obviously personal values and preferences, the nature of the office sought, incumbency, partisanship and ideology, local customs and belief systems, and so forth, help determine these decisions. The late Lee Atwater, the former head of the Republican National Committee, was famous for a "cut to the bone" style in campaigning; but his approach might be unacceptable, and unwise, for a local judicial candidate. In both cases, however, the campaign must make a conscious decision about the tone and message of the campaign, and how far it is willing to go in order to win.

Does this excuse campaign excesses? Of course not. Any campaign—and those responsible for it—should be fully accountable for what happens. The point that critics must remember is that campaign organizers and administrators will reach to the very edge of acceptable practices to find some way of appealing to voters, grabbing them on a hook, holding them there, and motivating them to vote. Anything less is tantamount to handing the election over to the opposition, because it will be out doing the same thing.

What's Behind All This?

During the course of the next several chapters we shall consider some of the reasons why modern campaigns have taken the form they do. Nonetheless, at the outset a few basic observations about the social and political context of modern campaigns in American life seem appropriate.

It is a central theme of this book that the modern political campaign reflects the values, preferences, styles, norms, and behaviors of contemporary American life; or at least those found in the region, state, or locality of a particular election. More important, if the campaign ignores these values and preferences, or runs counter to them, it is lost from the start.

This is a fairly stiff drink for many readers to swallow. On the face of it, for example, it suggests that it is American society, not the campaign, that causes any egregious behavior that takes place.

Remember, however, that the campaign bears the responsibility for what happens. But the campaign cannot bear the responsibility for larger questions of public values, taste, and preferences. These are formed through other mechanisms than political campaigns—although it is true that in reflecting them, campaigns may reinforce them—and the campaign takes advantage of them to try to gain the winning edge.

Where do public tastes and values come from? This is a huge question, one that goes well beyond the scope of this book. From our earliest days, individuals are socialized and influenced in terms of what to think, how to think, what is right and wrong, and so forth: families, churches, schools, government, peer groups, work groups, employers, valued friends, the mass media, national and international events—all of these work to shape us as individuals, communities, states, regions, and a nation.

For our purposes, however, the mass media and other forms of popular culture, especially television and movies, seem to have been particularly important in influencing what modern political campaigns do.

Consider the reasons. We know that most people are at best marginally interested in politics. We also know that most political information is gained through the mass media, especially TV. This is the same source that people use heavily for news, entertainment, and other forms of public information. Students of mass media tell us that the public is literally deluged with stimuli from TV, radio, newspapers, magazines, billboards, signs, mail, advertisements, flyers, and so forth. We seem to live in an age when a major problem for Americans is not to find information, but to sort out the enormous amount of material thrown at them, make sense of it, and use what they can to their advantage.

It can be argued that much of the information available to people is nonsensical, trivial, half-truths, whatever. This is not the point. The point is that every day, from the moment they wake up to read the paper and put on the morning news until they retire at night, Americans face a superabundance of stimuli thrown at them by the media. Some they perceive; some goes unnoticed; some lodges in the unconscious mind. But the barrage is constant, daily, overwhelming.

Thus, the problem for the political campaign is to break through all this and somehow register in the public's mind. A campaign that does not penetrate the voters' perceptual screen will be unnoticed, and surely a loser. So the campaign adopts the latest in marketing and mass entertainment techniques in order to ensure that it is heard. It has to compete, willingly or not, with all the other messages directed at the voter and stimuli received—car ads, beer commercials, real estate deals, investment opportunities, news, "infotainment," wars, police beatings, taxes, marital problems, sick children, bank balances in the red, job insecurities, and a myriad others. Is it any wonder, then, that the campaign will often resort to techniques that can try to force their way into the voters' consciousness, somehow "educate" or inform them, and induce them to go out of their way, perhaps inconvenience themselves, to vote on election day?

There is more to it than even this. The campaign must somehow take advantage of changes in, and the current state of, public taste and acceptability in order to ensure that its message gets into the voter's consciousness. As anyone who watches TV, goes to the movies, or reads newspapers and magazines knows, what is permissible and acceptable has changed dramatically in the past decades. Prime-time TV shows—not just daytime soaps—have become almost as explicit as movies in showing violence and sexuality. "Infotainment" programs, in which the most private lives of celebrities—political and otherwise—are revealed have become some of the most popular on TV. Newspapers and magazines print gossip and stories about the lives of public persons that a generation ago would have been inconceivable.[8] Movies and books, too, have in recent years seemingly shown no restraint in terms of the graphic violence and perversions which they explicitly show and describe. Indeed, matters have reached such alarming proportions that a major vehicle and arbiter of popular taste and culture, *Newsweek* magazine, published a lengthy cover story about the new explicitness and its impact on American sensibilities.[9]

The previous paragraph describes facts of contemporary American life. It is not an editorial. The modern political campaign cannot be oblivious to acceptable standards of taste. Like them or not, candidates and campaign architects and administrators must understand that if the public craves innuendoes and exposés of the private lives of public people—in the manner of *Entertainment Tonight, A Current Affair,* or *People* magazine—the campaign must in some measure accommodate this type of public taste if it is to break through citizens' perceptual screens, stand out from all the other stimuli, and motivate them to vote. Seen in this light, at least some of the reasons emerge why negative campaigning, in which the campaign criticizes the other side and shows it in a poor light, rather than focusing on the merits of its candidate or issue, has become so prevalent. Following this same line of argument will illuminate a host of other modern campaign practices, as well.

But, it will be objected, does not the campaign have a "higher purpose"? Are not voters somehow "different" from other people, and thus it is not necessary to pander to them in order to attract their attention, or motivate them to go to the polls?

We have already dealt with the first question: yes, campaigns do consider their public purpose, but they also are designed to win. They will reflect and take advantage of, not run counter to, public preferences in order to do so. The answer to the second can best be provided by an anecdote—perhaps apocryphal—from one of Adlai Stevenson's presidential campaigns. After completing one of his highly polished speeches more suited to a university seminar than the campaign trail, Stevenson heard a supporter cry out, "Good for you, Governor, you're the thinking man's candidate." He is said to have replied, "Thanks, but I need a majority."

To sum up, then, the successful modern campaign reflects dominant values and tastes. It must also find a way to break through the voters' consciousness, using those same vehicles of mass media by which the public secures information about the world around them. It must do so in a way that does not offend; but by the same token, it cannot afford to be ignored, or to bore the public. It must, in fact, entertain them as much as inform them. Sometimes this does mean targeting the campaign at the lowest common denominator, a feature which causes great hue and crying from some critics. The reader should remember, though, that the campaign will do what it takes in order to get through to the voters. If this means appealing to more than "thinking men," then that is what it will do.

Even if the campaign does this well it does not guarantee victory at the polls; too many other things influence electoral outcomes. On the other hand, to do otherwise—to treat the campaign as purely an exercise in civic education, or to ignore what the public really wants—is to bring about almost certain defeat.

The Plan of the Book

Having established the framework of the book, we are now ready to examine the workings of the modern political campaign from the inside. We shall examine older campaigns, as a point of departure for assessing the rise of the modern campaign. Then we shall look at individual parts of the campaign, including the candidate and voters, issues, money and PACs, media (especially television), negative campaigning, and so forth. At the end, we will reflect on the nature of the modern campaign, particularly with reference to its consequences for contemporary American democracy. We will especially focus on the question so many people have posed: is the modern campaign really so bad, and so bad for us?

PART I

Old-Style Campaigns

2

Mudslinging:
As American as Apple Pie

H. Rap Brown, the militant black separatist of the 1970s, once noted that violence was as American as apple pie. While his remark irritated and alienated many people, in fact he was on to something important: there is a dark side to American social life that distasteful as it may be, has been around for a long time, and is very much a part of the American character.

Happily, we need not pursue the line of inquiry to which Brown directed us. Still, Brown's comment forces us to ask whether there might be other aspects of American life, especially in political campaigns, that suggest that there is a side we may not always like, or even care to recognize, but which is very much with us.

The previous chapter argued that political campaigns are a reflection of American life, culture, and tastes—warts and all. In this chapter we shall pursue this matter further, along the lines Brown pointed: namely, that negative campaigning in all of its manifestations—mudslinging, character assassination, sloganeering, absence of issues, dirty tricks, and so forth—is nothing unusual. It's been around a long time. It's an accepted part of our campaigns. Public outcries against it and calls for reforms have been common, and essentially gone unheeded. The practices continue.

Is negative campaigning the norm? Do all political campaigns, no matter how high-minded they begin, ultimately become mired in mud?

It is impossible to answer the questions when phrased in this manner. It is easy to think of campaigns where personalities played a secondary role to issues, and where the general tenor of the campaigns was civil and polite, sometimes even friendly. Later in the book we shall look at the reasons why negative, mudslinging campaigns emerge, sometimes inevitably so.

For right now, then, we will sidestep these questions to focus on other ones: How deeply embedded in the American political tradition are negative, mudslinging campaigns? How far back can we trace the kind of campaign that arouses the ire, and righteous indignation, of so many citizens?

The answers—and this will dismay some readers—are, respectively, very much so, and virtually to the beginning of the Republic. Negative campaigns have been around a long time, and have been the primary feature of crucial political events that ultimately shaped the political destiny of our nation. To paraphrase H. Rap: negative campaigns are as American as apple pie.

In this section of the book we shall look closely at the two questions just posed. Our task here will be to look at some major negative campaigns in our past, to establish the long history of this type of campaign and to acquaint the modern reader with the conduct of campaigns "back then." In the next chapter we will dissect these campaigns to see what made them negative; later this analysis will help us place the contemporary campaign in the grand—or, perhaps, not so grand—tradition of American politicking.

We shall examine presidential campaigns exclusively, although it is possible to select others at the state and local levels that would establish precisely the same points. Presidential campaigns, however, have been selected for two reasons. First, their importance and visibility are paramount. No one can dispute the significance of a presidential campaign to the political life of the nation; the same is not true of a state or local campaign, no matter how visible it is across the nation. Second, because discussion of state and local races necessarily is limited to particular geographic areas, readers living elsewhere might not find them as interesting, or persuasive, as presidential politics.

Founding Fathers, Velvet Pants, and Powdered Wigs:
Federalists and Republicans, 1800

The modern reader might be surprised to learn that the fourth presidential election in our nation's brief history was one of the nastiest on record. Our impression of the Founding Fathers—formed, for most of us, in grade school—is all too often that they were "above" politics, especially petty, negative politics of the kind all too familiar to us. Washington, Adams, Jefferson, Madison, Hamilton, Jay, Marshall: these sons of the Enlightenment have achieved virtually semi-deific status as our nation's secular prophets, and their writings (including the *Declaration of Independence,* the *Constitution,* the *Bill of Rights,* and *The Federalist Papers*) our sacred texts. Surely they didn't sling mud!

But political intrigue had entered national politics even as Washington stepped down from his second term as president, and John Adams was inaugurated. It grew rapidly during his four years in office. Washington's death in 1799, moreover, ensured that any restraint on political hostilities that the nation's *éminence grise* might have been able to exert in the campaign of 1800 (in which he planned to participate) simply evaporated. The result, as First Lady Abigail Adams was later to write, was that the campaign unleashed enough "abuse and scandal to ruin and corrupt the minds and morals of the best people in the world."[1]

Her husband, John, had his troubles as president. A vain but morally incorruptible man, Adams sought on the one hand to continue the fundamentally Federalist policies of his predecessor, Washington, but also to restrain the excesses of the more militantly conservative wing of his party, headed by Alexander Hamilton. He did this by steering a moderate course designed to defuse growing Republican sentiment fueled by his own vice president, Thomas Jefferson.

Adams was in some respects successful. He kept the nation from a foolish war with France, even at a time when anti-French fever swept the nation as a result of the infamous XYZ affair. But, as more than one analyst has noted, this remarkable act of statesmanship cost Adams his political career.[2] Adams's problem was that the war would have been a popular one, and he was viewed as weak and indecisive because he opened peace negotiations with Napoleon in 1799.

Additionally, the infamous Alien and Sedition Acts, forced through

Congress by radical Federalists and unenthusiastically signed by Adams, gave great credibility to the Republican position that the Federalists sought to undo the great American experiment in democracy. The Kentucky and Virginia resolutions, authored and sponsored by Vice President Jefferson, were popular, and their potentially insidious impact on the Union was overlooked, as most saw Adams and the Federalists as overtly trying to quash opposition through the Alien and Sedition Acts. The arrest and conviction of prominent Republican politicians and journalists under the Acts strongly fueled anti-Adams fires throughout the young nation.

And Adams could not get along with his own Federalist party. Hamilton resented Adams deeply, and seemed to delight in stirring up intraparty strife designed to embarrass the president. Matters came to a head when, in the spring of 1800, Adams angrily dismissed Hamilton sympathizers from his cabinet. But Adams often made things worse by alienating his own party through personal stubbornness and a seeming unwillingness to bend on patronage issues. While the Federalists could not deny Adams renomination, neither was there much enthusiasm for him at a party caucus in May 1800; Charles C. Pinckney of South Carolina was chosen as the vice presidential candidate, and Hamilton openly thought, and hoped, that he might run ahead of Adams in electoral college balloting.[3]

There were clearly issues to be aired in the campaign of 1800: the meaning of the First Amendment, national versus states' rights, economic policy, the nation's place on the international stage, relations with France and England. Virtually none of this saw the light of day. It was all submerged under an avalanche of scurrilous attacks, character assassination, charges and countercharges, allegations of corruption, and worse.

No quarter was spared. Adams had been assaulted in the Republican press over the Alien and Sedition Acts (causing editors to be prosecuted and convicted). But a letter came to light in which Hamilton, leader of the Federalist hawks, himself viciously attacked the president. Adams, in his opinion, was "petty, mean, egotistic, erratic, eccentric, jealous-natured, and hot-tempered." He continued, "he does not possess the talents necessary for the *Administration* of Government, and . . . there are great and intrinsic defects in his character which unfit him for the office of Chief Magistrate."[4]

Republicans openly flaunted this letter once Aaron Burr (the Republican vice presidential candidate) got his hands on it. For his part, Adams returned the views of Hamilton: the latter, he stated, was "an intriguant, the greatest intriguant in the world—a man devoid of every moral principle—a bastard."[5]

But the barrage of ill will was not reserved for an internecine fight. Republicans and Federalists attacked one another without regard to decency or decorum. Jefferson was attacked without mercy. He was called a "Jacobin," an infidel, an atheist, and worse:

> Can serious and reflecting men look about them, and doubt that if Jefferson is elected, and the Jacobins get into authority, that those morals which protect our lives from the knife of the assassin—which guard the chastity of our wives and daughters from seduction and violence— defend our property from plunder and devastation, and shield our religion from contempt and profanation, will not be trampled upon and exploded?[6]

"Murder, robbery, rape, adultery and incest will all be openly taught and practiced, the air will be rent with the cries of the distressed, the soil will be soaked with blood, and the nation black with crimes" if Jefferson was elected, according to the *Connecticut Courant.* Jefferson's religious beliefs were repeatedly and viciously attacked by other Federalist journalists and leading clergymen throughout the campaign. He was also alleged to have led a debauched life at Monticello, including siring mulatto children; toward the end of the campaign Federalists even spread a rumor that he had died, but it turned out the dead Thomas Jefferson was a slave of the same name.

Republicans attacked Adams with equal fervor. He was a "fool, hypocrite, criminal, and tyrant . . . his presidency was one 'continued tempest of *malignant* passions.' "[7] Critics claimed he wanted to establish a monarchy and dynasty for his family. They even claimed that he had sent Pinckney to England to secure a string of mistresses for himself; even Adams, who was devoted to Abigail, had to laugh at that one.

In the end, political maneuvering elected Jefferson president. He and Burr had tied with 73 electoral college votes each; Adams was a distant third, with 65. The election went to the House of Representatives, but after thirty-five ballots Jefferson and Burr were still deadlocked. Finally, on the thirty-sixth ballot a crack developed in Federalist ranks, and Jefferson was selected. Hamilton, caught between a rock and a hard place, favored Jefferson. Burr, he thought, was "the Cataline of America," and while Jefferson was a "contemptible hypocrite" and a "concealed voluptuary," he at least had "pretensions to character," and ultimately would do less harm than Burr.[8]

This was the last presidential election in which the Founding Fathers participated in an active and preeminent way. If nothing else, this election showed that they, too, could compete with anyone in mudslinging. The tone and style they showed in this election were far removed from the courtly etiquette, manners, and civility of eighteenth-century drawing rooms. But this was the first national election of the new century; it established a pattern that was repeated in many presidential elections afterward.

Ins and Outs: 1828

The presidential election of 1828 featured another Adams: John Quincy, the son of John Adams. Whether through bad luck, a personality and style that made him an easy target (as was his father), or something else, the younger Adams found himself in the middle of a presidential election that, by all accounts, was the nastiest since his father's in 1800.

John Quincy Adams had been elected president in 1824 through a deal. No one of the four candidates that year received a majority in the electoral college, and as was the case with his father, the election had to be decided by the House of Representatives. The choices were Adams, war hero Andrew Jackson from Tennessee, and William Crawford of Georgia. Henry Clay of Kentucky, who had been the fourth candidate but who was eliminated from consideration after receiving the fewest electoral college votes, was the speaker of the House and the man in the best position to broker the outcome.[9]

He chose Adams, and when John Quincy appointed him secretary of state, the Jacksonians cried foul. It was a "corrupt bargain," they said, and it colored national politics for the next four years.

Jackson spent the Adams years planning his revenge. With his allies Martin Van Buren of New York, Thomas Hart Benton of Missouri, and John Eaton, a fellow Tennessean, he assembled a national political coalition of disaffected politicians and citizens the likes of which had not before been seen in America. Jackson himself proved to be a shrewd and capable political organizer, and he took full advantage of his national reputation and image as a war hero. At first his supporters called themselves "Friends of Jackson." Later they became the "Democratic-Republicans," and finally "Democrats."

More important than the name was the nature of the coalition. Using the increasingly unpopular Adams as a rallying point, they created an organization of southerners and westerners who felt ignored and left out of politics in the eastern, establishment-oriented Adams administration. They agreed on few matters—the "Tariff of Abominations" of 1828, which Adams signed, actually threatened to split the coalition—but issues were not important.[10] Of greater significance in shaping the dynamics and outcome of the election were the images of the candidates the Democrats were able to shape and maintain throughout the campaign: Adams, the candidate of old, powerful money who wanted to keep political power away from the people, and Jackson, the hero on a white horse who championed the cause of the people. It was truly a battle of "ins" versus "outs."

There were issues, to be sure. Adams was clear about favoring a national bank and the protective tariff. Jackson waffled: "My real friends," he said, "want no information from me ... but what my public acts have afforded, and I never gratify my enemies. Was I now to come forward and reiterate my public opinion ... , I would be charged with electioneering for selfish purposes."[11]

Jackson's political instincts perhaps told him that the outcome of the election would not be determined by a discussion of issues: organization, mobilization of public opinion, image, and character assassination would be much more important.

Indeed, the Jacksonians proved masters at organizing and mobilizing the public. They held rallies and parades throughout the states, with Hickory Clubs passing out leaflets, handbills, and other paraphernalia. Voters were approached in their homes. Campaigners passed out hickory sticks and brooms, and planted hickory trees everywhere (the Adams campaign, caught off guard and unable to match the groundswell of popular support for Jackson, tried to match the arboreal effort with oak trees, but the effort never quite succeeded).

All of this cost a lot of money—upward of one million dollars, according to some estimates.[12] It was the first presidential campaign in American history in which money played a key role. But in spite of the "common man" theme of the Jacksonians, the campaign never lacked for funds; there were enough monied interests behind Jackson who were anxious to rid Washington of Adams and his group of insiders that they bankrolled the whole thing.

The Jacksonians successfully kept issues out of the campaign; image was everything. Still, the candidates and their supporters had to say something. When they did, it rarely rose above invective, and generally descended into the gutter.

Adams, as noted, was an easy target. Jacksonian Democrats claimed he lived in splendor in the White House, and they pilloried him with an untrue story that he had purchased a billiard table with public funds. He was called, besides a monarchist, a "squanderer of the taxpayers' dollars on silken fripperies, Sabbath breaker [allegedly for riding on Sunday], and pimp": this latter because Democrats alleged that while he was minister to Russia he had acted as a procurer of American girls for Tsar Alexander I.[13]

The Adams forces returned the charges. Part of their strategy was to so anger the irascible Jackson that his temper would blow up and cost him the election. They tried, but failed. They called him ignorant, reckless, inexperienced, a blasphemer, bastard, and adulterer: Jackson had married his wife before she was divorced, and thus much was made of her bigamy and his living in sin, although the public record documented that they had gone through another ceremony to legalize the marriage. Still, one pamphlet asked, "Ought a convicted adulteress and her paramour husband to be placed in the highest offices of this free and christian land?"[14]

The biggest charge against Jackson was that he was a murderer. So-called Coffin Handbills were circulated purporting to show that Old Hickory had killed some of his own men in cold blood. While the facts were otherwise, as the Jackson campaign made clear, the handbills received wide distribution and currency.

They, along with the charges against his wife, made Jackson livid. He did not, however, publicly respond with anger or lose his temper. Rather, he allowed a committee to be established in Nashville to refute the charges, answer mail, and throw mud at Adams. He himself said relatively little during the Campaign. He didn't have to.

The result was predictable. As James MacGregor Burns wrote, no Adams could win a campaign based on invective and personality.[15] Jackson won the electoral college, 178 to Adams's 83. Adams won only the states his father had in 1800, and like him, lost the presidency.

This election was crucial in American history. It firmly established the presidency as a "popular" office, that is, one belonging to the people, not an elite group of insiders. It shaped national party politics—especially the role of party organization in presidential campaigns—for 150 years. Political operatives—managers, strategists, fund-raisers, get-out-the-vote specialists, local organizers—were extensively used in the campaign, and while previous campaigns had seen some of this activity, never before had they played such a broad and intensive role. And the 1828 campaign saw the emergence of big money and the necessity for expensive financing of presidential elections.

But in spite of this tremendous legacy—the phrase "watershed in presidential politics" is entirely appropriate for the campaign of 1828—it was not carried out on a high plane by moral or intellectual giants. The significant developments happened out of public view, by shrewd political operatives and politicians. What the public saw, and what the newspapers underscored, was mudslinging, character assassination, and other forms of negative campaigning unparalleled since John Quincy Adams's father ran a generation earlier.

Tippecanoe and Tyler Too: 1840

The presidential election of 1840 was less a contest than a circus. It was characterized by hucksterism, overt image making by candidates' handlers, deception, lies, character assassination, and an immense array of paraphernalia designed to excite the population into voting. It was the first presidential contest in which at least one of the candidates actually campaigned on the stump; previously it was considered unseemly for the candidates to do much, and their followers and allies did most of the work for them. (John Quincy Adams remarked during the campaign that "this practice of itinerant speech-making has suddenly broken forth in this country to a fearful extent."[16]) And if the presidential campaign of 1828 had served to popularize the contest for the White House, the campaign of 1840 was the first to deliberately broaden electoral participation throughout the nation, even to the smallest towns and most remote hamlets.

Whigs sensed victory in 1840, after eight years of Jacksonian democracy and four more of Martin Van Buren. The latter was blamed for virtually every problem experienced by the nation, most especially the Panic of 1837. His presidential style came under considerable criticism (he persisted in riding around Washington, D.C., in a large green coach with liveried footmen), and his daughter-in-law, an elegant woman fond of European fashions who served as White House hostess, enhanced his reputation as something of a dandy.

In part Van Buren was a victim of a bad (and undeserved) image. But he also followed the charismatic Jackson, and after twelve years of Democratic presidents the Whigs served as a haven for virtually every anti-Jackson, anti-Democrat sentiment or group looking for a place to land. As the election of 1840 loomed, it was difficult to see how the Democrats could maintain power; the midterm congressional elections, for example, saw them lose their majority in both houses.[17]

The Whigs' problem, though, was that they didn't have a candidate. Henry Clay was the obvious choice, and he fully expected to be nominated and elected president. But Whig leaders in New York, Pennsylvania, and Ohio (keys to a Whig victory) knew Clay was a loser. They saw that they needed to do to the Democrats what had been done to them in 1828: find a "candidate of the people" whose popularity would propel him to victory. Ideally also, the Whig nominee should be a man with little or no public record (thus nothing to defend), who would say little, whose image and even behavior could be manipulated by professional politicos, and who could somehow serve as a rallying point for the variety of anti-Democratic groups who were uncomfortably settling in the Whig nest.[18] This person was assuredly not Clay.

Whigs found their man in General William Henry Harrison, who was a hero of the Battle of Tippecanoe during the War of 1812. Like Jackson, he had successfully fought Indians. He had a modest record of public service, was sixty-seven years old, and had been born into a distinguished Virginia family on a wealthy plantation.[19]

None of this bothered Whig handlers. Harrison was rapidly transformed into a candidate of the people, a true westerner and rough-and-ready defender of popular rights.[20] Other than his wealth and military service, he had nothing in common with Jackson; but the Whigs made him out to be the epitome of Jacksonian democracy. It was a masterpiece of image making, smokescreens and deceptions, and outright lies.

Democratic bungling actually gave Whigs the key to victory. When Harrison was nominated (John Tyler, a Virginia states' righter, was the vice presidential nominee, to balance the ticket and satisfy southerners), the *Baltimore Republican* sneered, "give [Harrison] a barrel of hard cider and . . . he will sit the remainder of his days in a log cabin."[21] This remark was picked up by Whig strategists and turned into a powerful campaign gimmick. Suddenly Harrison was born in a log cabin (he certainly was not), and his drink was the hard cider consumed by everyday people, in contrast to the wine drunk from silver goblets used by the effete Van Buren.

The truth didn't matter; Harrison apparently didn't even like hard cider. Almost overnight the country was inundated by campaign artifacts associated with log cabins and hard cider: there were hundreds of varieties of souvenirs and pictures featuring one or the other, or both.[22] Portable log cabins were constructed and transported from place to place. Transparencies—a new medium of popular entertainment—even purported to show Harrison seated in front of a log cabin. Hard cider—plenty of it—was featured at campaign rallies. There were other kinds of campaign gimmicks as well. Songs were sung proclaiming the virtues of Harrison's common-man touch (in contrast to Van Buren), such as the following verse:

> Let Van from his collers of silver drink wine,
> And lounge on his cushioned settee,
> Our man on a buckeye bench can recline,
> Content with hard cider is he.[23]

Large balls—eight to ten feet in diameter, made of paper, leather, tin, or other materials—were rolled from village to village, accompanied by appropriate chants and ditties about getting the ball rolling for Harrison. And of course slogans were widely used, the most famous of which was "Tippecanoe, and Tyler too," an obvious attempt to exploit Harrison's military career.

All of this activity had a serious political purpose: to rally the voters for Harrison. Whigs learned the lesson of Jacksonian democracy well: as a prominent Democratic periodical later remarked, "We have taught them how to conquer us!"[24] Whig strategists and operatives proved masterful at organizing and appealing to voters. No village was too small for them to locate, hold a rally or parade, and line up voters for the general. Mass meetings were routinely arranged, and the size duly reported by the press not just in terms of numbers of people attending, but of acreage they covered. It was the first time in American politics that a substantial effort went into active mobilization of the electorate, and ways found to maximize the participation of everyday citizens during the campaign up to and including election day.

Of great importance to the campaign was the amount of printed material available on the candidates to the general public. It has been estimated that there were over fifteen hundred newspapers covering the campaign; Horace Greeley's *Log Cabin* had a weekly circulation rate of some eighty thousand copies. The papers were supplemented by a vast array of other printed material: circulars, pamphlets, newsletters, and the like. No citizen, and no voter, regardless of where they lived, was far removed from campaign-oriented literature in 1840.

Beneath all the hoopla and handbills and torchlight parades and rallies and sloganeering, were there any issues? Scarcely. The Whig convention at which Harrison was nominated specifically avoided drafting a platform. Throughout the campaign Harrison was told to follow the rules laid down by banker Nicholas Biddle: he should "say not one single word about his principles or his creed—let him say nothing—promise nothing."[25] In fact, of course, Whigs saw that their coalition was based on little but opposition to Van Buren. Any airing of policy choices would threaten it, and perhaps cost them the election.

In previous campaigns muzzling candidates was relatively simple, since they did not take to the hustings. But Harrison was trotted out before the public in part to convince citizens that his age was not a handicap, but also because showing the old war hero in public was good for rallying them behind him; this in fact was an essential ingredient to a "people's campaign." His first appearance was in Columbus, and he limited himself to platitudes. He seemed to like it, however, and his caravan moved on to other Ohio cities, where massive rallies and parades were scheduled in conjunction with his stump speech. He did not, however, bother with issues, nor did any of the other members of his entourage; this in spite of the fact that some of the rallies went on for hours.

Democrats were on the defensive throughout the campaign. They were completely outflanked by Whig strategy. Given Van Buren's reputation as a sybarite and snob, they could not portray their candidate as truly more democratic than Harrison (though, in fact, he was). Their efforts to debunk the log-cabin myth fell on deaf ears; it so rapidly became a part of popular culture that it achieved a life of its own completely apart from reality. They never could get out from under the charges and views of Van Buren current at the time, and expressed most vigorously by Congressman Charles Ogle: "How do you relish the notion of voting away the hard cash of your constituents" on "silk tassels, gallon, gimp and satin medallions to beautify and adorn the 'blue elliptical saloon' [in the White House]?"[26]

The attack on Van Buren and the Democrats was murderous. Whigs urged voters to place "their seal of condemnation upon a band of the most desperate, aspiring and unprincipled demagogues that ever graced the annals of despotism, a band of bold and reckless innovators calling themselves the democracy of the land, at whose head was Martin Van Buren, a monarchist in principle, a tyrant and despot in practice."[27]

Democrats even adopted some of the Whig strategy. While Van Buren did not campaign, they did bring a number of important Democrats out in front before the public, including Thomas Hart Benton and tired, sick Andrew Jackson in Tennessee. Even he bungled one of his appearances, however: he criticized Harrison's war record, which served to emphasize that Van Buren had none at all.

And Democrats threw verbal grenades at Harrison. They claimed the Whigs were an unholy alliance whose purpose was to exploit labor and poor people. Harrison, they said, was really "Old Tip-ler," a "sham hero," a blasphemer, and seducer of Indian women.[28] Perhaps the editors of the Philadelphia *Public Ledger* best summed up the Democratic view of Harrison and the whole Whig effort:

> The log cabin campaign was a "national drunken frolic" and a disgrace. The worst part of it was, said the *Ledger,* that many ladies went to the open-air meetings, strained their voices shouting "Huzza," drank hard cider from gourd shells, and devoured baked beans with their fingers from barrels. "Was this the proper sphere of women?" demanded the editor of the *Ledger.* "Was this appropriate to her elevating, refining influence? Did such things improve men? No. They merely degraded women, and made men still more degraded than they were before."[29]

Degraded or not, male voters chose Harrison in a landslide. He received 264 electoral college votes; Van Buren, only 60. Whigs won in Congress as well. It was the high-water mark for Whigs in America. Harrison died a month after the inauguration, and under Tyler (who was more southern than Whig) the coalition that had won the election immediately started coming undone. Indeed, the set of issues that underlay the campaign of 1840 but were not aired, namely national economic policy and the democratization of politics, largely disappeared in favor of those that ultimately rent the nation: national expansion and slavery.

As boisterous and even comical as was the 1840 presidential election, it proved important. In a sense, it was the first modern election, because it mobilized vast numbers of people throughout the nation, relied heavily on political organization (a characteristic it shared with the election of 1828), was heavily fought in the popular media, and deliberately created a candidate's image by recreating the facts and selling them as the truth.[30] It was even the first election in which the outgoing president received the winner from another party in the White House, and sought to improve the transition from one administration to the next.[31]

And it was a presidential election of remarkable negativity. True, some of what happened seemed funny at the time; certainly in retrospect much of it was comical. But there were bitterness, an avoidance of issues, and personal attacks of a vicious sort that underlay the hoopla and rowdiness. While both Harrison and Van Buren were gentlemen, the campaigns run by their followers, handlers, advisers, and organizers reflected none of their basic decency. So much for political gentlemanliness in 1840.

1884: Rum, Romanism, and Rebellion

Some analysts have argued that the 1884 presidential election between Democrat Grover Cleveland and Republican James G. Blaine was the nastiest in American history. If this is an overstatement, it is not by much. The mudslinging and character assassination and public questioning of the candidates' integrity may have been matched in other campaigns, but not exceeded. In the end, ethnic and religious bigotry—at play throughout the campaign, but front and center in its closing days—may well have made the difference in the final outcome.[32]

The Republican Party, in disarray that year, met in June to select its presidential candidate. Chester Arthur was the sitting president, but in spite of some significant accomplishments he had not managed to solidify his leadership of the party. A good deal of support—sentimental, as well as hardheaded political savvy—was behind James G. Blaine of Maine.

Blaine was a controversial figure. A founder of the Republican Party, he had served as Speaker of the U.S. House of Representatives. A man of considerable charisma, he was an obvious choice to become the eventual leader of the GOP. But in 1876 some letters came to light—the so-called Mulligan letters—demonstrating that Blaine had sold his influence to save some private railroad interests. Because of his obvious guilt—and in spite of the fact that he squarely faced up to the letters on the floor of the House of Representatives—the Republicans passed him up for the nomination in 1876 and again in 1880.

He retained considerable personal popularity, however, and was regarded as a power in the Republican Party. When his name was placed in nomination at the convention of 1884—the language used was, "the white plume of James G. Blaine, our Henry of Navarre"—delegates went crazy, and dumped Arthur for him. "A mass meeting of maniacs" was the way one periodical described the proceedings.[33]

The nomination split an already fragmented party. Prominent Republican intellectuals and reformers promptly abandoned ship, becoming known as "mugwumps," although some—such as the young Teddy Roosevelt—stayed loyal. Blaine's problem was that he could not shake the "character issue" even among his own party followers. Some regarded him as a great leader and man of destiny; others felt that while his private life was above reproach, his public reputation was so besmirched that he was unworthy of the nomination, let alone the office. Roscoe Conkling, a New York lawyer, Republican powerhouse, and rival of Blaine, when asked for his support replied, "I do not engage in criminal practice."[34]

The Democrats met in July, and found a candidate who had a meteoric rise in politics, and whose rock-solid personal honesty and integrity seemed just the antidote to Blaine. Grover Cleveland of Buffalo had been, in rapid succession, sheriff of Erie County, reform mayor of the city, and then reform governor of New York. Compared with Blaine he was dull and phlegmatic; but he was nobody's fool, was a very hard and honest worker, and refused to play politics as urban and party bosses wanted. "We love him for the enemies he has made," one convention delegate shouted, a direct comment on Tammany's opposition to him.[35] The *New York World* listed four reasons to support him: "1. He is an honest man; 2. He is an honest man; 3. He is an honest man; 4. He is an honest man."[36] Democrats began calling him "Grover the Good."

Immediately Democrats began to attack Blaine on the character issue. They were merciless. To make matters worse for Blaine, other letters came to light in which he had written to the broker who had handled the sale of some nearly worthless bonds he had supported, and included a draft of an exonerating letter that the broker's secretary was to copy and send back to him. On the draft, in Blaine's hand, was the telling phrase "Burn this letter."

The secretary did not burn it, and when Blaine's correspondence came to light Democrats howled. It was simply more fuel for the fires blackening Blaine's already tarnished reputation. They released the letters, calling Blaine "Slippery Jim," and made up ditties that were widely circulated and shouted at rallies:

> Burn this letter!
> Burn this letter!
> Burn, burn, oh, burn this letter!
>
> Blaine! Blaine!
> The Continental liar
> From the State of Maine!
> Burn this letter![37]

Things looked good for the Democrats until late July, when the *Buffalo Evening Telegraph* printed a story with a banner headline: "A Terrible Tale: A Dark Chapter in a Public Man's History."[38] It seems that Cleveland, a bachelor, had had an affair with a young widow named Maria Halpin, who had borne a child out of wedlock in 1874. Although other men were involved, Cleveland accepted responsibility and, while not proposing marriage, made financial arrangements for the child. Later, he helped arrange for its adoption after it had been placed in an orphanage.

Democrats were stunned. Characteristically, Cleveland insisted that the truth be told. Republicans—especially the clergy and editors—were jubilant, and repeatedly told the story of Cleveland's moral laxity. They even made up their own nasty chant, to counter the ones about Blaine: "Ma, Ma, Where's my pa? Gone to the White House, Ha! Ha! Ha!"[39]

Interestingly, however, within a short time the furor seemed to die down. Cleveland's candor was a refreshing contrast to Blaine's evasiveness and self-servingness.[40] But the public was confused and uncertain: one candidate had a spotless public life but had stained his private one; the other had a clean private record, but his public life was certainly not. One mugwump, after surveying the wreckage of both campaigns, seemed to speak for many when he concluded: "We should therefore elect Mr. Cleveland to the public office which he is so well qualified to fill and remand Mr. Blaine to the private station he is admirably fitted to adorn."[41] Lord Bryce, the great English student of American politics, was dumbfounded: the campaign, he said, was "over the copulative habits of one [candidate] and the prevaricative habits of the other."[42]

As the election neared, it was clear that New York would be the final battleground, and both candidates made major efforts in the Empire State. On Wednesday, October 29, just prior to election day, Blaine forces made not one but two colossal mistakes. They probably cost Blaine the presidency.

Early that morning, Blaine attended a rally in New York held by several hundred Protestant clergymen. The Reverend Samuel Burchard, waxing eloquent, ended his address with the now famous words, "We are Republicans, and don't propose to leave our party and identify ourselves with the party whose antecedents have been rum, Romanism, and rebellion."[43] It was a clear slap at the Irish, whose votes were up for grabs, and who seemed to hold the balance of power in New York.

Blaine, tired and distracted, apparently missed the significance of the remark. But a Democrat in attendance wrote it down, and immediately forwarded it to headquarters. Within hours Democratic handbills quoting the reverend were distributed throughout the city; later the slur appeared in the press. Blaine eventually disavowed the remark, but it was too late. The dark forces of prejudice and bigotry were already at work by the time he did.

That same evening Blaine attended an elegant dinner at Delmonico's, one of the swankiest restaurants in town. The occasion was a fund-raiser attended by Jay Gould, John Jacob Astor, Levi Morton, Cyrus Field, and other moguls of finance, business, and industry. It was a remarkably tasteless event, in view of the depression then wracking the nation. The Democratic press had a field day, calling it "the royal feast of Belshazzar Blaine and the money kings," and repeated similar views about it during the ensuing, and final, campaign week.[44]

Cleveland, on the other hand, stayed relatively quiet, but did make two speeches at rallies in Buffalo and New York City. The latter included a large parade that featured repeated chants of "Blaine, Blaine,

James G. Blaine, the Monumental Liar from the State of Maine."[45] On election day, Cleveland won New York in a plurality over Blaine by 1,149 votes, out of 1.2 million cast.

Did these egregious errors cost Blaine the election? They contributed heavily, as did the heavy rains on election day. The bolting of the mugwumps from the GOP was also critical to Blaine's defeat. Equally important was the failure of the Republicans—and to some extent the Democrats—to come to grips with the economic malaise in which the nation found itself.

But issues never played a role in this campaign. As one analyst noted, there was no incentive for either side to try to formulate firm policy positions. The issues of the day—labor unrest, farm problems, public lands, railroad and monopoly and trust regulation, tariff reform—were controversial and divisive.[46] The Democratic coalition behind Cleveland was at best tenuous. The Republicans, already fragmented at their convention, had great difficulty keeping their wheels on throughout the campaign because of the cloud surrounding Blaine.

Thus, neither campaign looked for issues. Instead, they found it more productive to wallow in dirt, innuendo, and slander. Voters, finding no substance, voted their partisan attachments, and gave the presidency to Cleveland, whose public character was stronger than Blaine's, and who in any case emerged from the mudslinging and character assassination slightly less brutalized than the white-plumed man from Maine.

The Cross of Gold: Presidential Politics, 1896

There were plenty of issues in 1896—farm prices, interest rates, business credit, monopoly and trust regulation—and they were again largely ignored during the presidential campaign. All of them together received scant attention relative to the single dominant issue of the election: monetary policy, in particular the free coinage of silver in contrast to strict adherence to the gold standard. And while the campaign became highly personalized, bitter, and acrimonious, and saw Republicans engage in strong-arm tactics of near fascistic intensity, even the negativity ultimately played second fiddle to the overriding, burning question of federal monetary policy. It was one of the few times in our history when a single issue dominated presidential electoral politics to the virtual exclusion, and subordination, of everything else.

William McKinley, governor of Ohio, was the Republican nominee that year. His nomination had been engineered by Mark Hanna, a wealthy industrialist from Cleveland who had become a powerhouse in the national Republican Party. He allegedly spent, by some estimates, over $100,000 of his own money to ensure that McKinley would be the nominee; but in fact there was much more to it than that, as Hanna had spent several years building coalitions in the party in support of his man.[47]

McKinley had considerable appeal as a presidential candidate. He even looked presidential. William Allen White wrote that McKinley "walked among men [like] a bronze statue . . . determinedly looking for his pedestal." [48] For much of his congressional career he had not advocated the gold standard; indeed, on some votes he sided with free silver. He was a trade protectionist, and actually had hoped that the tariff would become a major issue in the campaign. But his wishes and views didn't matter. Hanna and most of the other Republican leaders—especially those from the East—insisted on a gold-standard plank in the party platform. Some Republicans from the West walked out, and when they did, the GOP position was sealed: retention of the gold standard meant a tight money policy, one not favored by either the South or the West, which wanted an easing of credit and an inflationary monetary policy brought about by free coinage of silver.[49]

Democrats met in St. Louis a month after the Republicans. They had become disenchanted with their sitting president, Grover Cleveland.[50] But they were confused as to where they should turn. Part of the Democratic problem was the increasing popularity of the Populists; since their first convention on July 4, 1892, a wave of enthusiasm for them had swept the country. Meeting in St. Louis four years later, Democrats knew they had to come to grips with this growing western and southern threat; but they were unsure of what to do, especially as the party was split over the free-silver issue. Who the nominee would be was uncertain prior to the convention's opening gavel.

But all became clear when William Jennings Bryan took the podium and delivered his now famous "Cross of Gold" speech. It was an electrifying moment, one that irrevocably committed Democrats to free silver, found them a nominee and a hero, and set the stage for a vigorous, and vicious, campaign. It also was the death knell for Populism as an independent political force; Populists had been completely coopted by the Democrats.[51]

Republicans were actually caught off guard by Bryan's nomination.[52] They had anticipated a campaign in which they could heap scorn on the Cleveland administration and advocate higher tariffs as the vehicle for economic recovery. But since the Democrats had repudiated their own administration, obviously they had to take a different tack. Democratic-Populist insistence on free silver gave them the opening they needed. McKinley, who was prepared to discuss tariffs and downplay the gold/silver issue, suddenly found himself the center of a one-issue campaign in which he didn't fully believe but the people around him, including Hanna, thought was gospel.

More than that, Hanna and the Republican chieftains thought Bryan was a dangerous radical. They attacked him without mercy; no quarter was spared. Socialist, anarchist, communist, revolutionary, lunatic, madman, rabble-rouser, thief, traitor, murderer were just a few of the terms used. The *New York Times* called him "an irresponsible, unregulated, ignorant, prejudiced, pathetically honest and enthusiastic crank." The *New York Tribune* said he was a "wretched, rattle-pated boy, posing in vapid vanity and mouthing resounding rottenness;" in fact, much was made of Bryan's youth (at 36, he was the youngest nominee for president up to that time) during the campaign, none of it complimentary. He was even shown in cartoons as a mere baby. The *Philadelphia Press* thought his followers were "hideous and repulsive vipers."[53]

But this vicious and vituperative name-calling would have had less effect if it had not been accompanied by a well-conceived campaign engineered and directed by Mark Hanna. He understood better than most that the gold/silver issue was really a front for much more fundamental cleavages in American life: economic clashes between the haves and have-nots, sectional ones pitting the West and South against the East, and questions of the basic values and direction of American life as contrasted between agrarianism and the industrial excesses of the Gilded Age. For Hanna, then, the contest was not just between McKinley and Bryan, or even between the gold standard and free silver; it was about the type of nation the United States would become in the century soon to dawn. More pragmatically, it was also about the type of policies to be pursued in Washington: would the government continue to allow big business, big industry, and big banks to load their coffers, or was government to become redistributive, interventionist, and an opponent of capital?

Accordingly, Hanna threw his considerable energies into convincing voters that the way of Bryan was the road to disaster. Part of his effort was purely symbolic: never before in American political life had so many gewgaws been produced for a campaign. Plastic campaign buttons were invented just before it started; Hanna and the Republicans produced hundreds of varieties, and they numbered in the millions.[54] But there was more, to remind voters of the importance of gold to America: tons of gold elephants, gold bugs, gold hats, gold sheaves of wheat, anything gold to remind people of its importance to civilization.[55]

More important than the paraphernalia was the organization of the campaign. Hanna had Bryan followed everywhere, no small chore considering that the silver-tongued Nebraskan crossed the country four times by rail, traveled thousands of miles, and made more than six hundred speeches.[56] Every time he turned around, however, there was a group of Republicans to "set the record straight" following his appearance. Other speakers were dispatched to counter the Democratic-Populist message.

In addition, Hanna sent out over one hundred million pieces of campaign mail, and produced a great deal of other printed publicity. It was not the first time by any means that mail and publicity had been used in a presidential campaign, but no one had ever seen them used on such a scale before. Even Hanna's parades were bigger than those before: just before the election he arranged for 150,000 "solid citizens"—businessmen, industrialists, clergymen, bankers—to march up New York's Broadway in a "sound money" march; they all wore sober black. Readers might recall that in 1884 a parade of 40,000 in the city for Cleveland was considered a huge throng.

There was a dark side to all this. To pay for his campaign, Hanna used extortion and other strong-arm tactics. He personally shook down major Wall Street corporations for campaign contributions; the fee was a quarter percent of their profits; Standard Oil alone "contributed" $250,000 to the Republican war chest. Those who tried to get off cheap he called a "lot of God-damn sheep." Hanna himself estimated that he raised about $3 million this way; others said the total was closer to $16 million.[57]

Moreover, he encouraged employers to make clear to their workers what the consequences of a Bryan victory would be. Some even put warnings in pay envelopes: "If Bryan is elected, do not come back to work. This plant will be closed."[58] Bankers told farmers and small-business men that mortgages would be foreclosed and loans called if Bryan were victorious.

All of this was frightening to working men and women. But it was not surprising that Hanna took this tack: he, after all, once had told a politician that "no man in public life owes the public anything."[59] While he was in some ways a kind and even generous man in his private life, public-interest considerations did not motivate him when pushing his political agenda.

Bryan chose not to respond, but kept pounding on the need for eased credit and free coinage of silver; the message stirred the masses, but Bryan could not alleviate their unease. McKinley, for his part, stayed on the porch in Canton. He received delegates of citizens and other groups, whose public remarks had been previously approved by Republican headquarters. McKinley's own public comments were also studiously rehearsed; mostly he talked about the "full dinner pail."

In the end, Hanna simply wore Bryan down. He could not translate his charisma and excitement into victory; the Republican campaign was too negative, and had far too many resources, for him to counter it successfully. Still, Bryan received over 6.5 million popular votes, and lost by a mere 95 in the electoral college (271–176). He would not do so well again in 1900, when he and McKinley once more did battle.

3

Distilling History:
Lessons from Past Campaigns

What can we learn from the preceding chapter? Do these historical examples have anything to do with modern political campaigning?

If we return to the question with which we began Chapter 2, we can readily see that the point has been well established: mudslinging in campaigns is indeed a part of the American political tradition. It may not be one of which citizens are especially proud, but to suggest that the extent or quality of negativity in contemporary campaigns represents a departure from the past is erroneous.

We can also conclude that, based on these examples, mudslinging and other forms of negative campaigning have been functional—it seems to have worked. In not every case did the side throwing the most dirt win: Andrew Jackson in 1828 probably took more abuse than did John Quincy Adams, although both were badly smeared, and in any case it is hard to measure the quantity flung from a distance of 170 years. On the other hand, mudslinging proved to be an effective campaign tactic in these instances, and certainly when one side threw and the other did not—as in 1896—the throwers won. Perhaps McKinley would have won anyway—the depression was ending, the economy was improving, and foreign affairs were beginning to reshape the American political agenda—but Bryan's failure to respond to the repeated attacks against him, or to return the charges in kind, undoubtedly hurt his chances.

Are there other lessons to be learned from these early campaigns? Let us look briefly at a number of relevant aspects of the campaigns, for they will serve as introduction to some key matters to be discussed in later chapters.

Issues

Issues—defined as a concern with public questions—were present in all campaigns. To put the matter another way, in none of the campaigns were important issues missing. Indeed, in most of the campaigns—perhaps 1884 was an exception—the issues in the campaign were truly monumental. In most cases, they constituted what we might call "watershed" issues, those that define the political identity of the nation, and shape (or reshape) its future course.

We need scarcely revisit the campaigns to justify this point. The campaigns of 1800, 1828, and 1840 each dealt, fundamentally, with the distribution of power in American democracy, the growth of the party system, and popular participation in politics. There were other, less abstract issues as well: civil liberties, foreign relations, defense, monetary policy. Economic policy also enveloped the campaign of 1884 (although, in truth, it was hard to find), but it was explicit in 1896.

Two points need to be made about the presence of issues in these fundamentally negative campaigns. One, they constituted a part of political discussion; both participants and the public as a whole were aware of a public agenda and the existence of public concerns. In other words, the campaigns—understood as candidates, organizations, hoopla and activity, and voters—recognized that issues existed as part of the campaign, not something removed from them.

The problem was—and this is the second point—that issues were submerged under mud. They seldom, if ever, came to the fore. If they did, they became a medium of negative campaigning, a way of attacking the opposition not from a cognitive or an intellectual standpoint, but from their utility as a means of slinging dirt.

Chapter 5 will deal specifically with issues in campaigns. In it we will be able to make a number of observations about how issues are used in campaigns, and the circumstances under which they stand on their own during the campaign, or are used as part of a fundamentally negative campaign strategy.

For now, let us point out what is often forgotten: that issues can and may well be present even when campaigns seem mired in mud and unable to rise above character assassination. But campaign participants may sometimes sense and understand that they can attract greater support among the public by a strategy that resembles a street fight more than a national, rational debate over policy alternatives, and will behave and speak accordingly.

There is one additional point to which we must allude now, but will pursue at length later: the potentially divisive impact of issues. In at least two of the campaigns studied—1840 and 1884—strategists of at least one of the parties involved recognized that the success of their candidates hinged upon maintaining a working, reasonably cohesive coalition. They also understood that resounding articulation of positions on key issues of the day could threaten the stability of those coalitions. Better, therefore, to say nothing, or to engage in platitudes that would offend no one. Issues then become subsumed in self-interested coalition politics.

Sloganeering

Slogans can provide a kind of substitute for issues. Their appeal is anything but cognitive. Often little more than ditties or catchphrases, they nonetheless can invoke (or provoke) feelings, and convey images, emotional symbols, and messages. As such, then, they are an important instrument through which campaigns seek to attract voters, or attack opponents.

They were widely used in the campaigns cited. It may be that in the nineteenth century slogans were especially important, because literacy rates were relatively low and knowledge of public affairs limited. Slogans, then, were a substitute for discussion of complex information. They gave voters readily understandable cues that helped them determine in whose corner they stood, even if they were uncertain or ignorant of specific policy issues.

The most famous of the slogans was undoubtedly "Tippecanoe, and Tyler Too." In one quick, catchy phrase it invoked a glorious past, firm leadership, military service and heroism, anti-Indian sentiment, the West, and the South, both of which were needed by the Whigs to beat Van Buren. The fact that most of the slogan was built on excessive historical revisionism was irrelevant. It sounded good and had the ring of truth. Nothing the Democrats could come up with rivaled the effectiveness of this slogan.

But in other elections the Democrats had good ones of their own. There were several about Jackson ("Old Hickory" was about as effective as "Tippecanoe"), and the attack slogans against Blaine in 1884 were merciless. Probably their best, though, was Bryan's "cross of gold" slogan in 1896, which provoked an extraordinary Republican effort to counter it.

This latter point is important. Not all slogans are devoid of substance. Brief and simplistic, they nonetheless can suggest something of policy direction, possibly even of content. The "cross of gold" was a marvelous slogan in that it captured, at once, religious symbols and emotions, martyrdom, Christian ideals—and a clear difference in policy orientation between Populist-Democrats and Republicans. Not all slogans reach such heights, but others do come close: Franklin Delano Roosevelt's "New Deal" and Harry Truman's "Square Deal" suggest something of rebuilding the policy process to include new, more equitable outcomes; John F. Kennedy's "New Frontier" and Lyndon Johnson's "Great Society" suggest bold new directions in government.

In fact, slogans and contemporary sound bites have a good deal in common. Much of what we said about slogans also applies to this relatively new, electronic method of conveying candidate information to voters. It may well be, then, that if the medium really is the message, the contemporary sound bite is little more than a continuation of the well-established nineteenth- and twentieth-century practice of political sloganeering.

Personality

The campaigns we have looked at were fundamentally personality based. This means that the character and style of the candidates was the primary focus of the campaigns. Other considerations, such as issues, or partisanship, played second fiddle.

But to say that the campaigns were personality based is the beginning of the question, not the end of it. What exactly does this mean? If we look more closely at the campaigns, we can see that "personality" actually has several components.

It certainly referred to qualifications for office. For the most part, any such discussion was of a disparaging nature. In each of the campaigns, very serious doubt was cast on whether one's opponent had the credentials to serve as president: this even included vicious attacks on sitting presidents (John Adams, John Quincy Adams, and Van Buren), as well as one of the chief American demigods, Jefferson; obviously many of his contemporaries did not hold him in the near reverential status he enjoys today.

Another set of attacks was to raise questions about what the opponent would be like as president should he win. Again, the idea of these assaults was to frighten the voters into thinking that the person in question was dangerous. Jefferson, Jackson, and Bryan particularly had to cope with these charges.

A third dimension to personality-based campaigns was pure character assassination. There seems no other way to describe the assaults of this nature. They were broadsides against the very soul of the candidate in question. Indeed, it is fair to say that in the examples cited above, virtually every campaign (with the possible exception of Bryan's) shelled the other side with such disparaging remarks that one would think that they viewed each other as the devil incarnate.

Indeed, what is perhaps most remarkable about the personality base of these campaigns, at least to the modern ear, is the language that was used to describe opponents. It was inflammatory, vitriolic, intemperate, caustic, unsparing. Even family members of the candidates were attacked in this way, as Jackson's wife and Van Buren's daughter-in-law found out. A brief perusal over the previous case studies reveals language that would not be used today, and which (while undoubtedly hurtful), did not strike anyone as especially odd: atheist, blasphemer, bastard, fool, criminal, hypocrite, murderer, are only a few of the terms that were employed to characterize one's opponent, and they were employed not just by hatchet men and party functionaries, but by candidates and their senior advisers. By contrast, today's political language—"Hey Buddy, you're a liberal"—pales.[1]

Why this is true is a matter of speculation. Slander and libel laws existed in the nineteenth century, but they were not even invoked, let alone enforced. Politics may well have been a wilder sport then than it is today. Inflammatory language—especially since only men could vote—may have been more socially acceptable. Certainly if the object was to bring attention to one's campaign, heaping scorn viciously on the opponent might help accomplish this. And there is no doubt that the onset of the electronic media—radio, and later television—forced a tempering of language, because of legal requirements and cultural norms of acceptability.

Whatever the reasons, there is no doubt that negative campaigns earlier in our history included language that boggles the contemporary imagination—and leaves ears ringing. At least on this point, then, we might conclude that old-time campaigns may well have been "worse" than modern ones.

Dirty Tricks

For many political observers, Watergate—the burglary of Democratic national headquarters in 1972—was the ultimate campaign dirty trick. Perhaps it was. That is not our concern here. What is important, rather, is that campaign dirty tricks have been part of our political tradition for a long time. They certainly figured prominently in presidential electoral politics long before anyone had heard of Watergate.

This is not a justification of or rationalization for campaign dirty tricks. They lie outside the pale of accepted rules—legal and normative—for campaign activity. They generally show contempt not just for law and social mores, but for political institutions and human beings. Dirty tricks cannot be morally justified.

They are, however, understandable. To return to a theme developed in the first chapter, politics is a serious, and sometimes deadly, business. When the stakes are as high as the presidency, each side looks to find whatever advantage it can in order to secure this ultimate political prize. Dirty tricks may well be a result. Indeed, the interesting point is not that dirty tricks have been utilized in pursuit of the presidency, but that they have not been employed as much as they might have, or as often and intensively as is found in some other countries. Perhaps there is an ultimate respect for law, institutions, and "the rules of the game" that governs all but the most amoral politicians and their supporters in this country.

In our examples, two kinds of dirty tricks stand out; both have contemporary analogues. Lies and fabrications is one; strong-arm tactics is the other.

Lies and fabrications are different from distortions or half-truths. The latter are incomplete or slanted views of reality, generally designed to make one side look good, and the other bad. Lies and fabrications are an attempt to create a reality that has no basis in fact. It is a deliberate attempt to deceive and mislead voters by attempting to create disagreeable—but credible—facts about one's opponent. Presumably, the bigger the lie, the more credibility it might have. That the lies show the perpetrators' contempt for both the opponent and the voter is seldom noticed.

Some lies and fabrications were more silly than anything else; attempts to make John Adams and John Quincy Adams into progenitors of a monarchy, and to paint Van Buren as a dandy, may have been effective campaign weapons, but did not reach depths of immorality.

Others were more serious. Jefferson was declared dead by some Federalists, at a time when communication was slow, and Republicans had great difficulty convincing legislators that he was still alive. Had Federalists succeeded, the outcome of the election—and American history—might have been different. Lies against Jackson's wife and the circumstances of their marriage truly hit below the belt. Assaults on the moral fiber of both Adamses—based wholly on fabrications concerning women—were of a similar level of indecency. The attacks against the character of both Blaine and Cleveland, while vaguely based on facts, went so far beyond reality that they were little more than lies and fabrications. And Bryan—a young man—had relatively little experience or record in public life; yet he was made into a monster who would bring disaster to America.

The interesting point about these lies and fabrications is the currency they had, and the credibility they achieved. Voters had very few if any independent sources of information to verify or disprove the allegations. Candidates and supporters continually repeated the stories. Campaign materials hammered away at them. The nineteenth-century press was far more partisan and slanted than today's press is in its campaign coverage; the media helped start and spread the falsehoods. Today, this is not the case; while the media do (perhaps unwittingly) spread untruths, both print and electronic journalists have as a major goal sorting out truth from fabrications, and are not hesitant to say so to their readers and viewers.

Are lies and fabrications still a part of campaigns, even at the presidential level? The most obvious example was 1972, when stories abounded that George McGovern, the Democratic candidate, advocated a thousand-dollar cash payment to citizens. It had no basis in fact, but served further to undermine confidence in an already doomed campaign. More recent presidential campaigns have lacked such overt fabrications; perhaps the watchdog media have served to prevent their dissemination. On the other hand, recent campaigns have witnessed distortions and half-truths front and center, and these have served in their own way to create a substantially negative aura about the campaigns. One wonders, for example, if the charges and countercharges Bob Dole and Bill Clinton made about each other's statements on Medicare, Social Security, and welfare reform during the 1996 campaign went beyond distastefulness into the realm of lies and fabrications.

The other type of dirty trick mentioned was strong-arm tactics. It was most notably used in the 1896 campaign, when Hanna overtly extorted money for the Republican war chest from Wall Street corporations. Intimidation of voters was also prominent in that election over the possible consequences of a Bryan victory.

Egregious raiding of corporate profits for political purposes is no longer permissible under federal and state campaign finance laws. On the other hand, there is a modern version, which we shall pursue in Chapter 7: political action committees (PACs), through which not only corporations but a host of other organizations are able to throw large amounts of funds at their candidates of choice. Moreover, the opposite situation sometimes obtains: PACs feel extorted by candidates, who insist on a contribution in order to ensure "access" once the election is over. In addition, candidates for office often create special "clubs" that the rich and powerful are "invited" to join; the entry fee is normally the maximum campaign contribution permitted under law. Also, while the publicity attendant upon overt or heavy-handed efforts by corporations, unions, or other groups to bully and cajole members or employees into supporting one candidate over another might prove embarrassing, only a political ostrich would pretend that more subtle, or at least less muscular, efforts do not exist at present.

Political Organization and Popular Participation

Even before political parties existed as recognizable entities in American politics, organization was crucial for seeking the presidency. The election of 1800 can best be viewed as a series of factional movings and shakings, as Jefferson, Burr, Adams, and Hamilton all maneuvered their followings into positions of advantage, or formed (and abandoned) factional coalitions as was needed.

By 1828 parties were well established, but it was in this election that they came of age as mechanisms or instruments for building popular support on behalf of presidential candidates. It was in this campaign, readers will recall, that Democrats used their organization—and money—to seek out prospective voters and persuade them to vote for their candidate, Jackson. Given Old Hickory's reputation and image, and the floundering administration of John Quincy Adams, a man almost completely devoid of popular appeal, the task was a manageable one. Still, the point is that in this race, for the first time, political organization in the form of a party—not a personal, factional following—became the critical mechanism for creating popular support and a winning vote total.

The election of 1840—"Tippecanoe and Tyler Too"—finished what 1828 began. We noted that 1828 popularized the presidency, as well as presidential elections. The campaign of 1840 saw the most extraordinary efforts up to that time to actively engage the population in the campaign, hence, to influence the outcome of the election. Parades, rallies, speeches, events, hoopla, bunkum: P.T. Barnum understood all of this perfectly, and so did the Whigs. Excitement and image—even if they had to be invented—got people involved. Issues were of much less importance, sometimes (as in 1840) none at all.

Political scientists also understand the nature of this activity. Long ago E.E. Schattschneider noted that the outcome of a political conflict—and campaigns certainly qualify—can generally be predicted, and understood, by finding out which side controls its scope.[2] In other words, controlling who is involved and what kinds and levels of resources are brought to bear in the dispute will largely determine how it turns out.

Both the Democrats in 1828 and the Whigs in 1840 understood this principle well. In both cases the winning strategies were predicated upon controlling the scope of conflict; in both cases, the idea was to enlarge the extent of popular participation by using party organization to identify likely voters, get them excited, and persuade (or induce) them to vote for their respective candidate.

The mechanisms by which this was done may strike the modern reader, and perhaps the modern political pro, as quaint. Hickory sticks, pictures of Jackson on a white horse, portable log cabins carried in rallies, giant balls rolled from one village to the next, hard cider: it's the stuff of a Currier and Ives print.

But underneath all of this early Americana lies a crucial point: the purpose of this activity was for the candidates and their parties to seek ways of controlling the scope of conflict, that is, who forms the candidate's and party's constituency, and therefore should be encouraged to participate, and who does not? Who is undecided, and might be persuaded? Who is on the other side, where do they live, and should they be ignored, courted, or discouraged?

These are precisely the same questions that underlie the modern campaign. Indeed, no campaign can possibly be successful if they are not carefully addressed from day one, and continually reexamined throughout the duration.

True, there are some crucial differences. Perhaps the most important is that the linkage between candidate and party is no longer as tight as it was. There are many reasons for this, involving the changing nature of American parties, the "personalization" of campaigns, and the need for candidates to create their own campaign organizations since they no longer can rely on the parties. This is a large topic that extends beyond the scope of this book.[3] Also, the mechanisms through which campaigns seek answers to the questions posed are different, and much more sophisticated, than they were in the early and mid–nineteenth century: market research, polling, focus groups all provide tools and information to candidates not even envisioned by political operatives 150 years ago. And there are far more possibilities, and opportunities, in the contemporary media for getting candidate messages out to the public, tailoring them to specific audiences, and controlling the speed and timing of those messages, than existed earlier. Indeed, the modern media, especially television, forge the linkage between the candidate and campaign and the voters closer and more intimately than it was during the nineteenth century.

Though this point has been made, the link between political organization (whether party or candidate centered) and control of the extent of political participation remains strong. It was certainly still true in 1896—Hanna's problem was to ensure that he kept the scope of popular conflict under control by intimidating corporations and frightening voters about the consequences of a Bryan victory. Bryan, using his charismatic personal appeal, tried valiantly to expand the scope of conflict beyond what Hanna and the Republicans wanted, but in spite of his personal magnetism he lacked the resources—and political organization—to pull it off.

And the link remains strong today. To take a very modern example of a presidential campaign in which issues played almost no role, 1988 can also be viewed as a contest between rival political candidates and organizations seeking to control the extent and scope of popular participation. George Bush continued the Reagan-Republican strategy of appealing to white middle- and upper-middle-class voters, and disaffected white Democrats (many of whom were blue-collar, lower-middle-class white-collar, and ethnic voters). He did so by concentrating on the popular themes of "family values," simple-minded American patriotism, the modern version of the full dinner pail (economic times were still good in 1988); by successfully painting his opponent Michael Dukakis in negative terms as not embodying or even caring about these feel-good themes; by calling his public record into account; and (to cement the whole enterprise) by condoning a television advertisement that had the effect of frightening people by featuring a fearsome-looking convicted black criminal, thereby arousing people's racial fears and concerns over their safety. It was a masterpiece of controlling the scope of conflict and defining who the participants in the contest would be. The Democrats never came close to countering the Republican strategy, but instead found that, wherever they looked, Republicans had already corralled constituencies which they needed, and whom they were not about to turn loose.[4]

Media, Publicity, and Popular Participation

The historical examples also document the heavy reliance placed even by early campaigns on the media and other forms—some printed, some not—of publicity. The printed word, in particular, was a crucial mechanism of spreading information about candidates, building support or opposition, publicizing issues (if there were any), and in general reminding citizens of "campaign season" and their need to attend, at least in some ways, to matters political.

Prior to radio and television, there were of course no real electronic media. By the middle of the nineteenth century telegraphs were in wide use, and by the end of the century telephones were becoming common in cities, although in general they were limited to businesses and wealthy citizens. Thus, the printed media became a primary source of news and information to most citizens about political campaigns.

What may strike the modern reader as odd is the considerable variety and number of printed media in the nineteenth century. Even early, when illiteracy and functional illiteracy rates were high, printed materials were common. Not only were there newspapers and tabloids, but political pamphlets, broadsides, posters, banners, mailings, and flyers were in wide use. It is worth remembering that as early as 1840 there were some fifteen hundred newspapers alone—many of them weeklies— covering the presidential campaign. They were not limited to large cities, but could be found even in relatively rural hamlets and villages. They were accompanied by a host of other types of printed material to such an extent that it has been argued that few people, regardless of where they lived or their degree of literacy, did not have access to printed information on the candidates and campaigns.[5] Mark Hanna, of course, became the nineteenth-century master at using the mass media, including mailings: in 1896 over one hundred million pieces of printed campaign stuff were produced in order to sell McKinley to the public, or to warn it against the dangers of Bryan. Figures like these are shockingly modern.

Newspapers and magazines during the period of the examples cited served a different purpose than they do today, and of course the way in which they conveyed news and information was significantly different. They were far more partisan than today, and overtly so. They carried their points of view and biases proudly and publicly. The news and information they provided was designed as much to persuade—one way or the other—as to inform. They may well have been more obsessed with sleaze and scandal than today's journalistic organs, with the exception of supermarket tabloids. "Investigative reporting," a hallmark of today's professional journalists, was essentially unknown, except to the extent that it served a partisan purpose, especially if it uncovered something unsavory about the paper or magazine's opponents.

None of this should obscure the importance of the media during nineteenth-century political campaigns. It may have significantly influenced the type of materials and sets of facts available to voters about candidates and issues. Media may well have sought to overtly manipulate the voter by playing more heavily on emotions than intellect. Having said all this, however, for people who could (or would) not attend a campaign rally or hear a political speech, the printed media were the primary source of political information.[6]

In a later chapter we shall look more closely at the relationship between the media and the modern political campaign. Let us note for the moment, however, that contemporary campaigns rely heavily on the media—although now most especially television—to publicize the virtues of their candidate and the weaknesses of the opposition. Indeed, in some recent California campaigns, well over 90 percent of candidates' time has been spent raising funds for buying media spots; virtually all other traditional aspects of campaigning, such as mailings and personal appearances, have taken a back seat to this critical function.

In addition, campaigns seek to manipulate the media to create "free" coverage on television. News conferences, photo opportunities, press releases, "making news" are all mechanisms whereby candidates and campaigns seek to entice members of the media to report a "story," thereby sparing the expense of yet another paid commercial. If done successfully, moreover, the story will be reported on the campaign's terms (as is a paid commercial or spot), rather than risking the possibility that the reporter will frame the story in terms unfriendly or unflattering to the candidate.

We have already noted the importance of nonprinted forms of publicity that were generated during the nineteenth century for campaigns. Torchlight and daylight parades, rallies (including those in which attendance was reported in acreage covered), campaign appearances, speeches, festivals and fairs: the list of publicity gimmicks designed, created, and organized to attract voters became extensive.

Events of this kind are still used today, although on a more limited scale. Television is simply too important at the presidential level, and even in many state or districtwide races, to waste candidate time on campaign appearances. On the other hand, they continue to be an important part of local political activity as a cheap, and personal, means of bringing candidates in close contact with voters. Also, local traditions, customs, and styles often demand that candidates participate in events that have achieved almost ritualistic status. Woe be it to the candidate for governor (or mayor) of New York who is not seen riding the subways, or the Florida politician who does not show up at a major fish fry. And of course these "events" can be turned into photo opportunities for the media, or even taped and used creatively on television ads. Thus, events will continue to be a part of political activity, most especially if they can serve as a springboard for wider forms of electronic or printed publicity.

It must also be remembered that contemporary use of the media is designed to help influence the extent and scope of popular participation. The overtly partisan printed media of the nineteenth century catered to very specific audiences. So do today's media—both electronic and printed. Through marketing techniques, polling, and other forms of voter analysis it is possible to target messages to very particular segments of the population, and to use appropriate media vehicles to zero in on precisely the right mix of the population needed to secure votes, and avoid those who are hostile or indifferent. Radio and television audiences, newspaper and magazine readerships, mass mailing lists can all be tailored with remarkable specificity to reach, and touch, the right campaign constituencies, and to avoid those that are not appropriate. In a very real sense, then, use of the media has become much more efficient, and more effective, than it was; but the basic roots of media importance and utilization in early campaigns can still be seen today.

Money

Money drives political campaigns. In a later chapter we shall examine more fully the relationship between money and campaign outcomes. We will be concerned not just with the amount of money—does the candidate with the most win?—but the sources as well. This question is important because it not only has implications for the candidates, especially the winner, but for our democratic system.

But there are several important points we need to address here. The most obvious is how quickly in our political history large sums of money were spent on presidential campaigns. The 1828 election, it will be recalled, was the first in which efforts were made to expand the pool of Democratic voters to include "everyday" men; previously, expanding popular participation, by either party, was not a part of campaign activity. It was therefore no accident that 1828 was the first election in which one of the candidates—Jackson—raised and spent more than a million dollars on his campaign.

By the standards of the day, this was an extraordinary amount of money. The Louisiana Purchase of 1803 was, by comparison, $15 million. Construction of the Erie Canal, finished in 1825, cost $7 million.[7] The entire expenditure of the U.S. Postal Service in 1828 was only $1.7 million; the administrative budget of the federal government in that same year was but $16.3 million.[8]

Political commentators of the day were not unaware of the significance of the amount of money that the Jacksonians had thrown at the presidency. As there was no requirement at that time to report either the origins or the disposition of the funds, speculation was rife as to how such a considerable sum had been raised, and what the political consequences would be; this became even more of an issue when it was clear that Jackson's support—and presumably the source of the funds—was in the South and West. Even at this early date one hears the first stirrings of what has become in the late twentieth century a serious problem, namely the cost of a presidential campaign, and the pounds of flesh that big donors and other "fat cats" might extract from the winning candidate.

In the 1896 campaign, money once again became not only the vehicle for success (in this case, for the Republicans), but also an issue in itself. While it is unclear exactly how much money Hanna extorted from Wall Street and other corporate and capitalist sources, a figure of $10 million may well be conservative, and this was by no means the only money available to the campaign. To put this figure in perspective, it is true that by 1896 the federal budget had grown considerably—it was $352 million that year.[9] But the actual cost of living in 1896 had fallen below that of 1828; the consumer price index for 1896 was 25, while in 1828 it was 33.[10] Many industrial and commercial products cost a good deal less in 1896 than they did in 1828.

Thus, the moneys which Hanna had at his disposal for the 1896 campaign were at least as significant as those which the Jacksonians had sixty-eight years earlier. Can we therefore conclude that in each case the parties were able, respectively, to "buy" the presidency for their candidates? In other words, holding all other factors constant— the quality and style of the candidates, public opinion, issues, quality and record of opposition—does the vast amount of money these campaigns had at their disposal account for the victory of their candidates?

This is assuredly as crucial a question today as it was then. It has achieved even greater salience with the rapid rise in the cost of campaigns (presidential and other) in recent decades. And with the emergence of Ross Perot as a major independent presidential candidate— one who has pledged more than $100 million of his own money to foster his candidacy[11]—the question can further be asked whether or not available campaign moneys have simply squeezed out all other factors as determinative of the outcome of presidential and other elections.

It is necessary to ask the reader's patience, for we will deal with these crucial issues in Chapter 7. For now, however, we must observe that on the basis of the historical evidence, money was indeed crucial in the victories of Jackson and McKinley—but so were other factors, including the politically wise use of the funds, overall campaign strategy, shifting public opinion, and disaffection with the other candidates in part as a result of the negative campaigns directed against them.

Length of Campaigns

A frequent criticism of modern political campaigns is that they last too long. The result is not just added cost, but increased boredom to members of the public, who have other demands on their time, and whose tolerance for politics is not great anyway. If, the reasoning goes, campaigns didn't last so long, there might be more incentive for candidates to focus on issues in an effort to get their message across to voters, and less incentive to spend valuable, limited time slinging mud.

A corollary to this view is that candidates themselves must spend great portions of their life gearing up to run for public office, often at the expense of other important aspects of their lives, such as doing their current job or attending to family, instead of focusing on their next race. This comment is especially heard in conjunction with presidential elections; preparation times of four to five years are common, and eight or more years not unusual.

The validity of these claims is open to question. Stephen Hess, for example, has persuasively argued that since no other office or experience in American public life is in any way similar to the presidency, the lengthy and arduous road to the White House is not only good training for the job, but candidates' behavior along the way provides some indication of how they might perform if victorious.[12] It has also been observed that in other countries, where formal campaigning is limited to a certain time period, campaigns are not necessarily any more issue oriented, or less personality based, than ours are. Moreover, other critics point out that those seeking the presidency, our most important public office, ought to be single-minded in their pursuit of it. The office demands that level of commitment, and certainly for the winning candidate there will be virtually no other life during his tenure in the White House. The presidency is all-consuming, demanding full and undivided attention; presidents do not get evenings and weekends off.

These positions have been debated back and forth, and probably will continue to be debated. What is of interest here is that even in the nineteenth century the pursuit of the presidency took years (with no guarantee of success going to the longest pursuer), and the campaigns themselves were lengthy.

A few facts from our previous discussion will underscore these statements. Jackson spent four years planning revenge against John Quincy Adams and the "corrupt bargain" that had cost him the presidency; much of the time was spent not in sulking or fulminating, but in sophisticated planning, strategizing, organizing, and fund-raising. Hanna also had a carefully devised, years-long plan to get McKinley nominated and elected; indeed, when convention time came in 1896, his carefully devised scheme on behalf of McKinley was like an unstoppable juggernaut.

That the length of time a candidate puts into pursuit of the office does not always pay off is borne out by Henry Clay. He was the nineteenth-century version of Harold Stassen.[13] Perhaps no one with a possible claim on the presidency ever tried harder than Clay to become president, with less success. He was an active candidate in 1824, 1832, and 1844, and waited in the wings during the in-between years. He was influential in determining candidacies and outcomes of presidential elections. But he never made it to the White House— only once, in 1844, did he come particularly close, in fact—in spite of his visibility, prominence, and twenty-year active campaign for the office.[14]

And, to conclude the point, the campaigns themselves were lengthy, lasting months and months. Even in the Adams-Jefferson battle the campaign went on for many months because of the role state legislatures played in selecting electors; these had to be carefully cultivated over time. Jackson, as noted, campaigned for four years until he was successful. In the later elections of 1884 and 1896, there was little public campaigning prior to the party conventions (especially in the party of a sitting president). But there was a great deal of maneuvering and coalition building, as well as efforts to discredit possible opposition, by mudslinging if necessary. Moreover, as is the case today, the party conventions were held during midsummer, and while September and October saw the most vigorous public campaigning, in fact the candidates took to the hustings virtually the moment the conventions broke camp. In this sense, then, the length of these campaigns was very similar to the modern presidential campaign.

Public Reaction to Campaigns

What did the public think of the campaigns we have investigated? Were they disgusted? amused? bored? persuaded by what they saw and heard? Perhaps we don't know as much as we would like about what everyday people in the nineteenth century thought of the mudslinging and character assassination that permeated at least these campaigns.

On the other hand, some things are clear. Especially in our first three elections of the nineteenth century, newspapers openly expressed their views about the campaigns. As noted, the newspapers were much more overtly partisan then than they are today, and thus were more inclined to vent their attitude toward the campaigns in colorful language than is typical now. Newspapers, of course, are not the mouthpiece of common, everyday people. But given their large circulation and readership, it is likely that they helped mold public views of the campaigns.

The campaign of 1840—circus might be a better term—provoked sharp reaction. We already noted the disgusted views of the Philadelphia *Public Ledger*, which decried the impact of the campaign on women. But by no means was this all. The *Wheeling Times* wrote, "right joyous are we that the campaign of 1840 is closed. Its character and incidents will furnish matter for mortifying reflections for years to come."[15] The *Public Ledger* further opined,

> For two years past the most ordinary operations of business have been neglected and President-making has become every citizen's chief concern. The result being uncertain, some have been afraid to engage in new enterprises, others have retired from business, others have not dared to prosecute their business with the old vigor. Millions of dollars will now change hands on election bets; millions of days have been taken from useful labor to listen to stump orators, and millions more to build log cabins, erect hickory poles, and march in ridiculous, degrading, mob-creating processions. . . . However high the hopes inspired by the election of General Harrison, they will prove to be elusive.[16]

John Quincy Adams had the last word. "Harrison," he wrote, "came in upon a hurricane; God grant he may not go out upon a wreck."[17]

Conclusion

This discussion should not be read for more than it is. There are significant differences between the nineteenth-century campaign for the presidency and the modern campaign. The scope and speed of the campaigns, the use of technological wizardry, scientific polling and focus groups, the decline of parties as primary campaign vehicles: these and other features of the modern campaign render it a different political organism from its nineteenth-century counterpart.

And yet we see the roots of the modern campaign in these early ones. More importantly for this book, aspects of the modern campaign that seem to bother journalists, politicians, academicians, perhaps even the public at large—such as mudslinging, negativity, character assassination, an absence of issues, and the role of money—have been around for a long time. They have actually shaped the color, quality, and character of our political campaigns. They may very well have molded our particular type of democratic politics.

This is not to excuse the excesses of what has happened. It is not, further, an apology for an absence of serious political discourse, something the public needs and deserves. It is to say, however, that we survived these campaigns as a nation. And it would be difficult to argue that the outcome of at least some of these elections did not produce capable, even distinguished, presidents. Whether these same conclusions still obtain for the modern campaign is a question to which we shall return much later in the book.

PART II

The Modern Political Campaign

4

Candidates and the Modern Political Campaign

The preceding two chapters were designed to demonstrate that negative campaigning is an entrenched, if unwelcome, part of the American political tradition. Indeed, like death, taxes, and the poor, the strong likelihood is that it will always be with us, although of course the level of virulence it takes will vary considerably from one election to the next.

It has been our additional purpose to suggest that, as distasteful as negative campaigning can be, it is probably not terribly harmful to our democracy. Given that politics in America is primarily a spectator rather than a participatory sport, negative campaigning may actually have the beneficial effect of breaking into the public's consciousness, alerting it to the onset of an election, and perhaps even motivating marginal voters to go to the polls. Ironically, negative campaigning may have a positive effect on our democracy, at least to the extent it provides information (even if it is skewed, or of marginal relevance) to voters and enhances the level of political participation.

There are other aspects of the modern political campaign in America that also give rise to concerns about their possibly harmful effect on democratic institutions and processes. In this chapter we shall explore one of them: the candidates who offer themselves for public office in modern campaigns. The theme to be developed in the chapter parallels our discussion of negative campaigning: people complain about the candidates from whom they have to choose, and that they pale in comparison to the "greats" of old. But in fact their fears and discontent are probably misplaced because there is no evidence that our democracy is in jeopardy on account of the quality of the candidates who offer themselves during campaigns.

Candidates I: Where Are the Giants of Old?

Buffoons. Clowns. Morons. Incompetents. Untrustworthy. Shallow. Unacceptable. Tweedledum. Tweedledee. These are only some of the more polite nouns and adjectives frequently used by disgruntled voters confronted by their electoral choices. The interesting point about these sobriquets is that they transcend partisanship. They are applied in identical fashion to candidates from the two major parties, and often to those from minor ones and those in nonpartisan elections as well. Indeed, not infrequently they refer to the whole list of candidates on the ballot, whether in a primary or general election. "None of the above" is a choice many voters say they would like to have, but don't get. It is more than idle speculation to think about what would happen if in fact "none of the above" were an electoral choice, and even more so, if this line on the ballot received the most votes!

What seems to be the matter? Why do so many voters feel that the candidates from whom they must choose are unworthy of them, that they deserve better, and that maybe they would take electoral politics more seriously if the candidates were "better"?

Leaving aside for the moment the question of who or what a "better" candidate would be, or look like, let us first observe that complaints about the quality of candidates are not new. Once the heroic George Washington retired from political life, the floodgates of criticism opened. Even candidates who subsequently entered our American political "hall of fame"—Adams, Jefferson, Jackson, Lincoln, the two Roosevelts, Wilson, Truman, Eisenhower, Kennedy, Reagan—were reviled during their campaigns as malicious incompetents, and worse. Candidates of lesser stature, who never were selected for our pantheon, were treated even more harshly.

It may well be that Americans are too hard on their candidates, expecting supermen and superwomen, and expressing disappointment when they turn out to be mere mortals, complete with foibles, warts, and weaknesses. Why we as a political community should have these unreasonably high expectations is worth a moment of our time. Citizens in other nations don't: the French, for example, start with realistic expectations of who their candidates are and what they can reasonably be expected to do if elected. They are neither surprised nor disappointed to discover that their candidates and officeholders live up to this low set of expectations.[1]

Americans are different. We want our candidates, even for local political offices, to embody the virtues we associate with the greatest of our leaders: strength of character, vision, charisma, the capacity to rise above petty politics, an ability to create consensus, the moral suasion to see and do what is right, the power to defeat the forces of evil (or at least the naysayers, grumblers, and carping critics), the skill to get the job done and at the same time to make the job look easy, while maintaining a sense of identity with everyday people. It seems pointless to note that such a person has never existed, and probably never will; American voters keep looking for one, and expecting their arrival in the next campaign.

This image of the supercandidate is undoubtedly rooted in our distrust of politics. We the citizens feel uncomfortable in the political arena, and we prefer to keep a healthy distance from what we think of as its sordid ways. Better to find a supercandidate to deal with things political; if we locate and identify this person of virtue, we can leave politics in his or her capable hands, knowing things will be well handled, and we can turn our attention to something else, something more seemly.

The consequence of this unrealistic pursuit of political supercandidates is not simply that we are disappointed to find that they invariably and inevitably have feet of clay. It is that we find ourselves pining for a past that never existed. "Where are the giants of yesterday who presented themselves for office?" is not a complaint found solely in the reminiscences of senior citizens in a retirement center. The question can be found in newspaper editorials and even in college classrooms, voiced by young voters already looking for the impossible. The irony, of course, is that the image of a glorious past held by too many voters is belied by the historical facts: the very candidates whose qualities and virtues they cry out for, and whose absence they so deeply decry, were reviled in their own time.

Is there any evidence that the "quality" of modern candidates is lower than that of days gone by? We will see in a moment that it may well be that there is a significant difference in the type of modern candidate offered for public office compared with previous eras. But different does not mean worse. Indeed, it is a reasonable argument that, given the overall level of education, professional experience, and civic and community involvement that modern candidates, even for local offices, present to voters, they may actually have better, more impressive résumés than did candidates decades ago. Even in the smallest, most rural communities, it is rare to find a candidate taken seriously (even one that does not ultimately prove victorious) who is not regarded as a "solid citizen" of the community, however that is defined locally. In sophisticated, metropolitan areas serious candidates must not only embody the local criteria for success, they must also look and sound good on television. One wonders whether Harry S. Truman, or even General Dwight D. Eisenhower, would have been successful in today's candidate-centered, television-driven campaigns.[2]

Of course, merely that modern candidates may have more impressive résumés than their predecessors does not inherently make them "better." But it does suggest that the people presenting themselves for public office are, collectively, neither dregs nor ne'er-do-wells. There is, to be sure, the occasional crackpot or know-nothing or person with nothing better to do who runs for public office. What is of interest, however, is how seldom such candidates succeed; they rarely attract much support, generally don't raise the money needed to mount a serious campaign (that they may have private funds available to them is another matter), and find that American voters have a way of generally sorting out the fringe candidates and leaving them in the "lost" column.

But impressive credentials and résumés are not the only indicator that candidates may actually be better than they were earlier in our history. The diversity and variety of people presenting themselves to the public is assuredly a strength, not a weakness. A generation ago, and not merely in the South, it was next to impossible to find an African-American running for office. Now it is common, all over. The same is true of Hispanic-American candidates (at least in Sun Belt and large metropolitan states in the North and Midwest), and Asian-American candidates in the Pacific rim states. Women candidates did present themselves a generation ago, but generally only for a limited range of offices: school board was acceptable, perhaps city clerk, supervisor of elections, or some other primarily ministerial office. Now women run for, and sometimes win, offices at all levels, except for president. But the point is that except for this latter office, the novelty of the woman candidate has largely worn off, and while people may take note of gender in a race, it seldom dominates campaign politics.

It could correctly be argued that there are not enough hyphenated-American or women candidates, that campaigns are still dominated by white males. But this is a different issue. The point here is that the range and diversity of the pool of candidates from which voters have to choose is vastly greater than it was just a generation ago. It would be hard to argue that this increased candidate variety is anything but a strength of the electoral system, as it offers more choices to voters and enhances political participation from a broader spectrum of the American population. It is in fact a measure of increased candidate quality.

But if even local candidates offer better credentials than those of years gone by, and even if the variety from whom we get to choose is greater than before, why do we still keep looking for supercandidates? Why do we yearn for the giants of old, and lament the quality of those from among whom we must choose in the upcoming election? Don't we see that we may actually be better off, from the standpoint of candidate credentials, than we used to be?

A major reason for our continuing search for the good old days, and our disappointment with the current crop of candidates, has less to do with those seeking office than with the performance of those occupying it. In this connection, the presidency is exceptionally important, and is a powerful influence on our perception not just of occupants of the White House, but of officeholders at lower levels as well.

What seems to have happened is that our search for the giants of another era rests fundamentally on our perception of who held the office capably, and was regarded as "effective" in it, especially the presidency. FDR, Truman, and Eisenhower are regarded, in differing degrees, as capable presidents. Therefore they must have been terrific candidates, or so we choose to believe. But our memories play tricks on us, and are assuredly selective. When Roosevelt ran for president in 1932, the dean of American political commentators, Walter Lippmann, regarded him as something of a lightweight. Even General Eisenhower, for all of his heroic stature in World War II, had to convince members of the Republican Party that he was a better bet than Robert Taft. And Truman was scarcely taken seriously, either as FDR's last running mate or as his own man in 1948.

Looking backward to see what we want to see is not unique to American politics, of course. But it is assuredly a powerful part of the American political tradition. What seems to have made the impulse stronger is our ongoing disappointment with the performance of recent presidents. Since 1960, no president has managed to keep a strong political hold on the public; even the martyred Kennedy (whose administration seemed to move from mishap to mishap, and in any case never realized the promise of the candidate's brilliant campaign rhetoric) and Ronald Reagan, who maintained personal, but not political, popularity, ultimately had performances in office that were dissatisfying to the public. The others either left office in varying degrees of disgrace (Lyndon B. Johnson, Richard M. Nixon), or were not reelected. Even Bill Clinton, who won reelection in 1996, never really convinced the public that he was a president as competent as those of days gone by. In fact he received a majority of the vote in neither 1992 nor 1996; yet Nixon in 1968 and Reagan in 1980, both of whom faced strong third-party candidates, still managed to secure a majority of the popular vote.

Analysts of the presidency understand perfectly why this happens. The occupants of the White House invariably and inevitably disappoint us because the demands of the office are too great, and too contradictory.[3] No one seems capable of successfully carrying out the necessary balancing act needed to perform adequately all of the presidential tasks; put more simply, no one has shown the capacity to be all things to all people, and to do the job of president in a way that satisfies everyone. The office and job of president have grown too much and become too complex and contradictory for a mere mortal to carry them off successfully. Yet we continually hope and demand that someone—the candidate chosen—do so, because the giants of old did; and never mind how the office has expanded and grown, or that our country and world are far more complex and unmanageable than they were forty or fifty years ago.

Does our perception of the presidency affect our view of other offices? Because of its centrality in our political system, as well as in world politics, undoubtedly it does. But it is also true that even lower-level political offices have grown both in expectations and complexity, yet the public still demands a superperformance in order to be satisfied. Students of governorships continue to note the rising set of responsibilities on governors, yet observe that their power to act or the resources available to them are in no way consonant with these expectations.[4] Even the jobs of school board members and city council members—once part-time, relatively stress-free undertakings—now involve both abrupt changes in the occupants' personal lives and massive political risks.

Even as the scope and tasks of our political offices, from president on down, have expanded, so have public expectations grown that they will be done well. If not, we the public are disappointed, and complain about "quality." In effect, we have put officeholders, and therefore candidates, in a no-win situation. Indeed, we the public will no longer permit or accept political failure.

All of this is relevant to the question of candidate quality. Just as there are citizens for whom the idea of public service is attractive, but who do not wish to subject themselves—and their families—to a privacy-revealing negative campaign, so too are there potential candidates of quality who recognize that at least in the public's eye they are doomed to failure, and choose not to run. They are unused to failure in business and professional life, and thus cannot and will not risk failure in political life. Thus, the public is left to choose from among those willing to take these risks, and face the rigors of negative campaigns. That is not to say that this pool of individuals is necessarily inept or incompetent—indeed, it is our argument that, at least on the basis of credentials, the members of this pool are more impressive than candidates were previously. But it is true that the pool of potentially able candidates is substantially reduced because we the public force out those unwilling to risk failure.

But the issue goes beyond those for whom the risks are too great. Since we have witnessed failure in office, we the public assume the fault lies with the candidates, that is, those seeking our vote so they can occupy it. Our disappointment in their performance is based on their failings and inabilities, not in our misperceptions and unrealistic expectations. It's much easier to blame them, even heap scorn on them, than it is to recognize that the fault lies more with us than with the candidates. Nor do we search for systemic problems, in which the faults and weaknesses lie within political institutions themselves, and their interrelationship; we assume, perhaps incorrectly, that our structures of government can meet the enormous expectations we put on them. But unless and until we bring our hopes and dreams into some level of consonance with the capacity of our political leaders to serve and our political offices to address public needs, disappointment will continue. If we don't modify our perceptions and expectations, we will persist in complaining about the quality of our candidates for office, and fail to recognize that in fact we really don't give them much of a chance to succeed in the first place.

Candidates II: Who Are These Guys, Anyway?

In his thoughtful 1991 volume, *The United States of Ambition*, Alan Ehrenhalt, executive editor of *Governing* magazine, offered a more searching critique of the quality of modern political candidates. He was not the least concerned about our previous question, namely, the search for "giants." Rather, he was concerned that our political system has become so "open" that candidates appear from virtually anywhere. No longer tied to political parties or even coherent ideologies as they were under the old "closed" system, candidates instead nominate themselves solely on the basis of personal ambition. As a result, candidates "move in and out of office on the basis largely of their personal ambition and energy."[5]

In effect, Ehrenhalt says, our political system has been taken over by a new breed of professional candidate-politician whose major vocation is exactly that: running for office and, if successful, holding it. Gone are the days when candidates for office had to prove themselves to a party (or some other political) organization by working their way up the ladder, demonstrating loyalty and a willingness to be part of a team, learning patience, and building consensus and a base of support among publicly active citizens and leaders who could form the basis for a governing coalition. The "closed system," the demise of which Ehrenhalt lamented, was not designed to shut people out, as the term sometimes connotes. Rather, it served as a training ground, a virtual apprenticeship, in which those taking part in it learned of the relationship between campaigning and governing, and came to appreciate the way in which building alliances and fostering a consensus needed to win elections would serve them in good stead once they were in office, since they had a more or less permanent base of support in the community that could help them implement their governing agendas.

Ehrenhalt's critique of modern candidates, based on self-centered desires to hold office, actually transcends his criticism of contemporary office seekers. In fact, it is a scathing criticism of our modern political system. Under the present structure, in his view, in which anyone can choose to run for office based solely on personal ambition, the ability to govern essentially vanishes: "We see the process by which power does not so much change hands as evaporate altogether."[6] But by power Ehrenhalt does not simply mean the political clout held in individual officeholders' hands. Power in this sense can be identified. Rather, it is power within the entire system itself that has vanished, for in an open system, in which virtually anything and anyone goes, there is little to tie one officeholder to another, and even less to tie them to the political community of private citizens. Thus, the system is unable to move in any coherent way. Leaders find themselves estranged from followers; the community feels no particular sense of attachment to its public officeholders.[7] To the extent that anything happens in the political system, it is because an especially ambitious and politically skillful officeholder makes it happen. It is highly doubtful, in Ehrenhalt's view, that pressure to make it happen came as a result of consensus developing within the population, since in the open system politics is purely a supply-side proposition: the population gets what candidates offer and want to have happen, not what citizens demand.

Perhaps most tellingly, according to Ehrenhalt, the talents and capabilities required to win elections have little if anything to do with the requirements of governing.[8] At least in the old days, under the closed system, candidates for office were well aware of the need to represent public needs during their campaigns, and act on them in office, if they were to perpetuate the political strength of their party or other organization. Without any organizational ties, indeed with no loyalties except to their own ambition, modern candidates fail to build ongoing coalitions of support, but rather seek to do whatever fosters their own careers. "The only way to win is to traffic in the commodities that make a difference in any open political system at any level—talent, enthusiasm, and time."[9] In Ehrenhalt's view, these are of only limited significance when it comes to actually governing.

Ehrenhalt provides a great deal of meat to chew on. His critique of our political system is especially provocative given the empirically demonstrable growing mistrust the public has of its officeholders and political institutions.[10] He is also right to point out the diffusion (in his words, evaporation) of power in the political system at all levels: gridlock in Washington is but one manifestation of the inability to aggregate power and use it in a way that permits government to respond to public needs and desires. The shutdown of the federal government during the winter of 1995–96 is merely the outgrowth of the incapacity of public officeholders, and government institutions, to locate and aggregate power for the public good.

There is also much to question in Ehrenhalt's discussion. One cannot help but wonder whether the old, closed political system was necessarily so superior to the modern, open one. True, it was assuredly based on a greater and broader set of consensual politics than is today's system. But its range of political agenda may well have been a good deal more narrow. While one may well find disturbing the presence in our modern political agenda of issues that were formerly regarded primarily as private matters—family values, prayer in public places, reproductive options—the fact is that the modern political agenda is far broader than it was a generation and more ago. In addition, while Ehrenhalt makes clear that his version of "closed" politics is not designed to discriminate against people or keep them out of politics, one nonetheless has the lingering suspicion that there is a fundamentally elitist, nonpopulist, even antidemocratic streak in these yearnings for the old days.

Moreover, and most centrally for the purposes of this book, one wonders whether the failings of our modern political system can be blamed so heavily on the personal ambition of our political candidates. Are there not systemic difficulties, including institutional weaknesses, that may account for our political shortcomings? Indeed, at this point we must wave farewell to this central and troubling theme in Ehrenhalt's book, because our purpose is not to lay bare the faults of modern American politics, or even to analyze their causes. Rather, we must examine Ehrenhalt's prior thesis: that there is a new breed of candidate in American politics driven primarily by ambition, devoted to a professional—but personal—commitment to the vocation of politics. Ehrenhalt of course feels that this individual detracts from the quality of our politics. Is it really so bad for us?

Before addressing this question, let us make certain that Ehrenhalt's position is clear. He does not deny that in the past there have been professional politicians. What he does point out is that the modern professional politician has few if any loyalties or attachments to the political *system*. The modern candidate, he contends, is frequently someone who has chosen politics as a vocation, not out of a sense of public duty or commitment, or even a desire to do good, but as a means of making a living.[11] Thus, decisions about politics are made not out of a sense of obligation to the political organization that has fostered the politician's career (there usually isn't any, except as may have been created by the individual candidate) or the system that operates on the basis of consensual politics among others sharing a loyalty to and belief in it (in Ehrenhalt's view, it's basically every man for himself).[12] Rather, decisions are made by candidates solely on the basis of private ambition, not public regardingness.[13]

Two points can be made that may serve to put Ehrenhalt's gloomy conclusions in a more positive light. In the first place, the argument that by pursuing personal ambition contemporary politicians ignore public needs and desires, and cannot wield power in order to address them successfully, is simply not true. Ehrenhalt filled his book with examples of modern politicians who, pursuing their ambition, ultimately failed as successful leaders and policymakers. True enough. But there are other examples to the contrary.

President Bill Clinton is one. Throughout his first term it was often noted that he was a much better campaigner than chief executive. Indeed, he was frequently criticized for running the White House as though it were simply an ongoing campaign, rather than attending to the business of governing. In truth, he often looked more successful when he was "campaigning" than when he was involved in the close, detailed, difficult work of consensus building for the purpose of governing.

But it would be unfair to characterize the first Clinton administration as unsympathetic or insensitive to public needs, or, for that matter, as one in which public questions were not addressed. One could rightly criticize things the Clinton administration did (or, in some cases, did not do); obviously many people disagreed with his version of what the public wanted or needed. But if the Clinton administration was viewed as out of step and out of touch with the public at large, it is unlikely that the Republican Party would have had as much difficulty as it did in trying to unseat him. Clearly, in this instance, the personal ambition of President Clinton ran parallel to what much of the public felt was in its interest as well.

Other examples can be found. Mayors Rudolph Guiliani of New York and Richard Riordan of Los Angeles may or may not have been motivated primarily by personal ambition. Both, however, used their substantial political skills to forge governing coalitions in their cities; as of late 1996, both have been regarded as effective mayors insofar as they have broad bases of popular support for their agendas. One has the decided feeling that there are other such politicians in less visible and glamorous locations; regardless of their motives for seeking public office, they have found that they can respond to public need given adequate political skills, a minimum resource base, and a public willing to follow.

Indeed, it may always have been this way, even under the lamented "closed system" of American politics. Ambition has always been a part of the motivation of political candidates; that it was cloaked under an organizational blanket (known often, but not exclusively, as "Democratic" or "Republican") does not disguise it from what it was. Moreover, while we cannot pursue the point too far here, as our goal is not to write a political history of the United States, it is also the case that politicians under the closed system could not always rely on their organizational base to help them. In many areas of the country—the South is an obvious example, but by no means the only one—party organization was too weak and inept to provide an aid in governance. True, there were not many "effective" politicians in the South in the first sixty years of this century, if by effective we mean those addressing public questions in a serious way.[14] But there were some—governors Charles Aycock of North Carolina, Frank Clement of Tennessee, and LeRoy Collins of Florida come to mind. Ambition—perhaps even personal ambition—was at least a partial element of their motivation. The point is, the United States of ambition is not a recent development, at least as far as candidates and officeholders are concerned. It's been here for a long time.

But this last point brings us to our second comment on Ehrenhalt. Let us concede that the modern version of ambition is different, somehow, from that shown by candidates and officeholders in earlier eras. What disturbs Ehrenhalt about this type of ambition is that it is practiced for its own sake, and the enhancement of the individual, not the body politic. In effect, he is complaining about the commitment to the vocation of politics that the modern candidate has.

We leave aside Aristotle's important point that politics is life's noble calling. We all know it can get pretty sleazy. What is peculiar about Ehrenhalt's criticism is that he complains about what in other aspects of American life would be considered a virtue: namely, that the modern candidate is an entrepreneur. Rather than spending a lifetime as a cog in a wheel behind a corporate desk, or pushing papers in a stifling law office, the modern campaigner strikes out on his own. In effect, modern campaigners invest in themselves, and stake their careers by taking a risk that they can succeed by deciding "to traffic in the commodities that make a difference . . . talent, enthusiasm, and time."[15]

In so many areas of American life—whether one is talking about Horatio Alger or Bill Gates—these are regarded as virtues. They are the stuff of American myth and legend—the young entrepreneur with nothing but talent, enthusiasm, and time (along with a healthy dose of ambition) is portrayed as the model for the next generation. Even today these myths and legends continue, as we find that significant economic growth in this country is rooted not in corporate growth but in the creation of new businesses by people striking out on their own as entrepreneurs. That some of these enterprises will not succeed is not the point; many of the entrepreneurs will try again, perhaps to succeed on the third or fourth or fifth try. The point is that we regard entrepreneurial behavior as worthy of emulation and often a matter of civic, regional, or national pride.

But somehow, not so in politics, at least in Ehrenhalt's view. True enough, perhaps in opening up the political system we have fragmented power, and made consensus politics difficult to achieve. But the price does not have to be seen negatively, as Ehrenhalt sees it. Rather, the entrepreneurial spirit that motivates many modern candidates—ambition, in other words—has also brought an energy and talent and enthusiasm and diversity of candidates (along with their views and agendas) to our modern political stage not previously seen. While Ehrenhalt may well rue this development, there is no particular reason to see it as a weakness. Indeed, this entrepreneurial spirit may well represent a have leap forward in the quality of our candidates, not a step backward.

Conclusion—Should We Be Happy?

Having said all this, are we justified in concluding that we can be satisfied, even proud, of the quality of candidates who offer themselves for public office? This is a very difficult question to answer objectively, because so much of our evaluation of candidates depends on how we perceive them viscerally and emotionally, and this can be highly idiosyncratic, varying widely among citizens and voters. Voters can evaluate the quality of candidates very differently even as they might agree on the adequacy of their résumés (or lack thereof) for the position sought. For example, in the 1996 presidential election the considerable, and often distinguished, thirty-five-plus years of public service offered by Republican nominee Bob Dole was not in dispute; but there was considerable variation within the electorate as to whether or not that résumé, coupled with the way he conducted himself during the campaign, provided a convincing argument that he should be elected president.

Even the concept of "evaluating" candidates is vague. The criteria which people use to decide on the adequacy and quality of their candidates are not objectively fixed. Rather, people seize upon what they think is important, or appeals to them, and ignore what they don't like or think is less significant. For example, just a few weeks prior to that same 1996 presidential election a significant bloc of voters (about 45 percent) had serious doubts about Clinton's trustworthiness, but more than 60 percent were convinced he was going to win anyway.[16] Obviously, with numbers like these, the concept of evaluating candidates can proceed along several tracks at once, even within the same person, and contain internal tensions and contradictions.

What then do we know about how voters perceive candidate quality? In this regard anecdotal evidence may be as insightful as difficult-to-secure objective criteria. How often does one hear a comment resembling something like the following: "I held my nose and voted for ———" ; "Are these the best we could find?"; "These guys are clowns"; "Tweedledum and Tweedledee"; "I couldn't stand either one, so I skipped that race"; "I would have done a write-in, but I forgot a pen"; "What about 'none of the above'?"; "The candidates were so bad that I just didn't vote at all." In contrast, how often does one hear something like "I could hardly decide; they were both so impressive" or "Too bad somebody had to lose, they were both pretty good."

What is it that people are really saying when they complain about the quality of candidates from whom they have to choose? For some, obviously, their expectations are so high that no one short of a giant of old (and virtually impossible to identify before the fact, prior to seeing how they perform in office) could possibly measure up. Others, like Ehrenhalt, may feel turned off by the candidates' naked displays of personal ambition.

But surely the voters are telling us more than this. It is a reasonable argument that when voters complain about candidate quality, it is as much a commentary on their assessment of politics, and the ability of the political system to respond to public need, as it is an evaluation of those running for office. Some might object that this statement puts the cart before the horse; if voters felt better about their candidates, they might place more trust and have more confidence in their political institutions to "do something," especially do something good and right and helpful.

There is assuredly some truth in this objection. But it is undoubtedly also true that the way we feel about the adequacy of government to solve public problems—to make our lives better, both collectively and individually—colors our view of the people who want to serve in public office. Doubts about the capacity of political institutions to improve economic opportunity, to create jobs, to create peace (or, in a more limited view, to guarantee national security), to provide children with a quality education, to clean up pollution—in short, to do all of the tasks that we heap on government—are widespread. Indeed, much of the political rhetoric of the 1980s and early 1990s about limiting government, getting government off our backs, reinventing government, or whatever was the slogan of the month, may well have stemmed from an increasing frustration with its capacity to do anything right. Even President Clinton, who rode into office in 1992 essentially focusing on the argument that government, while needing fixing, could have a positive role in the life of the nation, really did not begin to hit his stride until 1995, when he decided to pursue a more conservative, limited political agenda designed to secure the support of the middle class who seemed to have the most doubts about the ability of government to get any job done right.

To put the point another way, we are suspicious of those who want to engage in an enterprise—government, in this case—about which we have serious doubts. If we did not feel this way, why do we then feel so uncharitable about our candidates? Why else would we call them clowns, and worse? If we had more trust and confidence in the public enterprise, we probably would not belittle those who offer themselves to run it. Indeed, there would be less reason to find fault with those actually announcing for office.

Indeed, the matter goes further. If we had more confidence in what government was about, we might actually attract "better" candidates! It is a commonplace now to hear persons qualified to run for office, who might make both quality candidates and fine officeholders, decline to do so. Reasons given are legion: "I would not subject myself and my family to public scrutiny"; "I could not stand the mudslinging that campaigns have become"; "I have my children's future to think about"; "I value my privacy"; "I could never ask people to pay for my campaign, much less to vote for me"; "I couldn't take the salary cut"; "Why should I disrupt my family's life to move to Washington, D.C., (or the state capital) for a couple of years?"

Undoubtedly in many instances these reasons are valid. But in other instances they are excuses, or even smokescreens hiding what many people suspect, but few potential candidates want to come out and say: there is little to be gained in the way of esteem, prestige, or community stature in running for public office because even if they win, the public has a very dim view of, and perhaps is negatively predisposed toward, the enterprise they seek to enter. Indeed, if this were not the case, the strong likelihood is that more quality candidates would seek office; perhaps campaigns might not even be as negative and personally wrenching as they are if we the people felt differently about our government.

But, it might further be objected, what about the people who really do want to serve, who feel that they can actually do some good if their fellow citizens elect them to office? Fortunately, there are people like that. In virtually every community one finds the occasional candidate or two who runs for office out of a spirit of public regardingness and a desire to work in government on behalf of the citizens. It is possible to identify these persons, but voters don't always choose them—they sometimes make terrible candidates, find themselves unable to convince cynical voters that they are the genuine article, or turn out not to know how to cope with a withering negative assault directed against them. Our goal, as a political community, must be to seek out and encourage such candidates. It is a reasonable hypothesis that if we felt better about government, we might actually be able to do so.

All right then, what would it take to change citizens' minds, to make them less cynical and have more trust and confidence in government? This is a long and complex topic, one that takes us far afield from the more narrow confines of this book. Perhaps the best prescription for change is for government to improve its performance, to show citizens that it can do what needs to be done effectively, responsibly, responsively, efficiently, and accountably. But, it might be objected, does this not require better people in office, and better candidates seeking to run? Perhaps so. But a helpful first step would be for citizens to think less in individualistic, isolated terms than in terms of collective responsibilities and obligations. That is, when we begin thinking of ourselves in relation to the mutual enterprise in which we are all engaged, the creation of a sense of community, we will of necessity need to think of our public institutions designed to foster a sense of community—government—in a more favorable way.[17] Perhaps then we will start to welcome candidates for public office, and encourage them, instead of criticizing and belittling them as we do now. But unless and until we reestablish our commitment to community and our common enterprise, we will probably continue to hear the same old refrain, at least with respect to the quality of our candidates: we get what we deserve.

5

Issues in the
Modern Campaign:
Where's the Meat?

It is a commonplace for Americans to complain about the lack of issues discussed by candidates in political campaigns. Sandwiched among the caustic remarks about the emphasis on personality, the character assassinations, the questioning of motives and integrity, the lack of trustworthiness, the shallowness and self-serving quality of debate, the mudslinging, the photo ops, the thirty-second sound bites and all the other defects of the modern political campaign is the feeling, often wistfully expressed, that voters wish candidates would stick to issues, explain their positions, and then leave the decision to them, the voters. They rue the lack of content, of substance, of meat in the campaign, and claim they want more. Would that it were all so simple.

In the first chapter we noted that campaigns cannot be totally devoid of content. If they are, they cannot achieve their "civic education" function. In effect, what this means is that the campaign must provide some minimal level of substance in order to convince the voting public that it is legitimate, that it, or at least its candidate, needs to be taken seriously. Gone are the days when a candidate for county commissioner can stand up before a rally and say something like, "I'm your neighbor from Happy Acres. I ask for your support." Once upon a time this might have been enough to get elected, if people liked him enough and he had the right political connections. Nowadays candidates for county commissioner have to know about solid waste disposal, utility rates, growth management, transportation patterns, welfare programs, crime prevention, employment discrimination, and a host of other matters. Their campaign literature probably has bulleted lists of accomplishments in each of these areas and more, plus plans for the future. Still, it's not enough. Inevitably the campaign will be criticized as lacking in substance.

Did campaigns in the old days have more meat? We saw in Chapter 2 that presidential campaigns during the nineteenth century frequently lacked an issue orientation, but it would be wrong to say they lacked content. In fact, they gave a good deal of attention to what the candidates were like (and perhaps even more to illuminating the defects of opponents). This in itself is information that can help voters choose between candidates. It may seem deficient to modern ears—it even struck voters and political observers then that more could have been said—but it did represent substance of a sort.

Even our hypothetical county commissioner of a generation ago gave voters at least two useful pieces of information in his brief statement: he is your neighbor, and he lives in Happy Acres. That information provides enough substance to hook him into the friends-and-neighbors style of politics so characteristic of county government a generation ago. His mention of Happy Acres tells voters if he is a city boy, a rural candidate, or something else, as well as his relative standing in the economics of the county because of the place Happy Acres occupies in the pecking order of places to live; in turn that information could give some clue as to what sort of people were behind him.

Thus, it turns out there is a good deal of substance in our would-be commissioner's brief statement, perhaps even enough to get him elected. Merely because that statement would not suffice nowadays does not mean his campaign lacked substance, or meat. What has changed, then, in campaigns is probably less the need to provide some form of content to voters than the type of content expected by voters, as well as the amount of material that has to be presented, and its range of subjects. We the voters have convinced ourselves that we want more and more meat.

And yet we all know of examples to the contrary. The candidate who drones on dryly about tax reform or nuclear power is too often dismissed as a crank, and boring. Ross Perot, arguably the most content-oriented presidential candidate in 1992, amused the public, for a while anyway, with his peppery style, his charts, and his TV "infotainment" programs. By 1996 he had simply become a national bore, and was scarcely a factor in the presidential campaign until the very end.

Thus it may well be that Americans are ambivalent about content and issues in their campaigns. They want some, but not too much. In this chapter, we shall look at the role of issues in campaigns. We shall especially concern ourselves with the way in which candidates try to convey a sense of issues and substance to voters, and ask if in fact they are informing voters or shortchanging them through their bullets on campaign literature and sound bites on television. We shall also try to get a sense of the relationship between issues and candidates, and see how this might affect their appeal to voters. Our goal, as before, is to ask a very fundamental question: does this aspect of the modern campaign hurt or help our democracy?

Some Confusing Examples

Let us begin our discussion of issues in campaigns by noting some recent examples of how candidates tried using them.

In 1984, former vice president Walter Mondale had the honor of being the presidential candidate of the Democratic Party, and the unenviable task of taking on a very popular incumbent, Ronald Reagan. The Mondale campaign tried a number of gimmicks to build credibility for its candidate and to try to dent Reagan's numbers. For example, Mondale choose Geraldine Ferraro as his vice presidential candidate, making her the first woman to occupy that position in a major party.

Even more surprisingly, Mondale decided to attack the president on his economic policy, specifically both supply-side economics and vast deficit spending. He lectured the public on the dangers of Reaganomics, pointing (correctly, as it turned out) to the impact it would have on the public treasury. He even had the temerity to indicate at one point during the campaign that he thought, if he were elected, he would have to propose a tax increase in order to pay for the deficit.

It turned out the voters were not interested in his jeremiads; Mondale was soundly defeated in November 1984. His searching discussions of economic policy had fallen on deaf ears; those voters who bothered to listen decided the lectures didn't have the appeal of

Reagan's rosy pictures. Issues, even pocketbook issues, did not resonate with voters in this election.

Let us move forward to 1988. The Democrats were searching for a
way to break the Republican lock on the White House. Gary Hart was
the front-runner; he was glamorous and exciting, with a Kennedyesque
appeal, and was eventually to self-destruct when caught on a boat with
an equally glamorous female not his wife. Mike Dukakis was grim and
intense, but understood the rules the Democratic Party had established
for securing the nomination. Bruce Babbitt of Arizona was the braini-
est of the candidates, discussing environmental issues, tax policy, and
foreign affairs with knowledge and understanding. He raised little
money, and dropped out early. No one paid him any attention, in spite
of his insistence on dwelling on substance and issues during his brief
campaign.

Fast forward to 1996. The Republicans had an easy target, they
thought, in Bill Clinton, but could not find a candidate to run against
him. There was no shortage of possibilities, but of the eight or so
serious ones in the race most seemed more concerned with appealing
to Pat Robertson's religious right wing of the party than with discussing a broad political agenda or, for that matter, figuring out how to run
against Clinton. The lone exceptions were Richard Lugar of Indiana
and Lamar Alexander of Tennessee. They lasted longer in the Republican race than Phil Gramm of Texas (he of the $26 million who
dropped out after Iowa) but were never serious contenders for the
nomination. Their serious discussion of issues—foreign affairs in the
case of the former, domestic policy in the latter—fell on deaf ears
among Republican voters.

Forward a little further in 1996. In accepting the Republican presidential nomination at the party convention, Bob Dole, perhaps for the
first time in his long career in public life, provided an eloquent picture
of what he hoped America could be. He linked the strength of our
nation to traditional values of the past, and laid out the agenda he felt
would put the country back on the right track. The speech was full of
meat and substance, and it was regarded by some commentators as the
finest address he had ever made.

It disappeared. Within a very short time Dole was talking on the
campaign trail about two matters only: his proposed tax cut, and deficiencies in President Clinton's character. In his two televised debates
with the president, Dole seldom discussed issues—indeed rarely ad-

dressed systematically the questions posed to him—but instead reiterated his pledge for a tax cut, and repeatedly reminded voters that they could trust him but not the president. For all his efforts and hammering on these themes, Dole's standing in the polls and approval ratings continued to fall, and in some states were no longer on the same map with those of the president.[1] In the last ten days of the campaign, Dole moved virtually all of his resources to California, with secondary efforts in Florida and Virginia, to try to move his numbers up; he also abandoned the verbal assaults on the president, as he discovered they were hurting him.[2]

What conclusions are we to draw from these examples? The first few indicate the inability of candidates for the presidency who talked seriously about issues and substance to attract any level of support, even within their own party. The final example demonstrates the failings of a candidate not previously recognized for his ability to articulate a policy agenda who created quite a stir and considerable admiration when he did so, ultimately failing when he gave up all pretense of offering a serious discussion of policy alternatives in his campaign in favor of negative assaults on his opponent's character and a die-hard attachment to campaign sloganeering. Do these vignettes tell us anything?

The first lesson is the obvious one: Americans are ambivalent about issues in campaigns. In some instances, they want to hear a serious discussion of issues, but in others they prefer to listen to slogans and hear candidates tell them what they (the candidates) know they want to hear. As Alan Ehrenhalt has recently pointed out, in some campaigns the electorate acts as though it is asleep, or drugged into stupor.[3] In these instances, it is content to hear about morning in America and shining cities on hilltops. But in other instances—1996 was an example, in his opinion—the American electorate is very conscious, very alert, very sober. It will not be duped, either because there are urgent public matters requiring attention (Ehrenhalt did not feel this was the case during the '96 presidential campaign) or because it is fed up with the tiresome prattle and empty promises of candidates (a situation he believed applied in '96). When the latter exists, candidates who frame issues well and discuss public matters seriously will be rewarded; those who do not will be punished. The lesson of 1996 appears to be that this is indeed the case.

But how are candidates to know if the election is one in which the voters are asleep or awake? Can polling data help them tell? Perhaps, but in fact this question leads to the second conclusion from our vignettes. Candidates who succeed in defining the terms and territory through which the campaign proceeds and on which the battle will be fought have a major impact on the presence or absence of issues. Indeed, this question is key. In the examples cited above, none of the candidates were able to determine the substance and tone of the campaign. For all of Mondale's and Babbitt's cerebral abilities, they never could displace the frameworks that the popular and genial Reagan or the hard-nosed organizational strategist Dukakis imposed on the campaigns. Nor were Lugar and Alexander able to subvert the right-wing language and themes that Dole and Buchanan imposed on the Republican primary. Dole, in turn, chose to discuss matter during the campaign in which the public was not interested; more than that, he was repeatedly put on the defensive by the remarkable ability of candidate Clinton to steal his agenda and frame issues coherently and appealingly, neither of which Dole could do.

In a very real sense, then, each of these failed candidates was forced to fight campaign battles on the opponents' field. The opponents defined the territory, terms, and agenda of the campaign. To the extent that their opponents emphasized certain issues in a way that either captured what the public was thinking or framed them in a way the public found acceptable and appealing, so did they play a prominent role in these campaigns. To the extent that they stressed or emphasized something else, so did issues play a secondary role. In any case, in all of these instances the candidates we have discussed played a catch-up, defensive role in the campaigns on territory defined by their opponents. No one was able to overcome this severe handicap.

But what determines the ability of one candidate rather than another to define the campaign territory? One obvious answer is political skill, style, and appeal. At any given time, and in any given election, one candidate is better able to capture the attention and imagination of the public than others; that candidate usually wins. How and why this happens is generally a function of reading the mood of voters, assessing what is on their minds, and finding a way to touch their minds and hearts. We call this political skill, style, and appeal. But this does not explain why and how issues appear in campaigns, and what role if any they play. We turn now to this important matter, beginning with the most fundamental question: what are issues, and where do they come from?

The Public Mood and the Issues

Few words are used more frequently, but with less specificity, in campaigns than is "issue." Voters claim they want to hear about "issues"; candidates want to raise or explain their position on "issues"; sponsors of candidate debates and forums say they want to provide an opportunity for "issues" to be discussed; the media say they report on "the issues." What is an issue, anyway?

An issue is something the public cares about. It is a public concern that may or may not lie within the purview of government to resolve, or even address (indeed, the question of the appropriateness of government response or action is itself an issue). Thus, to the extent the public cares or worries about a matter, so could it become an issue in a campaign; that is, candidates will be expected to talk about it. If the public is not worried, or does not care, so will issues fail to emerge, or decline in importance. Indeed, they can become insignificant or even constitute sideshows in campaigns if the public is inattentive, not listening, or bored.

The public's role in deciding what is an issue is often misjudged. As we will see shortly, candidates can assuredly influence the issue agenda during campaigns, but it is rare that a candidate can successfully inject an issue into a campaign if the public cares little about it, or if the candidate fails to frame the issue in a way that grabs the attention of the voting public. The 1996 presidential campaign was instructive in this regard. Republicans tried to make "character" an issue, or at least President Clinton's alleged character defects. Polls continually showed the public to be mistrustful of the president; but they also were not the least bit interested in Republican railings against his character deficiencies. Indeed, the harder the Republican nominee, Bob Dole, tried to force the character issue in front of the public, the lower his numbers fell. Republicans also tried to make "the economy" an issue, complaining of slow economic growth and the need for a massive tax cut. The public did not listen to this message either, as polls continually showed that most people felt the economy to be in pretty good shape; nor did they any longer believe in the need for a tax cut or take seriously Republican promises to deliver one.

To be effective in campaigns, issues have to emerge from within the voting public's consciousness. They may be latent, they may be ill formed and essentially unarticulated. Smart candidates understand when and if the public has a concern (even if it is inchoate and implicit); their ability to frame these concerns in a way that is appealing to the voting public may well mark the difference between candidates who can capture the attention and imagination of the public, and thus improve their chances for electoral success, and those who cannot do so.

But how do issues then emerge in the public consciousness? Sometimes this question is easy to answer. Events can cause them: for example, when Iranian extremists took Americans hostage in the late 1970s, the public became deeply concerned about our role in world affairs, and the type of leadership President Carter offered compared to that proposed by Governor Reagan. While President Carter was defeated for other reasons as well, it is also clear that this international event injected foreign affairs and presidential leadership of them squarely into the campaign.

A single event is a dramatic way to push issues into a campaign, but issues can also emerge over time, through changing circumstances. For example, economic upturns and downswings rarely occur swiftly, but their evolution can assuredly affect the public's consciousness and perception of how the economy is doing. In the winter of 1996, there was considerable public concern about loss of jobs as large corporations downsized and shifted internal priorities; indeed, the public was so concerned that news programs and weekly newsmagazines ran major stories about how worried the public was, and the president even discussed with corporate leaders the need to preserve and create jobs, not eliminate them. Strangely enough, by the time the presidential campaign was in full swing, most of these public fears had been allayed even though it was clear that some of the underlying structural problems of the economy causing massive layoffs had not been addressed; indeed, as the presidential campaign wore on, many voters expressed satisfaction with and optimism about the economy.

It is also true that candidates, and for that matter the media, can create issues, at least in some circumstances. As noted, sometimes the public is concerned or disturbed, although in a very unfocused way. In this instance, the capacity of the candidate or media to articulate and frame the issue in a way that creates a collective "Aha!" will bring it front and center into the campaign. What is important is that the candidate, or the media, must be attuned to where the public's consciousness is, what its mood is, whether it is generally satisfied or restive (even if only inchoately so). Thus, issues can be created only to the extent that the candidate or the media identify and frame them in a way that resonates with and moves the public. The failure to do so means that their efforts to discuss "issues" will fall on deaf ears.

Examples of this last situation are legion. In the 1996 presidential campaign it may well be that "character" and "economics" were matters requiring public discussion. The problem is that the Republicans failed to frame them in ways that resonated with voters; it may also be that they mishandled them, especially insofar as Republican candidate Bob Dole repeatedly asked voters to trust him as they did not trust the president—but he never gave them a reason why they should trust him. Likewise, Dole's continued assault on the president's character backfired on him, whereas when Reform Party candidate Ross Perot started hammering the same theme with ten days left in the campaign, the voters started listening. Clearly Perot could make the issue resonate, whereas Dole could not.

Prior to the 1994 gubernatorial contest in Florida several of the state's leading newspapers, headed by the *Miami Herald,* formed a consortium to conduct a statewide poll and establish some focus groups to determine what was on people's minds. The thinking of the newspaper editors was that the results of the survey would determine what the "issues" of the campaign would be, and the leading candidates (Jeb Bush for the Republicans, incumbent Lawton Chiles for the Democrats) would have to address them seriously. The results of the poll were somewhat ambiguous; the lone exception was crime and prison construction, the one issue that drove everything else off the table. It was virtually the only matter the candidates discussed in their campaigns; it was certainly the only one the public heard. The newspapers' efforts to direct the agenda of the campaign were essentially a failure, because no other issues resonated with or moved the public in the same way that crime and prisons did.

It is often stated that candidates in elections simply tell the public what it wants to hear, instead of informing and leading it. While this is something of an overstatement, in fact the preceding discussion indicates why it is more true than not. Candidates who talk about issues—that is, public concerns—in which the voters are not interested are not likely to have much success. Those who are attuned to public moods and attitudes at least potentially can gain the attention of the public, a necessary if not sufficient precondition to getting elected. Of course candidates tell voters what they want to hear; to do otherwise is politically suicidal.

However, it is also true that candidates do have the opportunity to decide how they wish to conceive of and frame issues. It is in this sense that candidates can lead public opinion. If public opinions were sharply focused and articulate, candidates would probably merely parrot back the public's attitudes and views. But we know this is a rare occurrence in public opinion; it is usually ill formed, transient, nonspecific. What happens more commonly is that the public's sense of issues constitutes broad parameters within which candidates can and need to find ways to frame and articulate public concerns and worries. Thus, it is not quite correct to say that candidates simply tell the public what it wants to hear; rather, candidates vie with each other (and struggle within their own campaigns) to decide whether or not they even can or should raise an issue, and if so how it is to be done. They understand all too well that unless they do so in a way that resonates with and moves the public, the effort will be at best wasted, and at the worst dysfunctional for their campaign.

There is a further problem with candidate introduction of issues into campaigns: doing so may resonate with some voters—even an important bloc or segment of voters—but alienate others, perhaps even a majority. The experience of the Democratic Party during the 1970s and 1980s is instructive in this regard. To many people, the party during this time seemed captured by special interests; it appeared to articulate an agenda geared less to mainstream middle-class concerns than to satisfying the demands of particular constituencies. In responding to these pressures, the party may well have sown the seeds for its electoral struggles during the 1990s.

Much the same thing happened to the Republican Party during the early 1990s. As it began to focus on issues more important to the Christian right and other social conservatives, it lost the support of women and many traditional, conservative but nondoctrinaire Republicans; at least some of the party's losses in the 1996 U.S. House of Representatives races, and Dole's weak showing at the presidential level, can be traced to the narrowly based issue orientation it adopted in San Diego during its August convention.

Issues, then, are very much a double-edged sword. They may attract and solidify support in some wings of the party, yet cause other constituencies to waver, even abandon ship. Just as the party as a whole needs to determine what issues it wants to raise in its platform and how it wishes to frame them, so too do candidates have to decide whether the articulation of an issue position will attract voters or drive them away. It should not be too surprising, therefore, that many candidates say little or nothing about issues during campaigns, or do so in ways that can most politely be described as bland. To seem overly forceful, or to take positions the public may feel are out of step with its own concerns, is to invite disaster.

The Role of Issues in Campaigns

Are we therefore to conclude that issues are of little use in campaigns? Nothing could be further from the truth. In fact, they can be of profound importance in shaping the dynamic and influencing the outcome of political campaigns.

Let us begin by reasserting that there are elections in which the public is very much attuned to issues, and those in which it is not. As Ehrenhalt noted during the 1996 campaign, in some elections the voters seem little concerned about public questions, and are content with expressions of patriotic sentiment, and other drivel. At other times, however, the public is worried, or at least attentive. Politicians who fail to sense what is on the voters' minds, and speak to their concerns in a reasonably responsive way, may find themselves unsuccessful once the polls close on election day.

Thus, in a very real way the public decides how much or how little it wants to hear of issues during campaigns. The problem, of course, is that "the public," or even "the voters," are not monolithic. While the vast majority of voters may feel apathetic, indifferent, or bored, some segments of the voting population will be hot and bothered about something. To the extent candidates respond to the former, and say little or nothing, so will the latter feel cheated and complain that the campaign isn't focusing on issues; but if candidates focus on those with a pronounced issue agenda, they may lose or alienate the bulk of those who do not.

Assuming, however, that the voting public and the candidates are more or less on the same wavelength about what public questions and concerns need to be addressed—a situation that occurs fairly often, perhaps even in most elections—what role do issues actually play? Do they have any strategic and political utility, above and beyond addressing what the public thinks it wants to hear about? At least four such strategic and political values can be noted, as detailed below: issues can define a candidate's political persona; they can be used to define the opposition; winning coalitions can be assembled around them; and, increasingly, many campaigns are fought purely over issues in popular referendum votes.

Defining Political Personalities

In the first place, issues allow candidates to define their political personalities. Any honest candidate will readily admit that one of the most daunting tasks of a campaign is the creation of a political identity that can be known to and recognized by the voting public. Whatever the candidates may be like in private and professional life and however famous in their own living rooms, once in the political arena most people will never have heard of them, and will know nothing of who they are and what they might do if elected.

Issues—or at least slogans associated with issues—can actually help create this necessary political identity. "Pro-choice" or "pro-life" may not say very much, but the phrases give a clue as to the position of the candidate not simply on abortion but conceivably on other social issues as well. Other issue slogans do the same: "Protect Medicare and Social Security"; "Three Strikes and You're Out"; "Just Say No"; "Say Yes to Charter Schools"—the list is virtually endless, readily adaptable to virtually any elective office at any level. From the standpoint of voters desiring a lot of issue content in campaigns, these brief issue statements are of little use. From the candidate's point of view, however, they are of great strategic value. They commit him or her to virtually nothing, but they give some indication of what the candidate stands for, and how he or she might relate to other issues. Most importantly, they provide a handle for voters to grab on to; they give a sense of identity and persona to what otherwise is just a name on a campaign advertisement or on the ballot when they get to the voting booth.

Defining the Opposition

Issues can also help a candidate define the opponent. In this connection, issues are especially useful for painting an opponent into a corner by suggesting the opponent is "out of step" or on the wrong side of what the public wants and needs. During the 1970s and 1980s, for example, Republicans often ran roughshod over Democrats on crime issues. Whether true or not, Republicans managed to convince voters that Democrats were "soft" on crime because of a seeming concern with the rights of criminals instead of the victims of crime, an emphasis on rehabilitative programs instead of punishment, and the like. In these instances Democrats often ran away from the crime issue since it was clear that public opinion favored the Republican position, and it was not until President Clinton took the crime issue away from the Republicans during the 1990s that Democrats could again feel comfortable with it.

Issues of national defense also caused political embarrassment for Democrats. When President Reagan characterized the Soviet Union as the "evil empire," he articulated what many Americans felt about our cold-war opponent. Democrats, on the other hand, seemed to want to cut defense spending, or at least Republicans managed to define and identify them in this way. Polls repeatedly showed that the public often regarded Democrats as "weak" on defense; in the presidential election of 1988, the Democrats actually undermined their own position through an advertisement showing their party's nominee, Mike Dukakis, riding in circles in a tank.

Other examples that show how candidates can characterize their opponents as out of step are legion. In recent years certain moral issues have achieved the status of a litmus test, and candidates in particular areas and with particular constituencies can use them to embarrass an opponent, or suggest the opponent is on the wrong side of the issue and therefore is unacceptable to voters: the choice issue and affirmative action are two such examples. Sometimes it is not even necessary to raise a particular issue in order to make the point that the candidate is out of step: in the 1988 U.S. Senate race in Florida the Republican candidate, Connie Mack, successfully used an advertisement in which he claimed his opponent, Buddy MacKay, was "a liberal." There was no mention of specific issues or positions that MacKay held; he was simply stuck with this label, and his response was weak and ineffectual. The term "liberal" by itself was enough to conjure up feelings and attitudes in the electorate sufficient to undercut the support of the popular MacKay; Mack won.

Divide and Conquer, or Assemble Winning Coalitions

Issues not only define candidates, they can further be used to divide the electorate or, conversely, to build coalitions of voters. In the first instance, candidates (as well as sitting public officials) can use issues to create dichotomies and force the public to make choices as to which side they want to be on. Richard Nixon as president, for example, used to talk about not taking the easy way, but the right way, when he contemplated yet another move in the Vietnam War. Thus he forced the public to decide whether it wanted to be on the "good" side or the wrong side. When Ronald Reagan asked voters to decide in the presidential campaign of 1980 if they were better off than they were four years earlier, he also created a division in which voters either abandoned President Carter for him or remained loyal to an increasingly discredited administration.

In recent years the candidate who used dichotomies to divide the public most dramatically was probably Pat Buchanan, the populist Republican presidential candidate in 1992 and 1996. Buchanan was a wizard at exciting his followers by laying down a series of gauntlets as he summoned them to fight the culture war he felt was destroying America. These choices included not only moral issues such as opposition to abortion, but extended even into the abstract realm of international economics as he opposed the North American Free Trade Agreement (NAFTA). In each of the instances Buchanan chose, he continually painted the choices as black and white, with no middle gray areas possible. Voters had to choose; they were either with him, on the right side of the culture war, or against him, in which case they were the bad guys. Buchanan was not successful in capturing his party's presidential nomination, but his ability to frame issues in such a way as to divide the voters into "them" and "us" greatly influenced the Republican platform and presidential campaign in both years.

Issues can also be used to create alliances and coalitions of voters. Here too the experience of sitting presidents is as instructive as that of campaigners for the office. Lyndon Johnson's oft-cited phrase, "Come, let us reason together," is an example of an effort to create consensus on an issue; the fact that his phrase really meant "let's do it my way" does not undermine the point that issues can be used to bring voters together. His March 1965 speech to Congress and the nation outlining the need for the Voting Rights Act is a further example of the unifying and consensus-building role that issues can have, especially during the portion of the speech in which he invoked the anthem of the civil rights movement by stating, "We shall overcome."[4]

Issues can play the same role in campaigns. In his 1960 presidential race John F. Kennedy focused heavily on a perceived "missile gap" between the United States and the Soviet Union; in invoking this phrase Kennedy actually sought to create a winning alliance based on the need for increased defense spending and a hard-line cold-war policy. More recently President Clinton repeatedly urged voters to "build a bridge to the twenty-first century," an appeal designed not just to turn them away from the seemingly backward-looking campaign of his opponent but to create an alliance of voters geared toward future policy needs.

Issue Campaigns

Finally, there are some campaigns that are solely about issues. In recent years, American politics has seen a mushrooming of petition drives, legislative agendas, referenda, and constitutional amendments, all of them at state and local levels. The reasons for this unique political development extend beyond the scope of this chapter. What is important for our purposes is that they involve vast and expensive campaigns for the purpose not of electing or defeating candidates, but of approving or disapproving proposals on particular policy issues. The politics of some of these campaigns have become as complex, and heated, as those of candidates for public office; one need only think of the 1996 campaigns in California concerning the future of affirmative action in state-sponsored programs (voters rescinded its use) and the $30 million spent in Florida over a proposed tax on sugar growers to clean up pollution in the Everglades (it was defeated). It is too early to say whether or not issue campaigns will continue as prominently and expensively as they have become in American politics. What we can say, however, is that those pundits and voters who decry the absence of issues in American politics are ignoring what has grown well beyond a cottage industry into a massive political undertaking. Campaigns based solely on issues are now very much a part of our political landscape.

Candidates and Issues

We noted earlier that if a candidate's selection and discussion of issues is to resonate with the public, this discussion must be attuned to the public's overall mood and attitude about them. When this congruence is lacking, it is highly likely that candidates will feel as though they are talking to themselves; likewise the public might feel that such a candidate is out of touch with the electorate.

We also noted earlier that the requirement that candidates dwell on issues the public cares about, and ignore those it does not, often amounts to the candidate's simply telling the public what it wants to hear. But in fact the matter is somewhat deeper than this. Do the candidates simply reflect public opinion in their discussion of issues, or can they lead public opinion? More normatively, does not the candidate have an obligation to lead public opinion, since presumably he or she is in a position to be knowledgeable about public questions and thus has the responsibility to inform the public so that intelligent collective decisions will be made?

The answer to this latter question generally devolves into a resurrection of the old civics model of American democracy. The model looks something like this: citizens need to be informed about and interested in questions of public concern (that is, issues). Granted that most citizens lack the time and resources needed to fully inform themselves, it is incumbent upon public officials and candidates for public office to present the various sides of the issues and debate them intelligently, so that citizens can then weigh the options and rationally choose which one—and which candidate—they prefer.

The actual workings of our democracy look a good deal different from this model, as everybody knows. But that does not make the questions posed earlier go away: should not candidates get out front on public issues? Why don't we expect them to "lead" instead of reflecting what most of us already believe, or just want to hear? Is there not room for candidates to shape public opinion? Indeed, what would happen to a candidate who simply spoke from the heart and the head, told us what he or she thought in a forthright manner, and asked us to vote on that basis alone?

The latter might well be a refreshing change in American politics, but there is already enough experience to suggest that such a candidate is not likely to do well. For example, in 1984 Walter Mondale tried to start an intelligent and realistic conversation about American public finance. He even suggested that a tax increase might be needed, given the rapidly growing national deficit and debt. While there were many people who thought Mondale was saying important and necessary things, most voters preferred the rosy vision of Reaganomics; Mondale was trounced in the presidential election. And so it goes; political prophets, like spiritual ones, are often spurned in their own time and country. Refreshing candor, or even a clear and honest vision, is not always appreciated or understood by voters.

But, it might be objected, if this is true at least most of the time and candidates of vision and candor are often defeated, are we not therefore hurting ourselves? Do we not thereby weaken our democracy, and cause ourselves worse problems and difficulties in the long run because we did not listen to and vote for them?

The answer to these questions, like so many others in political analysis, is a definite "maybe." We probably would be better served if we would listen to and elect candidates willing to lead from the front lines, rather than the rear, as we so often do. But frankly there is little reason to think this will ever happen, given that voters prefer to be entertained more than educated, that they quickly tire of sophisticated and complex discussion of "issues," that they often have a wrong or distorted sense of the issue position of many candidates, and especially that they have increasingly cynical views of politicians.

This latter point may be of greatest importance. For a growing number of citizens and voters, candidates for public office are not to be trusted.[5] Even the most well-intentioned, well-informed, public-spirited candidates have become the object of public scorn, even ridicule. Our tolerance for near slanderous political advertising shows almost no limits. We scarcely believe anybody who runs for public office anymore; the exception may be primarily local candidates, since we are likely to know many of them personally. In an atmosphere in which we are mistrustful of our candidates at best, and at worst regard them contemptuously, it is unlikely that we can readily discern the thoughtful, informed candidate from the one with a good advertising firm helping with the campaign. As a result, why should we expect our candidates to inform us and lead public opinion? We wouldn't believe them anyway, at least as things stand right now.

Moreover, historical evidence suggests that many politicians who turned out to be quality public officials—even leaders—were mealy-mouthed as candidates, and even took positions at odds with subsequent actions. Readers might recall from Chapters 2 and 3 that a number of presidential candidates actually went out of their way to avoid any commitment to issue positions—Jackson and Harrison, for example. Candidates who espoused well-defined positions—Bryan comes to mind—lost badly. Very few of Franklin D. Roosevelt's public pronouncements during the 1932 campaign suggested the type of issue leader he would subsequently become. General Eisenhower promised in 1952 to go to Korea, but said little else, and was elected. During his presidential campaign John Kennedy raised the specter of a missile gap with the Soviet Union, which somehow evaporated during his inaugural ceremony. Richard Nixon told us he had a secret plan to end the Vietnam War; he didn't, and he expanded military action. George Bush in 1988 and Bill Clinton in 1992 promised various tax cuts; neither delivered in any meaningful way. No wonder the public did not believe Bob Dole in 1996!

Indeed, a somewhat different conclusion can be drawn from these and other historical examples. The absence of issue leadership during campaigns is not necessarily an indication that once elected the official (in this case, the president) will be incapable of dealing with public problems and concerns as they arise. They may in fact prove quite adept at issue and policy leadership; some of course were better at it than others (Eisenhower, Kennedy, and Bush, for example, arguably may have been less comfortable with and capable of issue leadership than Nixon, Reagan, or Clinton). The public may not always have agreed with the way they framed issues and directed policy, and presidents as well as other public officials may well have seen their initiatives defeated. Nonetheless, it does seem reasonable to conclude that the failure of candidates in campaigns to engage in a serious discussion of issues in no way implies that once elected the individual, as a public official, will be unable or unwilling to do so. For these reasons then, we cannot say that our democracy is necessarily imperiled because candidates don't seek to engage the voters in a sophisticated discussion of issues.

But we still have to address the more empirical part of the matter raised earlier, namely, is it not possible for candidates to lead public opinion on issues? The answer here, too, is a decided "sometimes." Much depends on the sensitivity of the candidate to the political environment: What's on the voters' minds? What are the people talking about? What are they worried about? If they are in one place and the candidate's agenda is somewhere else, they will be like ships passing in the night, scarcely noticing one another.

Also, the ability of the candidate to frame issues in a way that captures the public's attention and imagination is crucial. It's one thing to have a sense of the concerns and worries the public has, if any. It's quite another to be able to articulate them in a way the public finds credible and acceptable. This is not to say that the public has necessarily to agree with the way the candidate defines an issue; it is to say that the public has to agree that the candidate is at least addressing the matter in a serious and believable way. One of the very best examples of how this works to candidates' advantage and disadvantage came in the two 1996 presidential debates between Bob Dole and Bill Clinton. Dole seemed incapable of framing issues in a way that showed he knew what they involved, even though by most accounts he probably did; indeed, his discussion of issues was thought, by Republicans, Democrats, and independents alike, to be rambling, unfocused, often bewildering. In contrast, the president showed a remarkable talent for briefly and convincingly showing the parameters of issues, as well as some thoughts as to how they should be addressed. Even voters who disagreed with him, and who refused to vote for him, felt Clinton did a far better job at framing and explaining issues than did Dole.

Then, too, the political standing of candidates probably affects their ability to mold and shape public opinion on issues. Those perceived as strong and credible candidates—whether in office or not—may well have more capacity to influence public opinion than those deficient in these qualities. In 1980 President Carter, while respected for his strength of character and commitment to decent values, was no longer seen as either strong or credible on many public questions. His opponent, Ronald Reagan, came across to many voters as strong, decisive, optimistic, and direct, even as he struck others as superficial and incapable of hard thinking. It was the former set of characteristics that carried the day; Reagan proved to be stronger and more credible in the public's eyes and won the election.

A complicating factor in the ability of candidates to lead public opinion is the intensity of feeling the public has about an issue. Where the public feels strongly, candidates probably cannot make much of a dent in public attitudes. In 1980 Americans were so incensed about American hostages held in Iran, and the seeming paralysis of the Carter administration, and its inability to do much about them, that nothing Carter did or said made much of an impression on the public or convinced them that the problem was being dealt with. In contrast, Reagan, who offered nothing concrete in the way of a plan to extricate the hostages, simply rode the wave of public outrage into the White House. On the other hand, if the public lacks strong feelings about an issue, candidates have a greater potential to influence their views.

A complication also emerges when a small segment of the population is important to a candidate and has strong views, whereas most of the public does not or even holds lukewarm views at odds with the smaller group. This is characteristic of "wedge issues" such as gun control or abortion. In these instances, the candidate may well have to reflect the strong views of a relatively small segment of supporters, and at the same time try not to offend or antagonize a larger group needed for election. Republicans felt this problem keenly in 1996; the social conservatives and Christian right held fervent views about abortion rights, whereas many mainstream Republicans (especially women) felt uncomfortable about the party's position. Dole never did secure the right balance between those who cared deeply and those who were uncomfortable; the result was that he lost both the women's vote and the election.

An important question arises: how does the candidate know what is on the public's mind? Candidates for major offices—president, Congress, statewide positions—have access to public opinion surveys and focus groups that can help them divine what, if anything, is troubling voters. There are of course problems associated with these devices. Sometimes "public opinion" on an issue does not really exist unless and until a pollster asks about it, in which case the results constitute a constructed or artificial reality; it is not clear whether this "virtual" reality has the same political importance as one that is "really real." Polls and focus groups cannot always uncover the public's intensity of feelings about an issue, especially if the surveys constitute quick "tracking" measures rather than in-depth analysis, which is both time consuming and costly. For the same reason polls sometimes miss or skip over the important matter of whether or not the voters think an issue requires governmental action; it is one thing to regard a question as an "issue," and quite another to regard it as within the legitimate scope of government to deal with, and if so, how.

In spite of these limitations, surveys of public opinion are of great help to candidates for public office; that candidates often hide behind the data is, as we saw earlier, often regrettable but essentially beside the point, since their issue orientation in campaigns often seems to have little to do with their performance in office. A more serious matter arises in the case of candidates for primarily local (perhaps including state legislative) offices. Except in the largest metropolitan areas, polling is not economically feasible for many candidates for city or county offices. Readers must remember that the smaller the population, the larger the sample must be for the candidate to secure accurate results; commercial firms charge anywhere from eighteen to twenty-five dollars per interview, and thus it can readily be seen that many candidates are reluctant to spend upward of five thousand dollars to have surveys conducted on their behalf.

They must instead rely on their knowledge of the population and the area in which they reside. Indeed, it is a reasonable argument that a candidate for local or state legislative office who does not have a finger on the pulse of the community not only ought not to be in the race, but is likely to be exposed as unqualified. This does not always happen, of course; incompetents and unqualified candidates do win elections. But they are also often turned away by voters, and in fact it is a reasonable argument that in American politics the number and percentage of truly incompetent and unqualified candidates who do win is actually very small. Granted, our perception of who is qualified and competent may very well rest, in part, on whether or not the person happens to be "our" candidate. But even among those with whom we disagree or whom we dislike, it is possible to make a distinction between those who we feel are worthy of holding public office and those who are not. In many ways it is a tribute to the strength of our democratic system of elections that so often voters make this distinction, and defeat those unworthy of the public trust.

What Do Candidates Believe? Does It Matter?

We come, finally, to one last important question concerning issues in campaigns: the relationship between candidates and issues. Does it matter what candidates truly believe? Does it matter if they adopt positions in campaigns at odds with their own beliefs solely out of political expediency? Does it matter if they say one thing during the campaign and do something quite different once in office?

The latter question is the easiest to deal with. The answer is that the public does not seem to make a fetish of consistency. It is well aware that it is one thing to talk or make promises during a campaign, and quite another to govern. In 1992, as a candidate, Clinton railed against President Bush's Haiti policy; once in office, he decided that it was the best one after all, and maintained it. For most Americans Haiti was not an issue in the 1996 election, and it is unlikely that Clinton's reversal cost him many votes. On the other hand, candidates have to be careful about the extent of their commitments during campaigns, especially on pocketbook issues: as a candidate, Vice President Bush's 1988 declaration, "Read my lips, no new taxes," came back to haunt him in 1992.

Indeed, it seems likely that the public accepts that candidates who are turned into public officials will change their minds; they may even expect them to, since a public official who fails to have a change of mind may not have an ear close enough to the ground or be attuned to changes in the political environment. But it is also true that these reversals probably must be evolutionary, not abrupt; Bob Dole caused great wonderment and consternation when, after thirty-five years of advocating a balanced budget, he suddenly announced in August 1996 that he had become a devotee of supply-side economics. And of course reversals of principle—as opposed to policy—also raise questions about a candidate's backbone and give rise to possible charges of expedience. For most of his career George Bush advocated the "choice" position on abortion rights, until he was offered the vice presidential slot under Reagan; and Jack Kemp was a defender of affirmative action until Bob Dole called him in the summer of 1996 to join the ticket. It is not correct to say that these changes were merely abrupt shifts of policy; they were more fundamental than that, since both issues rest on moral principles as much as political analysis. The shadow of the shifts haunted both men, including among the right-wingers they were attempting to mollify, since the archconservatives were never quite convinced of the genuineness of their newfound convictions.

These considerations force us back to our earlier question: Does it matter if a candidate will say anything to get elected? Does it matter if he or she really has no beliefs at all, but is simply the product of whatever happens to be the latest politically correct conventional wisdom?

Put in this manner, the questions force us to recognize that dangers do exist when this happens. Even those who agree with the overall premise of this book—namely, that most of what happens in modern political campaigns doesn't do us any harm—have to recognize that ultimately democratic political institutions and processes must have a basis in moral principles and beliefs if they are to continue to work. Thus, candidates who believe in nothing, or will say anything to get elected, undermine the moral foundation of our democracy.

The reason a lack of commitment endangers our democratic system ultimately rests on the nature of trust. For our democracy to work, we must trust that the candidates, and those selected for office, will act on principles common to all of us, principles that transcend agreement or disagreement on particular policy issues. If these principles are lacking, then we have no basis for holding candidates and public officials accountable for their actions; nor have we any reason to think they will be responsive to public needs and desires. In short, the concept of "public trust" is much more than a fancy phrase in civics books. It is the very heart and soul of our democratic system. If we as citizens and voters lose our capacity to trust candidates and public officials—and data suggest that our levels of trust are very low, and declining[6]—and if by the same token candidates and officeholders fail to recognize that they have been given a public trust based on the assumption that we believe them to be people of principle, then in fact we are in serious danger of undermining our democracy.

Conclusion

In the end, issues occupy a very ambiguous position in the modern political campaign. Voters say they want to hear candidates talk about issues instead of personalities, but when candidates do so, voters lose interest rapidly. They may even vote against candidates who are too forthright in their articulation of issue positions, especially if those positions are outside of what is currently politically acceptable. Far more attractive are the candidates who tell the public what it wants to hear.

For candidates too, issues are very much a double-edged sword. Any given candidate may very well wish to bring matters to the public table because they are important; the question is whether it is possible to get anyone to pay attention, or agree that this is worthy of public discussion. To make matters worse, unless the issue is relatively non-controversial, or the candidate is especially skilled at framing issues in a way that builds consensus, candidates are all too aware that issues can be divisive: for every voter that espousing some position or other attracts, the candidate will likely drive away another, or more than that. No wonder it makes sense to talk in clichés and tell the public what it already knows.

Are we hurting ourselves because "issues" in campaigns often come out like overdone brussels sprouts: bland and mushy? Probably not fundamentally. We may be cheating ourselves out of a robust, vital public debate; we may be limiting our political vocabulary and perpetuating our fear of political discussion. But we probably are not injuring ourselves because of this. We have to remember that elections in this country are primarily matters of public spectacle and entertainment, the modern version of the ancient Roman bread and circuses. Issues, which can be both boring and divisive at the same time, are not central to the way we Americans choose to carry out our electoral needs and requirements. Put more elegantly, issue politics are not really a part of our tradition of political culture; our political campaigning rituals and norms are more oriented toward entertainment and titillation than substance. Indeed, it is a reasonable argument that given the way we view electoral politics, it is astonishing that we have as much public discussion of issues in our campaigns as we do, not that we have so little.

There is a danger, of course. It is that we will elect candidates of no principles, who will say and do anything to win, in the end lowering still further the trust we have in our candidates and public officials. A further loss of trust will be harmful to our democracy. And yet, there is every reason for hope. Rare is it that this sort of person—the totally amoral candidate—is successful. While there is no shortage of voters the day after the election who feel a great mistake has been made, and perhaps a major injustice done, our national experience is that we will survive until the next election, when the cycle repeats itself.

6

Media and the Modern Political Campaign

In the dying days of his failed 1996 presidential campaign, Republican candidate Bob Dole was heard several times to complain about the media coverage he was getting. In particular, he pointed to the *New York Times,* arguably the nation's most prestigious newspaper, as having shown him and his campaign in an unfavorable light while glossing over the errors and foibles and character weaknesses of his opponent, Bill Clinton. The story was widely reported, including in the *Times.*

In attacking the *Times,* and by extension all the news media, and blaming them for the failings and deficiencies of his campaign, Dole joined a long and perhaps distinguished tradition in American politics: when things are going badly, blame the media. It's been going on for a long time. Candidates going down to defeat regularly blame the papers, television and radio, and other forms of media for their alleged lies and distortions, the favoritism they show the other candidate, their mean-spritedness, their emphasis on "the horse race" rather than the issues, their attention to the trivial rather than what the candidates say and stand for, their obsession with fault-finding and reporting of "bad" or negative news rather than "good" or positive developments, their "bias."[1] The list of complaints is endless.

In putting forward these criticisms, Bob Dole and other whiners actually point to a critical aspect of the role of media in modern political campaigns: they believe that the media can make or break a candidate, and determine the outcome of an election, whether at the presidential or the local level. In so doing, these candidates ascribe enormous power and give considerable credit to the media, at least to the extent that this power shapes and molds public opinion in such a way that electoral outcomes depend on what the media do (or don't do), and how.

Is any of this true? The evidence is at best mixed.[2] Scholars investigating the role of the media in American political life, including campaigns, have noted for a long time that most people receive their political information through the media; they get it much less frequently directly from candidates themselves or from other sources. In the past two decades, television of course has become the major purveyor of political information during campaigns. While newspapers and magazines continue to be important for the depth of coverage and scope of information they provide, far fewer people read them thoroughly as a means of finding out about campaigns than those who watch television.

Moreover, the extent of available information about campaigns on television is nothing short of prodigious. Each of the major networks has extensive coverage of presidential campaigns, as well as of major state (and important local) races, even in nonpresidential years. Even local stations carry at least some news about races in the viewing area. Radio, too—whether it involves sophisticated news programs such as those on National Public Radio, or local call-in shows that allow listeners to sound off, toot their own horns, advocate the virtues of their favorite candidate, and blast the failings of an opponent—provides an avalanche of political news and information. Newspapers and magazines, whether national in scope or purely local, also cover political campaigns extensively, whether by sending reporters to follow candidates around or relying on wire-service stories.

There is, then, no shortage of information about political campaigns. That the information may be deemed trivial, one-sided, or superficial is not, at least for the moment, the point. We know that there is a great deal of information about campaigns available to citizens who choose to watch TV, listen to the radio, or read newspapers or magazines.[3]

But we also know that viewers and readers are very skeptical of what they see and read in the media. Public opinion polls repeatedly show that the public does not take the news as reported at face value.

While the public apparently can make the distinction between a news report and a commercial bought and paid for by a candidate, they often don't believe either one. Moreover, we also know that when viewers of news programs are subsequently tested on content, they often get the information wrong. The conclusion is not necessarily that the news report was confusing (although that is a possibility) or that the viewer is stupid (not always true), but rather that he or she was not paying close attention: dinner preparations were under way, the telephone was ringing, the children were noisy. Whatever the reason, their attention was distracted, and they could not focus sufficiently to grasp accurately the content of the news being broadcast. This is of course less true of newspaper readers, but we know that it requires far more attention and cognitive effort to read a newspaper or magazine story than to "watch" the news; relatively few people, compared with the number of TV viewers, are willing to make the effort. Indeed, it is reasonable to ask how many people claiming to "watch" TV really just have it on as background noise while they do something else, instead of focusing their full attention and energy on it.

Thus, in spite of the obvious availability of political information from TV and other media sources, there is still the matter of just what impact all of it has on the voter's perception of the campaign. Can we truly say that the media in fact shape the public's perception to the extent that the media determine the outcome? Definitive evidence would be hard to find, unfortunately.

Moreover, we also know that other forces shape how voters perceive campaigns, and affect their decisions on whom to vote for or indeed whether to vote at all. While various theories of voting behavior exist and none are wholly explanatory,[4] evidence from research indicates that such factors as partisan affiliation or identification, socioeconomic standing, peer and parental influence, perception of how one is faring economically relative to a few years ago, and specific situational or environmental conditions ("I'm worried about my job"; "Taxes around here are too high"; "Look, he's our neighbor"; "I refuse to vote for the guy who wants to build a cement plant in this community"; "I've never voted Democratic in my life, but I can't bear these Christian right types") all greatly affect what a voter will do when in the voting booth. That political scientists cannot fully sort out which of these factors are the most important in no way undercuts the point that voters make up their minds whether or not to vote, and how, based on any number of forces playing upon them. Moreover, the mix of forces shaping their decision may well vary from one election to another, depending on their level of interest in the candidates and issues, their personal or family circumstances, the existence of major environmental or situational problems, and so forth.

And of course the quality of candidate and campaign has an impact on the ultimate outcome of the election. Victory in politics, as elsewhere, does not always come to the strongest or swiftest, but candidates who fail to establish their legitimacy with the public, who are not taken seriously, who seem lacking by whatever standards voters think are important, or who make serious blunders, generally don't win. The media may well report the failings (and the virtues) of candidates and their campaigns, and in so doing reinforce what voters can see and perceive about them, but for the most part they do not present fictional accounts to readers, viewers, and listeners, nor do they make silk purses out of sow's ears. Candidates and campaigns, for the most part, stand or fail on their own; the media report and underscore what is happening in the political arena, and may influence what happens there, but seldom do they determine the outcome.

All of this calls into question the supposed role of the media in determining the outcome of political campaigns. That the media play a role, possibly even an important one, is beyond question. But we need to take a more detached view, even as we love to complain about the media, of what they really do during a campaign. Do the media actually harm us and undermine our democracy in reporting on (in an often maddeningly superficial way) political campaigns?

What Manner of Beast?

There is no shortage of conspiratorial theories concerning the role of the media in modern life, political and otherwise. Some see the media as a tool of capitalists intent on exploiting the working class, or at least of lining their pockets at the expense of everyday people. Others see the media as a propaganda tool of either government or big business (or both, if they are linked in some kind of government-press complex), determined to keep us from finding out "the truth."[5] Still others, less conspiratorial but no less outraged, decry the lack of diversity of the media, often arguing that what we get as news more or less all has a similar political view or agenda behind it. And of course there are those who just say it is biased, and especially shows a "liberal" bias.

We shall have occasion later in the chapter to address some of these concerns, although we shall leave the conspiratorial theorists alone, as they probably would not be satisfied with any explanation unless it involved finding evidence that confirmed their worldview under every shrub and bush.

Let us instead initially focus on what the media consist of, and what accounts for much of what they do.

We can readily adopt the traditional distinction in our discussion of dividing the media into two parts: electronic and print.[6] The electronic media are principally television and radio; the latter has achieved something of a renaissance for conveying political information (about campaigns and otherwise) owing to the existence of talk shows as well as highbrow news programs. Print media of course have the longest history of political coverage in newspapers and magazines. For the purposes of this discussion we shall largely omit handbills, flyers, and direct mail (all of which are legitimate examples of print media) as instances of overtly one-sided or propagandistic material, and not truly "news" oriented.

Let us also make a distinction between media candidates can control and those they cannot. The former involve commercial advertisements bought and paid for by candidates, produced by them to convey a message or information created entirely by and at the discretion of candidates (or their consultants). So-called photo ops (political and journalistic slang for photo opportunities), which are events carefully designed by candidates with hopes that the media will cover them, may well also come under the rubric of candidate-controlled media.[7]

Candidates cannot control the content of stories constituting coverage of campaign events. Most of these stories and reports, whether printed or broadcast, we call "news," although in some instances the use of the term may be questionable; we shall return to this point below. Candidates try hard to influence the content of these stories, but with few exceptions they are generally unsuccessful. These stories are the product of the journalist reporting on them, the editorial policy of the news outlet involved, and occasionally the influence of publishers or other powerful shapers of that outlet's modus operandi.[8]

In general, it is these stories that cause candidates the greatest grief, and generate the most complaints. While they may complain about their opponents' "dirty" or misleading advertisements, they also recognize that the political campaign game is played hard and will probably involve negative advertising. They tend to be most exercised, therefore, when they perceive that news stories portray them or their campaigns in unflattering or unfavorable lights, since in their view these stories are supposed to be, at worst, "objective." Readers should not be too taken in by this term, however, for in the midst of a heated political campaign the term "objective" becomes a synonym for "favorable," and anything short of that ranges in a politician's characterization from "not objective" to "biased" to "malicious and misleading" to "libelous" and potentially actionable in law. The latter, while often threatened by outraged candidates, seldom actually occurs.

Do the print and electronic media do the same things? Do they convey "the news" (leaving aside at least for the moment the purpose and content of candidate-paid advertisements) in the same way, and with the same impact? What are the advantages and disadvantages of each for modern political campaigns?

These questions have been well addressed elsewhere and require only a brief comment here. The print media are generally thought to provide a more complete and comprehensive set of news stories on political campaigns than electronic media; a printed transcript of a half-hour television news show does not contain enough words to fill up the front page of a standard-sized newspaper. There is room and opportunity in print media to include details not possible on a broadcast; the print media also permit a greater range of interpretation and analysis of events, especially to discuss the context of a news story. Print provides an explicit mechanism for conveying editorials and opinion seldom available to electronic media. Whether true or not, it is often said that print media offer a more cerebral and serious coverage of news than electronic media do, although the news programs on CNN, C-SPAN, National Public Radio, and the Public Broadcasting System might well qualify this statement.

By contrast, electronic media, especially television, wins kudos for the visceral quality of the impact it makes on viewers (at least those paying attention). While words may be less important on television than on radio, there is no doubt about the punch that pictures can convey. The speed at which television and radio can cover events is instantaneous; it is now a commonplace for them to broadcast live as events unfold, and indeed the electronic media are sometimes criticized if all they offer is a taped version later on the news. By comparison, the print media—in spite of *USA Today*—move at a snail's pace. In addition, the electronic media have the capacity—some would say an overtendency to the point of superficiality—to reduce complex issues to ones readily understood by just about anyone. On the other hand, this capacity makes it easy for viewers and listeners to follow the story and presumably get something out of it. The result may be that the electronic media have a broader, if more shallow, impact on the public than do the print media. Finally, of course, it is cheaper—in terms of time and money spent—to watch television or switch on the radio than it is to buy a newspaper or newsmagazine.

There are also shortcomings of each medium germane to campaign coverage. The slow pace of print media sometimes seems dysfunctional in today's rapid-paced world of political campaigning—in which transcontinental campaign stops in a single day are the norm, not the exception—and more geared to the whistle-stops of railroad train campaigns. Inaccuracies and distortions have sometimes characterized electronic campaign coverage, as the need for speed, beating the other networks, and parsimony of presentation force errors or compressions of facts. Both media are regularly accused of slanting their stories, of "making" news instead of reporting it, of focusing on the trivial or sensationalistic, and perhaps most seriously of lacking perspective, insofar as they overreact to the importance of today's story and bury it in tomorrow's broadcast or back pages as a new "major" story unfolds.

Shortly we shall look at whether or not some of these criticisms are deserved. Before doing so, we need to look at two other issues: the driving force behind the media and its relationship to political candidates.

What Makes the Media Run?

Money makes the media run.[9] Not money in the conspiratorial sense mentioned earlier, but in the sense that members of the media are business organizations as much concerned with their profit margins— or at least cutting their losses—as any other business. The fact that many print and electronic media firms are part of large national or even international business conglomerates does not detract from this central point. They are in business to make money, not to serve as fiscal drains for other, more profitable parts of the owners' corporate enterprises. They are not charities, nonprofit organizations, or, generally speaking, tax write-offs.

These comments also apply, at least indirectly, to National Public Radio (NPR) and the Public Broadcasting System (PBS). True, they are essentially nonprofit organizations relying heavily on public subsidies to exist. But increasingly their funding relies less on congressional appropriations than on private sources, both corporate and individual. In order to appeal successfully to the private sector, they must in some respects emulate it. Thus, while they do not have to show a "profit" in the sense that a newspaper or TV or radio station must, neither can they appear as a bloated, inefficient public bureaucracy reminiscent of those in the former Soviet Union. They must at least try to operate according to the norms and rules of modern private business organizations—which fundamentally means a concern with the bottom line.

That the media are in business to make money, or at least to concern themselves with efficient operations, has certain implications for the way they cover news generally, and campaigns in particular. In the first place, finances determine which campaigns get covered, and how extensively they are covered. For national news networks and newspapers and magazines with national readerships this is less of an issue than for local or regional media. National media cover campaigns nationally, and make a financial commitment to do so; indeed, some may vie with one another to provide more "complete" or "inside" coverage.

For coverage of local campaigns, however, lack of resources is a real problem. Candidates often complain that the local media are not covering their candidacies. Sometimes even the public (or at least parts of the public) complains that the local TV station and paper provide only the barest coverage and lack information about the candidates and their issues. Why don't they put more reporters on the political beat, and have more local political stories in the news?

Part of the answer is purely a lack of resources. Local media are rarely financially flush to begin with. Even the largest stations and newspapers in metropolitan areas have a limited staff of journalists. During the campaign season it is common practice for them to assign reporters to particular races—but they have other news to cover as well. Unless they are a national news organization, the media usually cannot afford to hire reporters solely to cover the political beat—and when there are numerous state and local races, the task becomes financially as well as managerially impossible. Often, too, reporters—and editors—perceive campaigns as too long and repetitive, so that a story once a week or so, until the very end anyway, is sufficient; unless there is some sort of revelation or bombshell or scandal in the local race, the story one week is often pretty much the same as it was the week before. Why keep reporting it over and over again?

The media also find that not everyone in their viewership or readership likes to follow politics—indeed, may find it distasteful. Political stories have a way of dividing the public; since voters have to choose from among different candidates and issues, they may decide that the way a favored candidate or campaign is portrayed by the media is somehow offensive, and turn off the TV or quit reading the paper. Since the size of the audience has a direct impact on advertising revenue, news outlets do everything possible to attract, not drive away, that audience. If politics is causing people to push the "off" button or to not buy the paper, the bottom line suffers. Better to reduce political coverage and keep the audience, even expand it!

This latter point may well explain why other news drives out political news, especially but not exclusively from local media. For reasons that go beyond the scope of this book, the public seems to prefer either soft news (sometimes called human interest stories) or more hard-edged news about murders, car wrecks, robberies, and so forth. And of course everyone wants sports and weather reports. The media respond to—and sometimes lead—these public demands by emphasizing sensationalist aspects of stories. Scandals, excitement, tragedy—the public eats them up, even as it gets bored by campaign and other news (unless of course it is sensationalistic). Again, the media cannot afford to alienate the public, because if that happens the bottom line suffers.

Some readers will object that all of this sounds terribly callous and cynical. Don't the media have a public responsibility—an obligation to inform the public about current events, and even educate citizens about the world around them? Does not the masthead slogan so proudly displayed daily on the *New York Times*—"All the News That's Fit to Print"—imply that there is a duty to bring to readers an account of what is going on in the world around them? Are not news organizations something other, something more, than moneygrubbing capitalist institutions?

The answer to these questions is, probably. On the other hand, readers cannot discount the importance of financial considerations as the media decide and which campaigns are to be covered (among the other available political news), how, when, and in what depth. It seems clear, for example, that the expansion of television news in the late 1950s and early 1960s into half-hour formats was based in part on changing technologies, which allowed more news to be covered faster, but also on the bottom line: viewers actually watched the news, and wanted more. Thus, advertisers were willing to pay networks and local stations for increased coverage, and news became, if not always profitable, at least financially viable.

Having said all this, however, has not made the question of the informational role of the media go away. Does it not affect any decisions? The answer seems to be that it does, but it plays a secondary role. The media will not sacrifice their bottom line to educate or inform the public, but they will seek to do so if they can generate a sufficient audience to justify charging lucrative advertising rates. This is not always as difficult as it seems. Those who read newspapers and newsmagazines regularly and who watch news programs attentively—that is, those who follow the news, including campaign news—are often relatively advantaged in levels of education and income. Thus, they are aware of, and even willing to support, advertisers who pay for the programs, newspapers, and magazines. The trick for the media, then, is to keep this segment of the audience happy, but not alienate other potential audience members by boring them.

No wonder, then, that so much news coverage is superficial! No wonder the emphasis in campaign coverage is so often the horse race (that is, who is doing what today, whose numbers are moving up or down, and which candidates made fools of themselves) rather than issues, implications, and consequences. Indeed, it is no wonder that campaign news is sandwiched in between the day's murders and traffic accidents, or follows the indictment of the local bank president. The media want to inform, but in the process they may well have to entertain because there is a need to recognize and cater to public tastes, desires, preferences, and priorities.

Although the point cannot really be proved, it may well be the case that individual journalists are more committed to providing a public service, in the form of education and information, than the news organizations for which they work. Modern journalists are highly professional reporters, conscious of the ethical as well as reportorial standards they must uphold. They want their stories to be substantively sound, accurate, and credible; they also want them to be read, heard, or viewed. As a group as well as individuals, they take their jobs seriously, and want the public to take what they say or write seriously.[10] Many apparently feel stymied by their jobs, because they cannot always report stories they are trained or inclined to cover, in the way and depth they want. Others either come to terms with these barriers, or move on to more sympathetic newspapers or electronic media outlets. What seems clear is that many feel a desire to do more than contribute to the profitability of their employers. They may well, then, have a very different view of the news, and coverage of campaigns, than the organization that pays them.

Candidates and Media: Oil and Water

To understand fully the role the media play in the modern political campaign, it is important to discuss the relationship between the media and the candidates and their campaigns. The fact of the matter is that they are like oil and water, or cobras and mongooses, or Montagues and Capulets: they don't mix well. In fact, there is a fundamental tension between them leading to irreconcilable differences. No wonder each complains about the other![11]

Candidates and the media have very different needs and expectations about what should be reported and how. These differences are so vast that conflict is inevitable. While individual candidates may have idiosyncratic views about the role the media should play, essentially all have at least the following set of expectations:

Favorable Publicity

We noted earlier that candidates expect reporters to be "objective," which for them means favorably disposed and sympathetic. It rarely occurs to candidates that reporters are supposed to write up or broadcast "the news," or that they may define objectivity differently than politicians do. They dislike intensely the fact that reporters and their editors may think there is more than one side to a story, and that all of those sides need to be presented. Instead, they see the job of a journalist as providing favorable publicity for their particular campaign; at a minimum, they expect to be put in the most favorable light. Anything less makes them nervous, at best, and angry or worse depending on how much of a hatchet job they think the journalist did.

Get the Facts Right

Related to favorable publicity is concern that the journalist regard the candidate's version of the facts as the true and right one. Candidates often have trouble with the notion that the journalist may actually try to be objective by calling the facts put forward by campaigns into question. As far as most candidates are concerned, their campaign facts should be treated as gospel, and reported as such. They become upset when reporters ask awkward questions about their facts, or even have the audacity to report other (especially an opponent's) facts as the true, or at least more credible, ones. It does occasionally happen that a reporter, heavily sympathetic to a particular candidate or opposed to another one, will go easy on the facts the favored candidate puts forward. But this is rare and definitely the exception; the norms and credos of modern professional journalists call for them to make independent assessments of facts, and not to report untested those presented by candidates.[12]

Embarrass the Opponent

Candidates want the media to make their opponents look bad. Rare is the candidate who is not clothed in self-righteousness and a feeling that this campaign is one of destiny. Not infrequently candidates identify so closely with their campaign or cause that they take it, and themselves, far too seriously. The result is that the campaign becomes one of good versus evil, of right against wrong. Under these circumstances, they often assume that the media will readily grasp the teleological significance of their campaign, and report it accordingly. They fail to recognize that, of course, the opposition probably feels the same way, and has the same expectations of the media. There is an assumption, sometimes tacit but too often explicit, in many campaigns that the media will portray the opposition's warts and defects as it reports stories; it usually comes as a surprise, even a shock, to discover that the reports reveal their soft underbelly as well as, even instead of, the opponent's. Modern professional journalists seldom serve as shills for individual candidates or causes, regardless of their personal views; yet candidates continue to assume that because right and justice are on their side, and wrongheadedness and nefariousness on that of the opponent, reporters will prepare their stories with this in mind.

The preceding paragraphs have suggested sharp differences between what candidates expect of journalists during their campaigns and what journalists are prepared to do. Rare are the journalists who accept anything a candidate says at face value; journalists by training, and perhaps by inclination, are skeptics, even cynics.[13] Rarer still are those who will orient their stories overtly to enhance or diminish the electoral chances of a candidate. They may well report on facts that seem to suggest that one candidate is gaining ground and another losing, or that one candidate has a problem or weakness another one does not. But unless they work for a paper or station that has an overt partisan or policy agenda, and irrespective of their own political views, the contemporary reporter dedicated to professional work will form independent judgments about the candidates, their facts, and their campaigns, and write accordingly.[14] The quality of journalists' work can legitimately be judged or questioned by how well they carry out the tasks of the professional reporter—how thorough is the coverage of a campaign, what facts are brought out, how informed and balanced are decisions about what to write, and how well are the stories crafted. The product that appears in print or on the air may well alienate and antagonize candidates; but unless the reporter has made some sort of mistake—which can happen, of course—there is no need for apologies to candidates or the public.

Candidates may ultimately have to face the reality that newspapers and broadcast stations are not going to do them any favors; and even if reporters seem cooperative, they will not simply eat out of candidates' hands or do what candidates want. Indeed, the best protection for candidates is to adopt as skeptical a position regarding the media as most reporters and their employers do regarding them. If they want favorable coverage, they very likely will have to pay for it in the form of commercial advertising.

What other forces are at play, from the journalists' perspective, that influence how they do their jobs, and serve to create incompatibilities between candidates and them? We have already noted the skepticism they bring to their jobs, and a professional commitment to making an independent assessment of facts and forming judgments about them. They clearly want to inform readers, viewers, and listeners, but to do so in a way that represents a third-party view, that of the detached onlooker, and not simply to parrot the candidates (although they may well quote what they say).

There is more. Journalists want to be noticed. They want people to read their stories, or watch and listen to them. Here is another basis for antagonism between journalists and candidates. Attracting attention may well best be accomplished by highlighting conflicts, antagonisms, arguments. Readers and viewers may well get bored if all the reporter does is relay the candidates' latest speeches at the Rotary Club or news conferences at a subway station. Big deal. They will notice, however, if the story involves a fight between candidates, or somehow focuses on the personal antagonisms and demeanors that candidates show one another. The clothes worn and the attitudes shown on the campaign trail thus become grist for the journalist's mill, because how many times can the same speech be reported, and the public expected to pay attention to it? Odd occurrences on the campaign trail, or at least events that somehow point to the successes or failings of the campaign, become more important than what the candidates say or do. The journalist wants to be noticed, and wants to create interest. The best way to ensure that this happens is to focus on conflict, or personal qualities of the candidates, or a campaign organization that is rife with dissension and falling apart, or views of citizens and other officials willing to comment on the shortcomings or virtues of the candidate, or his necktie or her wardrobe—anything but The Speech or The Message of the Day, both of which become shopworn and boring quickly.[15]

Thus, to candidates, the journalist may be focusing on peripheries and irrelevancies. They quickly become concerned that the stories reported do not include "their message," which includes how wrongheaded the opposition is. They feel that the media are ignoring the substance of the campaign and dealing with matters of no concern.

In fact, of course, they may be of real concern to the journalist, and the audience. It follows that totally different conceptions emerge of what the campaign is, what it is saying, and what is important about it. Candidates want to see their meat and substance reported, or at least something bad about their opponent—and they don't find it. Journalists want conflict, smoke and fire, something interesting that attracts an audience. It's like oil and water; they just won't mix.

Some candidates are aware of all this, of course. Some recognize that the best way to get the media's attention is to start a fight. No wonder they quickly resort to negative campaigning—at least it gives something to journalists that they can report, in a way that will attract an audience. There are costs to this, of course: the public does not always approve of negative campaigning, the reputation of the candidate might suffer, and once the bombs start exploding there is no telling who will get hurt the most, since negative campaigns are hard to control. But candidates embarking on such a course can be assured that journalists will notice them!

But what about candidates who will not or cannot engage in negative campaigns, who insist on "running on the record" or otherwise engaging in a low-key, substantive campaign effort? They might find media coverage scanty, and what does exist may focus heavily on personal or other nonsubstantive differences between the candidates. They might even find the media coverage seemingly designed to create conflict and antagonism even when none are present, by the way in which a reporter crafts the story and the perspective chosen and facts conveyed. This is almost certain to produce an antagonistic, hostile response: "Why is the reporter saying this—it's not the issue!" a candidate will complain.

The answer is that the journalist wants to find and report something interesting and provocative. Then, too, the media usually have the last word, at least as far as what reaches the public, unless the candidate decides to pay for yet another ad to refute the reporter's story. Otherwise all that can be done is to fume and stew about it. But these considerations raise another set of issues central to our discussion of the relationship of the media to political campaigns: do the media actually "create" the news, and is it biased?

Making Biased News?

Do the media make the news? Is there a bias, as is so often charged, in the coverage of campaigns, especially in a liberal direction? Do the media have an undue influence on the outcome of political campaigns, whether at the presidential or local level?

These are very common questions and complaints about the role the media play in modern campaign politics. It is not just losing candidates who voice them, either; winning politicians, academicians, even journalists themselves worry about them, especially the question of whether the media exert an inordinate amount of influence on the outcome of campaigns.

These are not simple questions to answer. Let us begin with the last question first, probably the easiest to address. Earlier in the chapter we noted that it is highly unlikely that the media alone determine the outcome of political campaigns. Let there be no doubt, however, that the media do influence what happens in campaigns; candidates and their consultants watch and follow how the media report what they are doing and how it is perceived, and make adjustments accordingly. But to reinforce a point made earlier, as the media report the successes and failings of a candidate's campaign, they convey to the public a sense of what is actually going on, and underscore it. To this extent, they clearly influence what happens. But there is no evidence to suggest that what they really do is replace the reality—that is, what the fortunes of candidate and campaign might be—with their preferred version of that reality, that is, one they concoct.

What we can say, then, is that the media act like a magnifying glass. By focusing on certain aspects of campaign activity and developments, they underscore the campaign's importance and presumably its impact on readers, viewers, and listeners. Candidates and voters may disagree with and perhaps disapprove of the choices made by journalists as to the subject to be emphasized and magnified. And there is no doubt that by making these choices as to what to write or talk about, journalists force us to focus on those aspects of the campaign that they think are the most important, and these may well be ones candidates would just as soon forget about, and ones the public regards as trivial or irrelevant. In this way, the media are very influential. But to then argue that this influence is undue or unwarranted is probably inappropriate; as we noted earlier, there are too many other factors influencing the outcome of campaigns to ascribe a determining or definitive role to the media.

These considerations lead to a somewhat deeper question: by acting as a magnifying glass, does not the media therefore actually make the news? Before addressing this important matter, it must be noted that it raises an equally difficult question: What is it that constitutes "the news" anyway? While presumably it is some event or situation that someone deems worthy of public consumption, the debate over what standards exist for making this determination takes us well beyond the scope of this book, even in the relatively limited world of campaign news.

Let us, instead, simply posit that there is something called news that is reported in the media. Do the media then "make" it? Can the public be assured that what is reported is really real, or is it merely a figment of a reporter's imagination?

We can dispose of the latter question quickly. Professional journalists try very hard to convey a sense of reality, of what actually happened. Most try to check and double-check sources and confirm their perception of what happened by questioning other eyewitnesses or participants. They pursue the truth as best they know it and as best they can.

But of course this is the beginning of the issue, not the end of it. The problem of whether the media make the news actually has several parts. Probably the most fundamental difficulty is that reporters have to reconstruct the reality of an event they may have witnessed. Even if the reporter actually watched what happened, it is well known that one person's account of an event can be considerably different from another's. If the reporter was not present but must rely on secondhand sources, the problem of describing what "really happened" is augmented. Professional reporters will assiduously check and recheck their version of what happened with other sources, but in spite of all their efforts the basic problem does not go away: how can a verbal or written account truly reconstruct the reality of a past event or circumstance, even one that occurred only moments previously? At best, we can approximate, and while those approximations can come close to accuracy, like Zeno's arrow they never quite get to, much less become, the really real.

In a sense, then, the difficulty in reconstructing events for the public forces us to conclude that, yes, the journalist does indeed "make" the news.[16] The mere fact that the journalist reports something means that a construction of reality has occurred, thus, it is "made." Likewise, a nonreport is even news; lack of a story does not necessarily mean that nothing happened—it simply means there was no construction of a reality that may or may not have taken place. Even on-the-scene reports by television cameras and radio stations have to be recognized as constructions or reconstructions of events. In a very real sense, the camera and the microphone become instruments through which the reality of the event or activity is conveyed, thus, constructed.

Matters don't end here, however. Earlier we noted that the media serve as a magnifying glass, and that journalists have to choose which facts to report and which to omit. Not only does this involve judgment (which of course can be questioned), it also involves selectivity. The magnifying glass by definition enhances some facts, while diminishing others or leaving them out of the reportorial field altogether. In this sense too the journalist "makes" the news, by presumably putting together a selection of facts into something that is intelligible to others.

Thus, journalists select and sift and probably truncate what they saw, or heard about, and investigated. In the process of reporting on it, they actually construct a reality designed to give the public a sense of what it was all about—but it is not the event itself. Moreover, journalists and editors at some very critical point ask the audience to make a leap of faith that their reporting is according to the highest standards of accuracy, and that they are willing to vouch that it is as close to a true reality as is humanly possible. It is that leap of faith, of course, that causes candidates and the public trouble. Many are simply not willing to make it. Many are unconvinced that what is presented to them is really what happened, or really what is important. Many are convinced that a journalist simply made it all up. What has happened, of course, is that at some level a journalist did "make" the news; but it was not done so in the sense that many people think it was. As a result, many people are convinced the journalist is either lying or writing pulp fiction.

This leads to out remaining crucial question: are the media biased? The term "bias" is thrown about casually in discussion of media coverage of campaigns. Dictionaries define bias as "prejudiced"; in this sense, bias means distortion, leaving out facts, operating on the basis of stereotypes and incomplete information, and unwillingness to open or change one's mind.

On the basis of these definitions, it would be hard to sustain an argument that the media are biased.[17] Modern professional journalists seek to uncover more facts, not bury them. It is in their interest, and that of their employers, to ensure that the stories presented are not distorted and do not deliberately ignore important material that can illuminate further the matter under consideration. Some readers may object that the act of magnification, as discussed above, inherently injects bias into the reporter's story. But magnification does not necessarily mean distortion: it can actually clarify and bring into sharp relief obscure facts or those difficult to grasp when not specifically illuminated. Here too the judgment and professionalism of the journalist come into play; but for some audience members the level of professionalism is simply never high or rigorous enough.

As evidence of the general lack of bias in most campaign coverage, it needs to be pointed out that reporters usually report everything. Whether they actually like or approve of what they see is not a part of their decision on how to prepare the story. Reporters regularly cover candidates they have no intention of voting for; by the same token, even if they write about their chosen candidate or issue, they take pains to make certain that they don't thereby prejudice the story. One example may well clinch the point. Late in the 1996 campaign, after holding his tongue despite the personal and political criticism leveled at him by Bob Dole, President Clinton snapped back during a speech at Ohio State University. The *New York Times,* which endorsed the president, ran a series of stories about the president's counterattack, some of which made it clear that the reporters felt he had made a mistake; he had avoided such attacks previously, and data from polls and focus groups indicated that his "presidential" style in carrying himself above petty bickering was helping his campaign.

The *Times,* which at least some observers felt had made up its mind sometime in the spring of 1996 that President Clinton should be re-elected, generally gave the president favorable coverage throughout the campaign. If the *Times* had been biased, as Dole and many others claimed, the paper might well have quashed the stories about his lashing out at his opponent, or downplayed their significance. In fact, the paper did the opposite. Far from ignoring facts, it actually trumpeted them, even as it disapproved of what he did.

This example is not atypical. The media have favorites, to be sure. But that in no way means they have a bias. Journalists are good at reporting what they see and hear, irrespective of their own views or, for that matter, the editorial position of their newspaper or station. It is sometimes further alleged that because reporters tended (in 1992 anyway) to have voted overwhelmingly for Clinton that they have a liberal bias. Leaving aside the issue of whether or not Clinton is actually a liberal, critics making this argument have therefore to present evidence that these voting patterns are reflected in the stories prepared by journalists. While assertions are often made about the connection, hard evidence (for example, in the form of content analysis) is harder to come by. It is more likely that the critics just don't like the content of stories written, or agree with the way they are put together, than that they can convincingly demonstrate that the voting patterns of reporters bias the stories they craft.

Moreover, the advent and popularity of very conservative talk shows, at both national and local levels, would seem to give the lie to the argument that the media are biased in a liberal direction. If they were, Rush Limbaugh and his ilk would not have found such ready access to the airwaves. The fact is that they make money for radio stations, and regardless of the editorial position of the station the decision to include them in the programming is a result of economics, not political bias.

Finally, of course, critics of the "liberal bias" of the media have short memories. During the Reagan years there was a frequent complaint, from the opposite end of the political spectrum, that the president had a Teflon quality—that the media liked him and let him off easy, that he did not get hard questions at his infrequent news conferences. The alleged bias in the 1980s apparently was in the opposite, that is, conservative, direction. The conclusion to all this is that bias is in the eye of the beholder; as noted before, many in the public are not willing to make the leap of faith that journalists or their employers are doing a professional job of reporting what is really real.

But even if the stories presented are not biased, are they not selective, and thus do they not have a slant to them? The truth is that, in fact, this is the case—it is another aspect of the way in which journalists "make" the news. The very process of crafting news stories about campaigns means that certain perspectives are chosen. No story can cover everything; choices have to be made about what to cover, what words to use, what phrases to employ. Language and words themselves convey certain meanings, and have certain nuances beyond what the content of the story might be. As journalists write or speak, they must be very conscious of these nuances and meanings, for they automatically convey a slant to their story. And this is aside from the perspective or slant a journalist chooses for preparing the story in the first place. Pictures do the same thing, as photographers have to decide at what moment to snap the shutter or roll the tape, and editors determine which of the photos available to them will be used, if any.

One can, then, legitimately ask if it is possible for a reporter to be completely "objective" in preparing a story. The answer is, probably not. Language and words, as well as the slant chosen for the story or photos, convey meanings to the public above and beyond the particular content of the story. The fact that selectivity has entered the reportorial process probably undercuts all pretense of complete objectivity.

Is this bad? Does this mean that the news reports of campaigns are worthless? Are the media undermining our democratic system by their failure to reach objectivity? The answer to all of these questions is a decided no, as long as one understands what the media are capable of doing, and as long as one understands that the media attempt to uphold high standards of accuracy (even as one may disagree with what those standards are and how they are implemented). American journalists, in fact, do quite a fine job of accurate reporting and striving to convey in their stories a sense of a reality the public otherwise has no knowledge of or access to.

Furthermore, objectivity may be less important, at least as far as the news about campaigns is concerned, than responsibility. On this, journalists score high. Responsibility here means not simply getting the story right, but being accountable for it—to the candidates they write about, to their editors, to the public, to themselves and their peers. Rare is the journalist who abjures his or her own story; equally rare is the newspaper or TV or radio station unwilling to redress and correct errors when they are made. One can legitimately ask if every story about political campaigns found in the media really constitutes "news." But it virtually never happens that the journalist or media outlet will fail to take responsibility for running it and for its content. This is assuredly a sign of health and vitality, not of weakness or a tendency to undermine our democratic system.

What Are the Media Doing, Then?

While recognizing that the media can have a significant but not determinative impact on political campaigns, is there anything else we can say about their role? If the media are not busy prejudicing the public about one or another candidate, or leading a stampede toward one and away from another, is this an implication that they are simply inert purveyors of information?

The answer is of course not. The media are active players in the politics of campaigning. As noted earlier, they provide a mechanism for people to get information about candidates and campaigns. This role, by itself, is a highly active, even proactive one.

While different news outlets play different roles—depending on where they are located; their editorial posture; their national, regional, or local scope; the energy of reporters; and so forth—there seem to be two roles all media play in the politics of the modern campaign. The first is that, like other players in the political process, they look for winners and losers. While the media cannot elect anybody, they can and do search out who is ahead, who is falling behind, who looks strong and is building momentum, and whose campaign has peaked too soon or, worse, never got in gear. This is a natural part of the American political process; it is how the campaign game is played. By their very nature, campaigns result in winners and losers, and the media want to know who each are. They may of course pick the wrong horse; in spite of their polls and focus groups editors and journalists may be politically out of touch with voters.

On the other hand, the media's search for the winners and losers of election contests strongly influences the stories carried and their content. The complaint is often heard that media coverage of campaigns rests too much on "the horse race," and not the issues. Why should the public expect anything different? The horse race is ultimately what the contest is all about, once we clear the field of often indistinct, muddied differences in policy positions or promises the candidates offer. Setting all this aside, ultimately the voter has to choose between individual candidates or ideas. The media very much want to convey a sense of which candidate is ahead at the start, in the backstretch, and in the final dash to the finish. Like everyone else, they are concerned with which candidate crosses the line first.

The other major role the media play in campaigning rests primarily on their broader role in American society. Put most succinctly by H.L. Mencken, that role is "to comfort the afflicted, and afflict the comfortable." As skeptics and even cynics, reporters find it part of their job to poke pins into overinflated personages, mainly but not exclusively public personages. Candidates for office (whether incumbents or not) are just too easy as targets for not infrequently misanthropic reporters to pass up. If journalists seem to spend their time poking holes in candidates' balloons, or even just poking fun at them, this too is part of the grand tradition of American campaign politics. Indeed, it is likely that in the nineteenth century journalists, especially cartoonists, were much tougher on candidates than they are today.

This tendency of journalists can be pushed too far, of course. The one quality that candidates for office probably all share is an overdeveloped sense of self-importance, but aside from that they deserve more credit than they often get for their willingness to run for public office, endure the rigors and hardships and expense of the modern campaign, and serve as public servants if elected. On the other hand, by setting themselves up, candidates have to expect a few slings and arrows to be shot in their direction, not just from their opponents, but from the media as well. It is how the game is played in America.

Paying for It

Most of the preceding discussion has dealt with media coverage that candidates cannot control easily, or even at all, because it is in the hands of journalists and editors. But what about campaign information which is prepared and delivered directly by the candidate, campaign, and supporters? This of course refers to paid advertisements, which presumably provide exactly the message and tone candidates want to convey to voters, in the form they want and generally when they want. Do these vehicles solve the problem of the media for candidates, insofar as they can simply buy space or time to give the desired message directly to voters, negating the impact of uncooperative or unsympathetic journalists and their editors?

There is a vast literature dealing with campaign advertising and its impact on the election process.[18] Paid advertising is frightfully expensive, not only in design and production, but even more so for putting it on television or buying substantial newspaper space. Radio is cheaper, but the audiences reached tend to be more specialized, and unless the radio buy includes the drive-time hours it is unlikely to have much impact.[19] As a result, the costs of media act as a hurdle that many candidates cannot negotiate successfully; they simply do not have the resources to pay for adequately getting their message out to the public through the media. Thus, less well funded candidates are at a competitive disadvantage, at least as far as media buys are concerned.[20]

There are some other problems with paid use of the media that need to be mentioned besides cost. Media campaigns and advertisements may not be well designed and executed; while it is commonly thought that those for local races sometimes show an amateurish or parochial quality, an examination of ads in gubernatorial, congressional, and presidential campaigns sometimes shows remarkable naïveté, silliness, and downright stupidity.[21] Also, advertisements sometimes fail to resonate with the public regardless of how well they are done; Bob Dole's repeated assaults on the character of President Clinton in 1996, and his continuing promise of a tax cut, actually hurt him in the first instance, and were ignored or not believed in the second.

Indeed, the 1996 campaign, from the presidential level on down, raised questions about the future of campaign advertising. No one is pretending, or even proposing, that it will go away; candidates will still need it, and the media make too much money from it to flush it away. There is some evidence, and increasing suspicion, however, that the public has pretty much caught on to campaign advertising as it has existed, especially on television, since the early 1950s. It is overtly manipulative, and often highly negative. Given the public's increasing mistrust of anything candidates say or the media report, voters may well be resisting these ads, or regarding them so skeptically as to raise questions about their effectiveness. The future may even see something different in the way of campaign advertising; a greater emphasis on "soft sell" and issue-based ads that avoid the in-your-face style that has become so common and, apparently, increasingly disliked.

There is an additional aspect of modern campaign advertisements that needs to be addressed: the ten-, fifteen-, or thirty-second spot on radio or TV, and the "fast-back ad" in print consisting mostly of a picture, a few words, and empty space. These have come in for very heavy criticism, especially the quick sound-bite advertisements so common on television and radio. Superficial, misleading, incomplete, insulting—these are some of the more polite words used to describe such commercials. Are they, in fact, as bad as all that? Do they really do us harm?

The answers are, probably not and no. In the first place, one needs to remember the purpose of paid advertisements: to provide exactly the message the candidate or campaign wants the voters to see or hear.[22] In this sense, the 30–second spot is a terrific mechanism for allowing a clear, concise, uncluttered message to be delivered to voters. In such a short time period, content must be stripped to the very essence in order to achieve maximum impact. Subtleties and nuances have to be swept aside or avoided as content is reduced to the most fundamental level (some would say lowest common denominator). Thus the "substance" of the thirty-second spot, if it is done right, may well serve as a synopsis of the major message a candidate seeks to convey to the voters. In this way the spot can help the voter differentiate one candidate from another.

It will be objected that many times thirty-second spots are fundamentally negative, often attack ads. They are devoid of content, insofar as they are designed more to make an opponent look bad than to say something positive or favorable about the candidate producing the spot. True enough, the thirty-second format probably lends itself more readily to attack ads than to positive ones. But it does not have to be this way. They are often used to attack because negative ads are easier to put together than positive, content-oriented ones. It is hard to effectively reduce a positive message to bare bones, and many candidates—and their advertising consultants—either cannot or will not make the effort to do so. Moreover, if one of the goals of the thirty-second spot is to differentiate one candidate from another, or to throw an opponent off balance, then it is hard to argue that there is something fundamentally wrong or harmful about them. Some voters may not like them and may find them distasteful. If so, it is a reasonable argument that such ads are effective—they were noticed and digested, and they caused a reaction. In a very real sense, that is exactly what the candidate wants. An ad that is ignored, or produces no reaction at all, is of no help whatsoever. On the other hand, if the ad is wrong, or based on incorrect information, or simply offensive, voters reject it; voters do have the capacity to differentiate what is true and credible from what is not.[23]

Critics of thirty-second spots and fast-back ads also claim that they cannot really offer any substance. How can the policy and political views of a candidate really be offered in thirty seconds? The best we can expect is superficiality, and at worst they are misleading.

It is certainly true that in thirty seconds (less, actually) ads can offer little meat. But that is not to say that they are devoid of content, or that they cannot provide clues as to the political views of the candidate. Pictures—even if they are but snippets or flashes or tidbits—can have a substantial impact on viewers, and give them a real indication of how the candidate feels about schools, or pollution, or care for the elderly, or whatever the particular content deals with. In the case of radio and newspaper ads, where words and not pictures are important—and even in the case of the words and phrases used to complement the pictures on television spots—if the words are carefully chosen and the phrases well crafted a good deal of meaning can be conveyed in a short space. In fact, they can give a good sense of the issue orientation and priorities of the candidates; in this sense, neither pictures nor words are trivial or superficial. True, they may not commit the candidate to a specific course of action or tell the voters exactly what the candidate intends to do. On the other hand, given that candidates so often find, once in office, that what they thought they could accomplish is outside the realm of possibility, it is probably better—and healthier—for voters and candidates that they give a sense of what they want and expect and hope to do, rather than lock themselves into a specific course of action.

Finally, it may well be that in our rush-rush society, thirty seconds is about all that most people are prepared to give a candidate. Many people are not all that interested in what the candidate has to offer, or in politics generally. They know that they are supposed to be informed about issues and candidates, but lack the time or interest to make a thorough study of either. They feel an obligation to vote, but feel competing pressures for their time and attention from family, jobs, and the myriad other forces that buffet them daily. A thirty-second spot or fast-back ad does not tax them; if done well, it will give them a little information, provide a sense of candidate priorities and orientations, differentiate the candidate from opponents, and presumably leave some sort of reasonably lasting impression—all without intruding unduly on the voters' busy lives.

Moreover, for the voter who wants more, there is no shortage of political information available. The voter determined to be as informed as possible need only buy a few more newspapers and magazines (or go to any public library if cost is a factor), call candidate headquarters directly (even local candidates in small places now use answering machines, and will return calls promptly), or turn on certain specialized television and radio programs on CNN, PBS, C-SPAN, and NPR. For the more technologically advanced, the Internet already offers huge quantities of political news and information, and will undoubtedly offer more, with easier access, in the future. There is no shortage of political news and information available to those wanting it; in fact, it is a reasonable argument that even the most avid political junkie could not read and absorb even a small fraction of it. Voters who claim they are not sufficiently informed about candidates and issues, in this day and age, are probably not making a sufficient effort to take advantage of what is available to them. While of course it is the business, and in the interest, of candidates to make voters aware of their candidacies and campaigns, voters too have an obligation to inform themselves. There is a surfeit of material available to those willing to do so.

Conclusion—Can the Media Do Better?

There is no shortage of suggestions and recommendations to improve the performance of the media in covering political campaigns, or in reducing their supposed impact on the outcomes. Some people want more attention to "issues" and less to personalities and the horse race. Others want more "depth," whatever that means. Some suggestions are fairly concrete—the media ought to offer free airtime or newspaper space to candidates, to level the playing field and reduce the problem of costs; others suggest that media coverage of campaigns stop a week before the election, to eliminate "the late October surprise" when an opponent airs or publishes charges (well founded or not) to which a candidate does not have time to respond.

Most of the suggestions floating around about improving the media's role in the modern political campaign ignore some fundamental realities this chapter has discussed: most people, even voters, are not all that interested in candidates and their campaigns, and have limited patience and attention spans for them; the media are fundamentally business organizations concerned with their bottom line primarily, and informing voters only secondarily; and First Amendment rights allow the media to cover campaigns more or less as they want to.

In the end, those advocating major changes need to ask some fundamental questions: Are we ill informed about candidates and their campaigns? What else would most voters like to know about them, given that in today's invasive approach to journalism we learn virtually everything about candidates, including details of their private lives?

Probably the most reasonable criticism concerns local races, especially in smaller communities with limited media outlets. Often local candidates complain, with justification, that media coverage is spotty, irregular, and often irrelevant. They complain that they cannot get a news story to cover them, and then when one occurs it isn't what they want.

There is no easy solution for this. The latter problem is easier to deal with than the former: candidates probably never will get the story they want, and need to learn from the outset not to assume that the media will carry their message for them in the way they want. The prior question is more serious, because media in local communities are understaffed and logistically cannot cover campaigns in depth, especially when there are numerous candidates and races. Moreover, they may not want to risk extensive coverage, out of fear of either boring audiences or alienating them. It may well be that the cost of running for office in small communities, while less in financial terms than in major media markets, is higher in the sense that the media just don't have the capabilities of providing ample coverage.

In the end, too, the best suggestion for improving media coverage of campaigns is for the public, and journalists themselves, to demand the highest level of professionalism. While it is futile to expect complete objectivity of coverage, we can expect responsible coverage. In this regard, there is reason for optimism. The media in this country have proved highly amenable to self-policing and self-criticism. A great deal of thought and effort and planning go into decisions about how the networks and newspapers—even small, local ones—will cover campaigns. It is not unusual to find journalists publicly discussing how they cover events and write stories, criticizing content and focus, seeking advice on what can be done better. Academic political scientists are often consulted by working journalists during campaigns, not just for answers to questions but for off-the-record discussions about the meaning and consequences of campaign activity and candidate behavior. After the elections are over, there are always numerous symposia and seminars in which the media assess their own performance, or listen attentively while others do it for them.

Ultimately, it is not the media's decision who will be an informed voter, or which candidate will win. The media are very influential, to be sure. But at the end, it is the individual citizen who must decide whether to vote, how much to be informed, and for whom to vote. It is the voters who pick winners and losers, not the media.

7

Money and the Modern
Political Campaign

The theme of the book up to this point has been essentially this: much of what happens in the modern political campaign is rooted in our political tradition. While there is much that is distasteful in modern political campaigns, and they don't always seem capable of producing an informed citizenry according to the model of American democracy proposed by many civics books, in fact the campaigns probably are not injurious to our political system either. The way our campaigns go forward is largely a function of the position they—and politics generally—occupy in our culture; in a sense, it is our way of taking care of political business that many of us don't really like very much, but know we have to do anyway. In this way, campaigns become a form of mass entertainment, like circuses or baseball.

When we come to the topic of money and the modern political campaign, the theme of the book must shift, however. Money presents a problem for the modern political campaign, and a real danger for our democracy. The argument we shall put forward is not a standard criticism, however.[1] Our concern is not with the amount of money spent on political campaigns. While already substantial, and growing steadily as the costs associated with campaigns continue to rise, in fact the amount of money we spend on political campaigning is virtually trivial, given the importance of the enterprise. The real worry is essentially threefold: the differential in the amounts of money available to candidates for the same office (largely, but not exclusively, a function of incumbency versus challenger status); the sources of political money; and the increasing evidence that the use of political money is out of control, especially (but not exclusively) with the rise of so-called soft money.

Some readers will observe that this is already old hat. Money, it has been noted, is the root of evil in politics as in so many other things.[2] It buys influence, it is corrupting, it puts our democracy up for sale. The first million-dollar presidential campaign in American history—the 1828 Andrew Jackson–John Quincy Adams contest—was widely condemned. The first million-dollar governor's campaign—in the largely rural, agricultural Florida of 1940, between Francis Whitehair and Spessard Holland—brought expressions of disapproval from citizens and editorialists alike.

While it is true that money and politics have often had a sordid past, we may be in the process of taking a qualitative leap in the role money plays in political life. In the past, our democratic system has been strong enough to withstand the pernicious influence of money, especially the occasional outbreaks of venality and corruption that have colored our political history. We can no longer be sure that this is the case. Differential amounts of money available to candidates, the extraordinary capacity of PACs to raise funds and inject them into campaigns, and the onset of soft-money expenditures pose challenges to our democracy that neither the Jacksonians nor residents of pre–World War II Florida nor anyone else could have anticipated.

In this chapter we shall look at the role money plays in the modern political campaign—first at the amounts of money we spend, and what that money buys. We shall then look at the three major problem areas noted earlier, and conclude by suggesting a major reform in the way money enters political campaigns. This chapter is not designed to be a comprehensive survey of money in political campaigns; other scholars provide that material very well.[3] Nor is it a survey and critique of available reforms for campaign finance, of which there are many; we shall allude to some, however. Our goal, rather, is to focus readers' attention on what the role of money in the modern campaign has become, where it is headed, and why it poses such a real challenge to us. The reform proposed is controversial, and probably will be widely criticized. But the problems and dangers money poses for the modern campaign, and our democracy, require nothing less than a substantial overhaul of the way we fund our campaigns. To do nothing simply perpetuates a system that is increasingly out of control.

The Cost of Campaigns

How much money do we spend on political campaigns? The 1996 presidential campaign reportedly was the most expensive in history, costing about twice as much as the 1992 race.[4] Through September 1996, all the candidates had spent about $237.2 million; during the same period in 1992, they had spent about $123 million; in 1988, the figure through September was $210 million.[5]

The previous figures are for money spent during the primary season. Presidential candidates raised about $245.5 million for primaries, of which about 23 percent came from public matching funds. Some 52 percent of moneys raised for presidential primary candidates came from individual contributions; contributions from individuals are important in primaries because those of $250 or less are generally matched by federal dollars. Contributions from PACs are not matchable, and accounted for about 1 percent of monies raised during the primary season.[6] Candidates in primaries accepting federal matching funds cannot contribute more than $50,000 of their own money; Steve Forbes and Morry Taylor bankrolled their own campaigns and did not accept any federal money, with the result that some 19 percent of the total funds spent during the primary season came from the candidates themselves.[7]

Once the primary and convention seasons were finished, the candidates became eligible for federal moneys to conduct the general campaign.[8] The Democratic and Republican candidates received $61.8 million each; Ross Perot, whose vote total of 19 percent in 1992 was just under half of the average for the two major candidates, received $29 million in federal dollars, but he was allowed to raise private moneys to reach the $61.8 million ceiling.[9]

On the face of the law, the major candidates were not permitted to raise additional moneys to pay for their presidential campaigns. The law does permit, however, the candidates to raise money for legal and accounting fees to comply with federal regulations. The Clinton-Gore campaign raised about $6 million for this purpose, and Dole-Kemp about $4.6 million.[10]

Candidates are also permitted to raise private moneys to use for campaign purposes, but these cannot be funneled through the actual campaign accounts. The parties, for example, spent about $12 million each, in conjunction with the candidates, advocating election of their party candidates. Parties spent additional funds on generic efforts to elect Democrats and Republicans to office. Other organizations can also spent money on behalf of their candidate or cause, including presidential candidates.[11] These moneys have to be reported to the Federal Elections Commission (FEC), but there are few restrictions on the amount that can be raised or spent in this connection; it is this possibility that has opened the door to "soft money" in campaigns.

All told, Republicans raised about $278 million in "hard" money during the 1996 presidential campaign; in 1992, Republicans raised about $146 million. Democrats in 1996 raised about $164 million, and $85 million four years earlier. Republicans further raised about $121 million in soft money ($106 million in 1992); the Democrats' soft money was $46 million in 1996 ($31 million in 1992).[12] On the basis of these figures, about $609 million was raised to fund the 1996 presidential campaign; not all of it was spent, however, as a portion remained in the hands of the political parties and other organizations, to fund activities during non-presidential-years.

Congressional campaign spending for the candidates on the ballot in the 1996 November election reached $469 million between January 1, 1995, and October 16, 1996. About $562 million was raised during that period; presumably the cash balance between the figures was spent during the last three weeks of the campaign.[13] These figures represent about a 4 percent increase in spending over 1994 totals, while actual fund-raising increased about 8 percent. Through September 30, all congressional candidates, including primary losers, raised over $617 million; they spent about $489 million. These figures represent an increase of 12 percent in fund-raising over 1994, and 10 percent in spending over the 1992 and 1994 totals of $445 million.

There is some difference between Senate and House of Representatives spending and fund-raising in the 1996 election. Many of the 1996 Senate races took place in smaller states that require less money than large, heavily populated ones. Senate candidates in 1996 raised about $188 million, and spent about $163 million. About $124 million of the Senate election money came from individual contributions, and $34 million from PACs. Funds for Senate campaigns loaned or contributed directly by candidates actually decreased in 1996 from 1994; in 1996 the total made available by candidates themselves was $19.4 million, down from $42.2 million in 1994. The latter figure was heavily influenced by the senatorial campaign of Michael Huffington in California that year.[14]

House races showed an increase of 27 percent in fund-raising, and 23 percent in expenditures, between 1994 and 1996. House candidates in 1996 raised $374 million, and spent $300 million as of October 16, 1996. Individual contributions to House candidates totaled $211 million, while PAC contributions came to $126 million, more than three and a half times the amount provided to Senate campaigns by PACs in 1996. House candidates bankrolled their own campaigns to the tune of $23 million.

PACs contributed substantial amounts of money to federal candidates in the 1995–96 election cycle, as they did in 1993–94.[15] Over all, between January 1, 1995, and June 30, 1996, PACs contributed $126.5 million. This represents about a $17 million rise over 1993–94 figures. Of this total, some $114.4 million went directly to federal candidates; the remainder went to debt retirement and future elections. In 1993–94, some $100.9 million went directly to candidates, out of a total pot of $109.9 million. None of these figures include funds contributed to candidates in state and local elections. FEC analysis of 4,430 PACs showed that, in the first eighteen months of the 1995–96 election cycle, they raised about $311.5 million, and spent $264.7 million. Incumbents in 1996 received $98.3 million of the $126.5 million contributed to federal candidates, while challengers got only $12.5 million (a nearly eightfold difference). Candidates for open federal seats received $15.8 million in PAC money. In 1994, incumbents received some $91.1 million, challengers $5.5 million (a sixteenfold difference), and candidates for open seats $13.3 million. Through June 1996, Republican candidates received $71.6 million in PAC money, while Democrats got $54.7 million. Through June 1994, Republicans had received $37.8 million, while Democrats got $72 million. The top fifty PACs, in terms of contributions to federal candidates, between January 1, 1995, and June 30, 1996, can be found on pages 146–47.

None of these figures include data for state and local elections, where by far the greatest numbers of candidates and races can be found. It is difficult to estimate how much money was spent at these levels during 1995–96. A total can be obtained by aggregating figures supplied to every county supervisor of elections in the country, as well as those for each state department of elections. The task of securing this information is nothing short of Herculean. It should be noted, however, that the range of contributions and expenditures for these elections is vast. In small communities, a few hundred dollars, maybe a thousand or so, is still sufficient to win a seat for city or county commission. But the cost of running for state legislatures has grown substantially; even in small media markets a state house of representatives seat can cost $150,000 or more; a state senate seat can quickly reach a quarter-million dollars. In large media markets, these figures double.

Increasingly, too, as various ballot initiatives and constitutional amendments are put before voters, costs reach astronomical proportions. In Florida in 1994, proponents and opponents of casino gambling spent about $20 million, the vast majority on the proponent side (it lost, 2–1).[16] In 1996, Floridians witnessed a tremendous political fight between sugar producers and environmentalists over a proposed constitutional amendment creating a sugar tax to clean up the Everglades; some $30 million was spent in about six weeks of intensive campaigning. Indeed, this campaign virtually drove all others off the airwaves, and in some respects was thought to contribute to the inability of Republican candidate Bob Dole to reach voters effectively.

All told, then, FEC data indicate that in 1995–96 the presidential campaigns raised about $609 million; not all of this was spent, of course, but at least $423 million was.[17] Congressional races cost another $469 million. Including soft money, and state and local as well as federal elections, it has been estimated in the media that a total of close to $2 billion was spent on political campaigns during this election cycle.

This figure is only an approximation. Still, it is a working figure. The question is, is this an absurdly large amount of money? Is the price of running for office too high? Do we spend too much money on political campaigns, giving support to the argument that public office is for sale in this country?

Put in this way, these questions are hard to answer. Obviously some people will be appalled at, say, congressional spending figures of $469 million, especially given what they see as a lackluster congressional performance. Still others rankle at a local sheriff's race in a small county costing close to $100,000, double that in a metropolitan area. The problem with answering the question in this way is that our perceptions of when enough is enough, about right, or too much, are highly idiosyncratic.

Top Fifty PAC Contributors in the 1996 Federal Elections

1. Democratic Republican Independent Voter
   Education Committee [L] $1,584,710
2. Association of Trial Lawyers of America Political
   Action Committee [T] $1,552,975
3. International Brotherhood of Electrical Workers
   Committee on Political Education [L] $1,321,600
4. American Federation of State County, and
   Municipal Employees [L] $1,311,222
5. UAW Voluntary Community Action Program
   (UAW-V-CAP) [L] $1,293,775
6. National Education Association Political Action
   Committee [L] $1,213,230
7. Dealers Election Action Committee of the National
   Automobile Dealers Association [T] $1,204,475
8. Laborers' Political League [L] $1,163,800
9. Build Political Action Committee of the National
   Association of Home Builders [T] $1,134,349
10. United Parcel Service of America Inc. Political
    Action Committee (UPSPAC) [C] $1,125,531
11. American Telephone and Telegraph Company
    Political Action Committee (AT&T PAC) [C] $1,019,183
12. American Medical Association Political Action
    Committee [T] $1,018,505
13. Active Ballot Club, A Dept. of United Food and
    Commercial Workers International Union [L] $1,007,901
14. NRA Political Victory Fund [T] $963,368
15. American Institute of Certified Public Accountants
    Effective Legislation [T] $958,675
16. Realtors Political Action Committee [T] $952,008
17. Machinists Non-Partisan Political League [L] $929,275
18. Carpenters Legislative Improvement Committee,
    United Brotherhood of Carpenters [L] $847,256
19. Transportation Political Education League [L] $840,000
20. American Federation of Teachers Committee on
    Political Education [L] $839,514
21. American Maritime Officers, AFL-CIO Voluntary
    Political Action Fund [L] $827,960
22. National Beer Wholesalers' Association Political
    Action Committee (NBWA PAC) [T] $812,242
23. American Bankers Association BANKPAC [T] $782,350
24. CWA-COPE Political Contributions Committee [L] $699,430
25. American Dental Political Action Committee [T] $689,721
26. Lockheed Martin Employees Political Action
    Committee [C] $681,750

27. United Steelworkers of America Political Action Fund [L] $674,650
28. National Association of Life Underwriters Political Action
    Committee [T] $638,500
29. Sheet Metal Workers International Association Political
    Action League (PAL) [L] $621,750
30. National Committee for an Effective Congress [M] $604,270
31. United Association Political Education Committee [L] $595,000
32. Committee on Letter Carriers Political Education [L] $570,009
33. Employees of Northrop Grumman Corporation Political
    Action Committee (ENGPAC) [C] $568,700
34. Air Line Pilots Association Political Action Committee [L] $565,000
35. Ernst & Young Political Action Committee [M] $550,365
36. Philip Morris Companies Inc. Political Action Committee
    (PHIL-PAC) [C] $549,730
37. Federal Express Corporation Political Action Committee
    (FEPAC) [C] $543,000
38. Seafarers Political Activity Donation (SPAD) [L] $538,950
39. Associated General Contractors Political Action
    Committee [T] $538,550
40. Union Pacific Fund for Effective Government [C] $517,290
41. National Association of Retired Federal Employees
    Political Action Committee [T] $516,100
42. Team Ameritech Political Action Committee [C] $506,390
43. National Restaurant Association Political Action
    Committee [T] $489,783
44. Ironworkers Political Action League [L] $474,965
45. RJR Political Action Committee, RJR Nabisco Inc.
    (RJR PAC) [C] $448,400
46. American Hospital Association Political Action
    Committee (AHAPAC) [T] $436,976
47. American Crystal Sugar Political Action Committee [V] $434,525
48. Tenneco Inc. Employees Good Government Fund [C] $431,475
49. General Electric Company Political Action Committee [C] $423,050
50. Independent Insurance Agents of America Inc. Political
    Action Committee [T] $422,057

Key
C = Corporate
L = Labor
M = Nonconnected
T = Trade/membership/health
V = Cooperative
W = Corporation without stock

Source: FEC, "Top Fifty PAC's—Contribution to Candidates January 1, 1995–
June 30, 1996"; Internet address: http://www.fec.gov/press/pac18ctr.htm .

There is another way to address these questions, however. It is to compare our campaign expenditures with other things that we Americans spend money on. The following is a partial but illustrative list.[18]

Health and beauty supplies
Analgesics, $1,300 million
Dentifrices, $836 million
Cold medicines, $778 million
Deodorants, $761 million
Shampoo, $751 million
Sanitary napkins, $536 million
Razor blades, $457 million
Vitamins, $418 million
Antacids, $398 million
Tampons, $359 million

Food and Household Goods
Juice in a box, $711 million
Yogurt, $1,182 million
Granola and yogurt bars, $343 million
Liquid cleaners, $294 million
Pretzels, $395 million
Cat litter, $392 million
Frozen waffles, pancakes, and french toast, $604 million
Frozen yogurt, $469 million
Hot sauce, $542 million
Toaster pastries, $440 million

Advertising
Procter and Gamble advertising (1991), $2,149 million
Philip Morris advertising (1991), $2,045 million
General Motors advertising (1991), $1,442 million
Sears Roebuck advertising (1991), $1,179 million
K-mart advertising (1991), $527 million
Anheuser-Busch advertising (1991), $508 million
U.S. Government advertising (1991), $253 million

These figures are revealing. Americans in 1992 spent about four times more money on health and beauty supplies than they did on electing public officials. They spent more on Mexican hot sauce than candidates spent campaigning for the presidency of the United States—not just our most important public official, but arguably the most significant state leader in the world. We spent about as much on frozen waffles as the candidates for the presidency raised, and much more than they spent. Philip Morris spent about as much money convincing us to smoke their cigarettes as we spent for all of our campaigns; Procter and Gamble, most of whose products may be slightly less injurious to the public's health, spent even more on advertising than did Philip Morris. The United States government itself spent more on advertising than did all the candidates in the 1996 presidential primary, and quite a bit more than it supplied to the three major presidential candidates in the general election.

Seen in this light, the question whether political campaigns in this country are too expensive acquires a different meaning. Too expensive compared to what? The cost of yogurt, toaster pastries, pretzels, and cat litter?[19] Given these data, it is a reasonable argument that the amount of money we spend on political campaigns is trivial. Moreover, to make an obvious point, the money we spend on most of these consumer goods is repeated on a continuing basis; we eat daily, and when we run out of toaster pastries or hot sauce, we go buy some more. The presidential campaign cycle only recurs every four years, however; for the Senate it is six years, the House, two; and for most state and local offices, two, three, or four years. Thus, our expenditures for these consumer items double, triple, quadruple, even sextuple during the cycles for electing public officials. The figures cited above, then, seriously underestimate how much money we spend on goods relative to political campaigns.[20]

Indeed, it is a reasonable argument that we probably ought to spend more money on campaigns, not less. The argument is not based on the premise that more money would get us better candidates, or more thoughtful campaigns; neither is likely to happen, at least in the short run. Rather, the argument rests on a matter of national priorities: is the race for the presidency more important than frozen waffles? As Americans, should we not put a higher priority on placing people in positions of public trust and trying to ensure a high quality of governance—after all, this is part of what elections are all about—than we do on trying to get people to smoke?

These questions, at least for the moment, are best left hanging; readers may well fear the results of a public opinion survey taken on the relative importance or priority in this country of cat litter versus congressional campaigns. Nonetheless, we shall return to the matter later, while noting now that in fact we as a nation really do spend a very small amount of money on political campaigns.

There are some dark sides associated with the amount of money we spend on campaigns, however. We already mentioned two above: it would be pleasant and satisfying to argue that if we spent more on campaigns, we would get better candidates and more uplifting campaigns. There is no reason to think that either would be true; these will only improve when and if we demand improvement.

There is another matter, however, that is beyond the realm of speculation and is in fact a very unpleasant political reality. It is that candidates—whether incumbents or challengers—must spend inordinate amounts of time raising the money needed to conduct an adequate political campaign. Data cited earlier note that PAC contributions to incumbents in federal offices far exceed those to challengers. Readers who take the trouble to survey the financial reports required of all candidates, even at the most local levels, find that challengers usually have trouble raising money from individuals, and in the past have not infrequently found that PACs all but ignore them, unless the incumbent is viewed as highly vulnerable.

But even for incumbents, fund-raising has become virtually a full-time business. In the past it has been estimated that candidates, as a group, may spend 60 percent of their time raising money; in recent years, as costs of campaigning have skyrocketed, this figure has increased to 70 percent, even higher. For U.S. House of Representatives members, and some state and local officials holding two-year terms, the search for money is simply a part of the daily routine, as campaigns for these offices never really stop.

One might think that senators, with their six-year terms, are spared the day-to-day grind of raising funds. Simple arithmetic shows this is not the case at all. A six-year term consists of 312 weeks; a modern Senate campaign, even in a moderate-sized state, with strong opposition could easily cost $6–8 million, and perhaps a good deal more. Taking the lower figure, to be conservative, the Senate incumbent must raise slightly more than $19,000 each week in order to have sufficient funds for his campaign. Of course, the incumbent does not really have 312 weeks; most of the money has to be in hand well before the election season starts (in part in an effort to scare off powerful challengers, and in part because there are considerable start-up costs for any campaign that must be paid up front). Thus, the incumbent's weekly fund-raising target is actually far higher than the figure cited. If the Senate candidate is lucky and faces a less expensive campaign, the fund-raising burden is alleviated somewhat. But if it turns into an $8–10 million spend-a-thon, fund-raising becomes an all-consuming task unless the candidate is exceptionally wealthy and willing to use private resources to fund the campaign. And all of this is true only for incumbents; challengers face even tougher fund-raising problems because generally it is much harder for a challenger to raise the money needed to unseat an incumbent.[21]

Candidates for the presidency face a similar problem, except that the amounts of money required are even greater. A serious run at the presidency cannot begin a year or two before the primary season: the search for money, as well as establishing the campaign mechanics, must begin years in advance in order to be prepared for the onset of primaries, to lock in supporters, to begin the search for popular visibility, and to find financial backing.[22] Unless the candidate is a Steve Forbes or a Ross Perot able and willing to spend personal resources on a campaign, running for the presidency is now as much a search for money as it is for support and votes.

Some might argue that this is simply a part of the political rules; you want to run for office, you have to prove yourself to be a good fund-raiser. Such an argument ignores the enormous costs associated with having to raise money. Not only does it distract from other parts of campaigning—spending time with finance committees and making phone calls for money are probably the parts of campaigning that candidates from dogcatcher on up least like—in the case of incumbents it is a liability insofar as it takes them away from their duties in governance and public service. Raising money is not the same as carrying out their constitutionally sworn duties and obligations. Moreover, there are potential conflicts of interest involved in raising money for campaigns when viewed in the context of the responsibilities of public service, as legitimate ethical questions can be raised about, say, candidates accepting funds from business or industry they are supposed to regulate; this problem especially, but not exclusively, arises when PAC money is involved. In a very real sense, the pursuit of money to run campaigns raises private and public ethical questions of the most profound sort. We shall return to this point later.

Thus, although it is a reasonable argument that the amount of money we spend on political campaigns in this country is so small as to be virtually insignificant, efforts to raise even this amount of money create hardships for candidates and put them in potentially ethically compromising positions. Were we to spend more money on campaigns, the problem would simply be exacerbated. Thus we need to consider a new approach to financing campaigns, a matter we shall address shortly.

What Does the Money Buy?

What about this money raised for and spent on campaigns? What does it do? Why do people and PACs contribute to campaigns? Are they being good citizens, or do they expect something from it?

There are several approaches to these questions. On the one hand, money literally buys the campaign. Without money, no campaign would get much beyond the candidate's front door. Whether the money comes from public or private sources, money becomes the mechanism or instrument by and through which the candidate reaches voters. Where this money is lacking, the ability of the candidate—or those pushing an issue—to get the message to voters is seriously compromised or even eliminated.

Like it or not, campaigning has become big business. Even candidates for local offices in small communities need to find a way to reach the voters; only in a few places can the candidate walk enough neighborhoods and ring enough doorbells to meet enough voters to secure enough votes to win. For the vast majority of candidates, surrogates must be found to establish communication linkages between themselves and the voting public; there is neither time nor opportunity to do so on a personal basis. This basic fact of modern political life means that money has to be raised and spent, because money allows these surrogates to be created. Often, indeed generally, this means use of the electronic and print media. They are all expensive.

It is well recognized and understood how much television costs; a thirty-second spot on a small local television station during the six o'clock news (a favored time, as voters are often news watchers, and news watchers are often voters) can cost well over a thousand dollars; in a big station in a major market, this figure rises to double, triple, and quadruple that. Cable TV is much less, but of course the audience reached is smaller and more specialized. Radio is the cheapest electronic medium, but unless the candidate buys drive-time spots (at premium prices), the message will likely be ignored. A quarter-page advertisement in a local newspaper can run hundreds of dollars; in a metropolitan daily it will cost thousands, and unless it is sufficiently splashy or otherwise designed to attract attention, it will be overlooked or overwhelmed by furniture store sales, grocery discount coupons, and other commercial advertisements. It is also important to realize that political advertising rates are generally not discounted, and often are priced at the maximum allowed by law. Political advertisements also must usually be paid for at the time of placement, whereas the furniture store or topless bar can often wait until the end of the month before payment is due.

The cost of media is principally responsible for the cost of campaigns. Even local campaigns increasingly emulate state and national campaigns; even in small communities, no candidate wants to be left out. A great fear among candidates is that they will awaken one morning to discover that an opponent is on TV or the radio, and they are not. Thus, they have to engage the media—because the other guy is doing so. Obviously, a cycle of media use ensues, and once the pattern is established it will recur and probably increase in the next election cycle.[23]

There are other costs associated with campaigns. From local campaigns in large areas to major state races to national offices, consultants of one kind or another are often used; fees up to hundreds of thousands of dollars can be paid to such firms, but even small local campaigns sometimes will spend a few hundred dollars to get some expert advice. The cost of producing advertisements for electronic and print media can easily run into thousands of dollars, depending on the size of the advertising firm chosen and the amount of production required. Bumper stickers, yard signs, magnetic signs, car toppers, and billboards and other large signs have large printing price tags; putting them up (and taking them down) are also costly. Direct mail, if done well, can be politically very effective; but it is very expensive, especially if one realizes that a single or even double mailing has little utility beyond a reminder to go vote, and a candidate relying heavily on mailing to get the message out must do a minimum of three, and preferably more, mailings. Polling is expensive; many professional commercial polling firms charge between eighteen and twenty-five dollars per interview; if the sample drawn is somewhere around four hundred people (as it would be even in a small area), the cost can exceed seven thousand dollars, and this is solely for a baseline survey; tracking polls add to the cost. Polls conducted on statewide or national bases are frightfully expensive.

There are small communities where face-to-face campaigning is still possible. For these places, some handbills, placards, and yard signs might be all that is needed. But campaigning, like so much else in American life, has gotten more complex. In not every place can one campaign door-to-door, so one must find other means to reach voters. Most are expensive. Moreover, experience suggests that candidates managing and running their own campaigns spend too much time on administration and not enough meeting voters. It makes more sense to hire a consultant to take care of business and allow the candidate to campaign. While the consultant need not be a high-priced Washington firm, but a cheaper local one, the cost still goes up. Consultants, too, have utility beyond whatever expertise they provide; they become part of the candidate's entourage, a symbol of the professionalism and dedication and prestige the campaign exemplifies.[24] Polling for local candidates can be prohibitively expensive, although costs can be cut if several candidates agree to pool their resources and commission a joint survey. At some level a poll may not be needed; a candidate in a small place who does not have a sense of the community's mood and needs probably isn't a viable candidate anyway. On the other hand, a candidate about to spend $75,000 or more on a countywide race, say, for county commission or sheriff, really needs a survey. The strategic information a good poll gives can help allocate the use of money effectively; without such data, the campaign is reduced to guesswork and judgment, and while these can work out successfully, they can also result in wasting a great deal of money and effort.

Money thus buys the actual campaign. But money does a good deal more than just pay for campaign posters and all the rest. For some people, donating money to campaigns satisfies certain needs. They may feel it is their civic obligation and responsibility to help defray the costs of the campaign of their candidates of choice. Others make contributions out of friendship or some other association, for example, church membership, business or professional association, or proximity of residence. For other people, a donation is a way to feel involved in politics without having to make much of a commitment beyond writing a check; it's also psychologically safe, insofar as there is little risk to the donor involved, whereas taking a more active stance not only requires time and effort but could cause embarrassment.[25]

Political scientists have noted for a long time that money donated to campaigns by individuals or PACs creates a bond between donor and candidate. They refer to this bond as "access." This is a vague term, and it is not always clear what it means. It can refer to anything from getting one's phone calls to candidates returned promptly to having a voice in decision making once the candidate achieves public office. Perhaps the meaning of access, at least in some of its senses, was best summed up by James Carville, the successful Democratic consultant, who noted that if he has two phone calls to return, the one with the dollar sign attached goes first.

The problem with the term "access," insofar as it is supposed to indicate what campaign donations buy for the contributor, is that it is too neutral and passive. Not every donor necessarily wants something; as noted before, people give money for all sorts of reasons, many of which never produce a payoff of even modest proportions. But others do expect something. It's been common practice for generations that ambassadorships, especially to glamorous capitals, often go to large campaign donors.[26] Other types of payoffs for large donors are also common.[27]

But buying ambassadorships or securing other tangible payoffs probably only accounts for a small percentage of campaign donations. Most donors, whether individuals or PACs, don't have the resources to contribute at the levels needed to secure an appointment to London or Paris, or secure some other good. Rather, for many donors, campaign contributions are seen not simply as a way of getting access, but as an entrance fee into the political game. In a sense, virtually everyone has some degree of access to public officials, but not every citizen is a player in the game of politics. Campaign donations allow the individual or PAC to be a participant in whatever type of political activity happens to be taking place, whether it is deciding on the wording of legislation, writing administrative rules, passing out political pork and other forms of patronage, or something else. The "entrance fee" concept is not unlike that required to enter high-stakes card games or various investment opportunities; it is the cost of the right to participate. It is not the same as buying a ticket to a show or sports event, where one just sits there and watches. In the political game, one can actually become a player by making a donation. Often too, the larger the contribution, the more active and powerful the player becomes.[28]

It is at this point, of course, that the act of donating money to a campaign becomes potentially pernicious. In the civic model of our democracy, money should not matter; all citizens are active players in public affairs, and all are equal. In reality, our system of democracy does not work this way. Money does talk in politics, and it buys influence and the right to be involved. It buys much more than access; it buys the attention of public officials and the ability to be right there, actively participating, as decisions are made. It is not just a matter of passively sitting at the table; money allows individuals and groups to play with the others, indeed, in some cases to determine the size and shape of the table, who sits where, and who else is permitted to play.

Seen in this light, the willingness of individuals and PACs to contribute money to campaigns becomes understandable. It is clearly in the interest of those who have a political or policy concern to become players, and the easiest, most direct way to ensure that this happens is to make campaign donations, the more and higher the better. Some readers may be appalled at the rank cynicism of this approach. But this is the present reality of our politics: money makes you a political player if you are not a public official or have secured by some other means a position of political influence.[29]

This is serious business. Readers feeling queasy about all of this are justified in their concern. Too much of our democratic way of governance is up for sale. The cost is not simply to undermine public confidence in our governing institutions—although that is bad enough—it is to reduce governance itself to an auction, one that denies entrance, or at least limits the extent of influence, to all but those willing to pay. It is this fundamental problem to which this chapter alluded above, when we talked about possible dangers to our democracy caused by the mix of money and politics. In fact, these dangers can be very real, and in the absence of mitigating forces—such as a watchful and constructively skeptical citizenry and aggressive media coverage—their impact can be pernicious, indeed. Regrettably, it is not always clear that the citizens are watchful or concerned about the health of democratic institutions, or that the media are sufficiently aggressive and forceful, to ensure that the impact of money does not seriously erode our democratic governing institutions.[30]

Three Fatal Flaws

At this point, some readers may be willing to throw in the towel, and regard the situation as hopeless. In fact, though, before reaching this conclusion we need to direct readers' attention to three major problems in the way in which money enters campaigns, and how it is used. These fatal flaws concern the advantage of incumbency, the role of PACs, and the increasing presence of soft money.

Incumbents and Challengers

Political scientists are increasingly discovering that money alone does not make a difference in the outcome of a political campaign. Rather, it is the gap between the money available to different candidates that very well may determine the final results. The advantage, then, goes significantly to the candidate with more money. The larger the gap, the greater the advantage.[31]

It is now virtually a commonplace to note that incumbents generally have a significant advantage over challengers in raising money. The exception of course was in 1994, when the Republican surge for the U.S. Congress and many state legislatures drew significant funds into GOP challenges against incumbent Democrats. However, 1996 saw a return to previous patterns. As noted before, of the $126.5 million given by PACs to federal candidates between January 1, 1995, and June 30, 1996, $98.5 million went to incumbents; only $12.5 million was donated to challengers. Looking solely at congressional campaigns, between January 1, 1995, and October 31, 1996, a total of 407 congressional incumbents (House and Senate) raised more than $314 million; however, 952 challengers raised only $127 million, a gap of close to $200 million. Incumbents raised about two and a half times the amount of money that challengers did.[32]

There were differences across parties and across chambers in the incumbent-challenger differential. In the Senate, the gap between seven Democratic incumbents and fourteen challengers was not great: $31 million to $27 million; among Republicans, however, thirteen incumbent senators raised $41 million, while eight challengers could muster only slightly more than $19 million. In the House, 171 Democratic incumbents raised about $92 million, and 209 challengers a little more than half that, $49 million. Among Republicans in the House,

213 incumbents raised $149 million, while 176 challengers could raise but $30 million.

Data from state and local elections were not systematically examined for this study. However, it is of interest that at least in Florida, some incumbent legislators raised so much more money in their campaigns than they needed to spend that they made substantial contributions to their respective political parties. Through October 31, incumbent Republican legislators donated some $476,532 to the state party coffers, while Democratic incumbent legislators gave $191,847.[33] Under Florida law, any excess campaign funds have to be either returned to donors, on a pro rata basis, or given to charities or the political parties; in the old days candidates could either keep the money or roll it over into the next, or even a different, campaign.[34]

These data suggest a significant imbalance between incumbents and challengers that cuts across party lines. In retrospect, 1994 looks increasingly like an exceptional election, not the beginning of a new pattern, since 1996 appears to return to the older pattern of incumbent advantage.

Does it matter? It does matter if elections are supposed to be competitive. The vigor and health of democratic governing institutions depend at least partially on robust elections in which candidates vie with one another on a more or less equal playing field. Given this significant imbalance in funds, a real question arises as to just how level the playing field really is. Incumbents—unless they are involved in some sort of scandal, or a peculiar environmental change takes place such as occurred in 1994—have the field tilted in their favor. It is no wonder that, prior to 1994 anyway, it was often estimated that U.S. House seats were more than 95 percent safe. There were other factors contributing to the sinecurelike quality of House seats (apportionment, for one), but the enormous advantage incumbents generally have in fund-raising assuredly contributed. If we are interested in making our elections more robust and competitive—and presumably thereby enhancing the health of our governing institutions, we probably need to find a way to reduce the incumbent-challenger money gap, and at least make that step toward a more level campaign playing field.

PACs

Everybody nowadays likes to beat up on PACs. They are too powerful, raise too much money, have made themselves indispensable in the campaign finance business, create a linkage of dependency between public officials and themselves that gives an advantage to private interests over the public's interest.

Undoubtedly there is some truth in each of these criticisms. They are not our focus of concern here, however. No matter what one's view of PACs, they are protected under the First Amendment (the right to petition the government is guaranteed), and their capacity to raise and contribute campaign money is also constitutionally protected, as campaign donations are an expression of political speech. PACs are not going to go away, not under present circumstances, anyway.

Moreover, the amount of money PACs contribute is, by itself, not especially troubling. We noted earlier that during the past campaign cycle, PACs contributed about $126.5 million through June 30, 1996. As election time rolled nearer, PAC contributions increased; we saw also that through October 16, 1996, PACs contributed $34.1 million to Senate candidates and $126.3 million to U.S. House candidates. But these sums, as substantial as they are, are dwarfed by individual contributions: Senate races received $124.1 million from this source, while House races got some $211.1 million from individuals.

The problem with PAC money is not the amount, therefore, but rather how it is distributed. Earlier we saw that it overwhelmingly goes to incumbents, not challengers, at a ratio in 1996 of nearly eight to one. PACs thus have become a major force tilting the campaign playing field in favor of incumbents.

But there is more. PACs have a long lead time and quick response time in fund-raising. Their efforts literally go on continually, allowing some of them, at least, to amass sizable war chests to be distributed as they see fit. They can also quickly funnel funds into favored campaigns that seem to need an infusion of money as election day nears; candidates relying heavily on individual contributors rarely can get donors to respond as quickly as PACs can. PACs also can "pyramid" money by soliciting and collecting funds from local PACs elsewhere, thus augmenting the amount of money available to favored candidates. And of course there is almost no limit to the number of PACs that can be formed; each PAC can contribute up to the legal limit, which can also serve to pyramid funds.

PACs have also become important forces in state and sometimes even local elections. While aggregate data on PAC involvement in these campaigns are hard to come by, a perusal of state financial reports of major PACs indicates that they are capable of injecting tens of thousands of dollars, and in some instances hundreds of thousands, even millions of dollars.[35] It should be pointed out that in at least some states corporations can donate money directly to political campaigns, although they cannot do so for federal elections. The result is essentially a double whammy; both corporations and any ancillary PACs they may have formed can independently donate money to a candidate or cause.[36]

But even these difficulties pale in comparison to an even more fundamental one. Because of the financial power of PACs, they create an insidious bond between themselves and officeholders. Each becomes so mutually dependent on the other that the relationship drives out other voices that have a right to be heard during campaigns, and during governance. The voices of individuals, in particular, simply get lost, or are never seriously heard, because of the this axis. Moreover, not even all groups of voices can crack this barrier, because not all voices are combined into PACs—or even if they are, the resources available to them are puny compared with those of the major corporate, labor, and other PACs. The voices of children come to mind as an example, but they are by no means the only politically disadvantaged group in this regard.

Perhaps what is most pernicious is that there are no mitigating political organizations or institutions to act as a buffer between PACs and candidates. Courts cannot intervene if there is no illegal activity. The political parties either cannot or will not do so: they benefit from PAC contributions. The media represent the only real possibility to expose cozy relationships and conflicts of interest between candidates and PACs, but their financial resources are limited, and the public's taste in investigative journalism seems to have moved more toward invasion of the privacy of prominent individuals than toward exposure of political shenanigans.

Yet ultimately our system of democracy has to operate through mechanisms of checks and balances. In the PAC-candidate relationship, it is hard to find either a check (except a financial one!) or a balance.[37] There is little to intervene in the relationship other than the moral fiber, character, and good sense of PAC leaders and candidates. Regrettably, the health of democratic institutions cannot simply rest on the rectitude and high-mindedness of the players: too often they are lacking. Rather, an organizational or institutional or even systemic checks-and-balances mechanism needs to exist that can inject itself between PAC and candidate, serve as a mediating force or buffer, and at least offer the possibility that other voices will be heard that can modify these PAC money ties. We shall return to this point shortly.

Soft Money

Soft money is essentially funds raised and spent outside of a specific campaign, whether for a candidate or a cause; it can be found at federal, state, and local levels. Theoretically, soft money is not supposed to be used to promote individual candidacies; to accomplish that purpose, money is supposed to be contributed to campaign organizations, with either federal or state laws governing the limits and mechanics of that contribution. But, as has been noted with increasing frequency, it is easy to subvert this purpose, and soft money is now regularly raised and spent under an only thinly disguised "generic" appeal.[38] Unless some limits are imposed, soft money may well become out of control by the next election cycle.

Examples of soft money are legion. We already noted the famous "Willie Horton" ad of 1988, paid for by an organization supporting the election of George Bush but not formally affiliated with it in any way.[39] In 1996, the AFL-CIO was thought to have spent over $35 million in soft money in an attempt to return the U.S. Congress, specifically the House of Representatives, to Democratic control. That its efforts were largely unsuccessful scarcely undermines the point that soft money can have a powerful impact. By mid-October 1996, there was reason to think that Democrats might actually retake the House, except that the Democratic party became embroiled in a mini-scandal over accepting campaign donations from foreign interests and individuals, which caused a shift in public opinion back to the Republicans.[40]

Soft money must be reported to either the FEC or state and local officials, depending on where it is spent. In this sense, it is accountable. What is important for now, however, is that soft money is not subject to any dollar limits. Any amount of money can be spent regardless of what restrictions are placed on contributions to specific campaigns. The reason is that, at least in theory, soft money does not go to any specific campaign—it is raised and spent separately.

Thus, accountability of soft money can quickly become a joke. As with at least some PAC money, if the money is spent near the end of the campaign, the accountability comes totally after the fact. Moreover, even though all advertisements are supposed to contain a disclaimer telling who paid for the ad, they are often spoken so hurriedly on the air (if at all), or the print used to flash across the screen is so small, that they are scarcely noticed. In print advertising this problem is somewhat alleviated—most responsible newspapers will not accept ads without a disclosure plainly printed—but television and radio seem to be the favored media of soft money, probably because of its proven effectiveness if executed well.

Was soft money a problem in the 1996 election? Probably not, unless viewers found watching the AFL-CIO ads, as well as others put on by different political organizations to push their cause, especially annoying. Both political parties aired advertisements; while this is not strictly soft money, in fact the parties can spend whatever amounts they want in fostering the campaigns of their candidates. In 1988 the Horton ad was well known and widely discussed, although no one seriously believes it caused the defeat of Michael Dukakis, because the problems of that candidacy far transcended any single TV spot.

But soft money could become a problem. The reason is that there are virtually no controls on how much money can be spent outside of candidates' campaigns. Any group can raise and spend virtually whatever it wants to promote its interest or message. Moreover, if 1996 is any indication, media specialists are already skilled at making sure that, while they do not specifically endorse any particular candidate or issue, in fact the message so strongly points in that direction that it can scarcely be missed.

What seems to happen is that once a door is opened that permits political money to flow, it rapidly becomes a gusher. That's essentially what happened once PACs were created in the early 1970s, and the financial cataract that ensued still has not crested. The likelihood is that now that soft money can so easily and freely be injected into campaign cycles, we will see more and more of it. But unlike PAC money, which must give obeisance to the rules, soft money can quickly get out of control.

Is There a Way Out?

Campaign finance reform has acquired the status of a mantra. There is no shortage of suggestions: Impose limits on money raised, on funds spent, on the duration of campaigns. Force the media to provide free access to candidates (would this mean every crackpot as well as the "real" candidates?). Force congressional and state legislative candidates to raise money only in their own states or districts, and disallow money from outside. Restrict PACs in some fashion. Eliminate all public financing of campaigns; make campaigns totally dependent on public funds. Limit the time period in which campaign money can be raised and spent.[41]

The list of suggestions is endless. Many of them are mutually incompatible. Often they ignore basic First Amendment rights, either the free speech provisions or those permitting petitioning of the government. All ignore political realities. The fact is, those in office are successful products of the system as it now exists. They have a powerful disincentive to changing it. Given that there is no agreement in the private sector (including in the media or academic circles), at any level of government, or in any groups of interested bystanders and participants on what changes should be made, and public opinion offers little more than "do something," it is no wonder that most campaign finance reform to date has been modest, to put it charitably. In fact, there has been little change at all that addresses the basic problems caused by money and campaigns discussed in this chapter, or the many others not discussed.

It is a reasonable assumption, moreover, that merely tinkering with the existing system of public finance will be insufficient to solve the basic problems of challenger-incumbent disparities, PAC insidiousness, and soft money discussed before. Fine tuning the adjustment knobs cannot attack the basic difficulty facing the existing system of financing campaigns: the money creates an unequal campaign playing field, establishes too much dependency between PACs and candidates, and is about to become out of control. Rather, a major overhaul of the way we do campaign finance in this country is needed.

With this in mind, the following proposal is put forward. As noted earlier, it is sure to be controversial and, if anyone pays attention to it, will be heavily criticized. Virtually none of the existing powers in the campaign finance business—incumbents, PACs, party leaders, soft-money advocates, professional fund-raisers, campaign consultants, and anyone else who profits from the system as it now exists—will like it. It is put forward with full recognition of the difficulties it has before it. But it is to be hoped that readers will give it serious consideration, and at least use it as a starting point for the national debate over campaign finance reform that incumbents and others have so far managed to keep under wraps.

The heart of the proposal lies in a point made earlier. There is currently no mediating institution or organization serving as a buffer between donors (specifically PACs) and candidates. If one were to exist, it could serve as an instrument of checks and balances so dear to American democratic theory; more immediately it would force accountability and responsibility on the part of contributors and recipients of campaign money—it would break apart the very cozy relationship that all too quickly develops between candidates and major sources of campaign money.

The question is, how to identify this mediating institution or organization? The likely candidates are our political parties, not so much as they exist now as what they would need to become. And what they need to become is what they used to be—major political instruments that play a powerful, even decisive, role in finding candidates for office, financing campaigns, conducting campaigns, and holding candidates accountable to the party organization and those composing it. If this sounds suspiciously like late nineteenth-century political parties, minus the corruption and graft, it is.

Parties nowadays are little more than shells of political organizations. In recent years, at state levels, they have shown some signs of life as state organizations have acquired funds that can be distributed to state and local candidates. What does not exist is the ability of parties to choose candidates, and directly finance their campaigns; the contributions they currently make, while not trivial, are usually only a fraction of the total the candidate actually requires. And of course there is virtually no accountability or sense of mutual obligation between candidate and party organization. Indeed, to the extent there is any relationship at all, it is likely to be antagonistic, as candidates regard the party as a meddlesome nuisance, and party officials often regard candidates contemptuously as little more than amateurs in the case of newcomers, and uncooperative ingrates in the case of incumbents.

It doesn't have to be this way, of course. This is not the place to discuss how parties and candidates need to refigure their relationship. If this proposal, or one like it, is adopted, that will come as a matter of course; indeed, money will make it happen.

Essentially we have to establish a system in which virtually all campaign money is funneled through political parties. We probably cannot completely prohibit contributions to individual candidates or causes because of First Amendment issues; but we can limit the size of them to, say, one hundred dollars. This would be a hard and fast rule that applies to individual contributors and PACs alike. But there would be no limit—as there is none now—on how much money could be given to political parties by private persons, PACs, corporations, unions, whatever.

Parties would then allocate money to candidates. For primaries, all candidates for the same office—including the incumbent—would receive the same amount. In the general election, parties would decide how much to allocate to candidates for the different offices. Candidates would not be permitted to use their private fortunes directly; they could, however, donate whatever they wanted to their party of choice, which would then decide on allocating the money as it enters the total pool. So much for the need for term limits: on a financially level playing field, one wonders how many incumbents will survive primary challenges or, if they do, a serious opponent whose financial base may equal or even exceed their own, depending on the allowance given the campaign by party headquarters.

Obviously this is a major change from what exists now. The direct tie between candidates and donors (individuals and PACs) would be broken. It would replace that tie with one between candidates and parties. But is not this potentially more healthy for our democracy? Parties in this country have played the role of mediating political organizations: they can be big tents, as the late Lee Atwater used to say; they can serve as a mechanism in which individual and group interests are articulated, aggregated, amalgamated, with the result that they represent at least a version of the larger public interest.

It will be objected that parties, as they exist now, cannot do this; they are not equipped to handle this level of responsibility, to make the decisions about allocating massive amounts of funds. No argument there; but an infusion of few hundred million dollars might serve as quite an incentive for them to reinvent themselves. Others will point out that this proposal runs counter to the whole Progressive movement and its effort to shoo parties out of the political process, and that we might reinstitute powerful political machines, even bosses. But as long as sufficient safeguards are built in concerning immediate and full disclosure of campaign finance information so that corruption and graft will be avoided, stronger party organizations may well serve to revitalize other political institutions,[42] invigorate our national political debate, create policy agendas that deal with real public issues, and so forth.

What would happen in local elections, including nonpartisan ones? The same thing: parties would allocate campaign moneys, and if that means getting rid of nonpartisan elections, so be it—because the evidence gathered by social scientists for years is that they hurt parties, permit interest groups to have unwarranted power in elections, and probably discriminate against less well educated citizens. What about issue referenda, constitutional amendments, and the like? Same thing: parties would decide to what extent they wish to fund campaigns for or against any of these proposals.

Would public financing continue, or be abolished? There's no reason why it could not continue. It has served, in some measure, to level the political playing field, so there is no sense in junking it. More abstractly, political campaigns ultimately have as their end the selection of people or ideas involved in governing, a public enterprise. Why not continue public funding for this public purpose?

Would soft money be permitted under this proposal? Citizens cannot be denied free political speech, which probably means that it is not possible to prevent soft money from entering the political campaign season. But greater levels of accountability could be required, and prominent disclaimers displayed. Candidates could be required to publicly report their association or relationship, if any, to those financing soft-money campaigns. Soft-money contributions could also be taxed, possibly at a high enough rate to serve as a disincentive for their use. Finally, limits could be imposed on total amounts of soft money that any given organization could spend; this might please those who were appalled at the amount of soft money that some organizations spent in 1996.

Would it not turn out that parties would play key roles even in the selection of candidates? Would this not be a disincentive for a uniquely qualified individual to run? The answer is that, right now, there are plenty of disincentives for qualified people to run; the woods are full of people who can be identified by their neighbors and other members of their community as potentially attractive candidates and valuable public servants, but who would no more run for office under the present system than they would lie down naked on an ant bed. Moreover, given reasonably competitive parties, there would be a continuing incentive for each party to find attractive candidates and the money to finance their campaigns; it would not be in their interest to continually put forward candidates the public regarded as dogs. Mistakes will be made, and no doubt parties will have to make trade-offs as to what they consider quality candidates. Too, individuals will still be able to nominate themselves; in primaries they will be assured of getting the same amount of financing as their opponents. There may well be an incentive for parties to minimize the number of challenges to incumbents in primaries, but clearly in the general election—whether the seat is open or not—the parties' interests lie in putting forward capable candidates.

Under this proposal, donors and contributors could indicate how they wished their money to be spent, and for which elections. The key point, however, is that their wishes would not obligate the party. All donated money would go into a single pot, to be distributed as the party wished, according to formulas and rules that it would create. Would there not be titanic, even epic, struggles within the party as to how money should be apportioned, and would there not be huge confrontations between large donors and party officials on the allocation of funds? Undoubtedly. But these power plays would take place on an internecine basis, within the confines of the party; they would not directly affect candidates, thus sparing them the tight bond of dependence that has developed between them and contributors. The bond would develop not between candidates and private interests, but between candidates and parties; for the sake of democratic institutions, this is a much easier relationship to justify.

Full and immediate accounting of all moneys donated, allocated, and spent by parties and candidates would be required to federal and state officials. Reporting would not be periodic as it is now. Computer technology exists to make reporting instantaneous. Indeed, these reports ought to go on-line, so they are instantly available to the media, interested groups, candidates, and the other party. Given the amount of money political parties will have at their disposal under this proposal, it is not unreasonable to expect them to pay for the additional facilities, hardware, and personnel that state and federal elections agencies would require in order to handle the increased load. Either political contributions and donations could be taxed to raise these funds, or a percentage of the parties' take would have to be turned over to state and federal officials for this purpose. Candidates for local elections would still file with local supervisors of elections (more frequently than they do now), who would have the additional responsibility of seeing that these reports were immediately forwarded electronically and by hard copy to state officials.

Does this proposal discriminate against third or minor parties? No more than the existing system does. There is nothing in this proposal to prevent a third party from finding a financial base in some segment of the population. It would prevent a Ross Perot or a Steve Forbes or some other zillionaire from bankrolling his or her own campaign (or that of someone else) through personal funds.[43] It would not prevent the formation of parties, solicitation of funds, recruitment of candidates, and launching of electoral campaigns, along with all of the other activities in which parties engage. The failures of third parties in this country to have much staying power only rarely rests on their inability to find funds; the rules third parties have to follow to qualify for the ballot, majority-vote requirements in many elections, the tradition of two-party politics in America—all these things and more weigh against the success of third parties. This proposal would not add unnecessarily to the burdens they already face.

Obviously this proposal is far reaching. Its impact on party and probably legislative politics is enormous. It builds a barrier—not an impregnable one, but a sturdy one—between private or PAC donors and candidates. Contributors will have little claim on their candidates of choice, except to the extent that their hundred-dollar maximum donation establishes some sort of tenuous relationship. The financial playing field will be significantly equalized between challengers and incumbents. We may even find that more campaigns are of the robust, vital, competitive sort that our elementary-school teachers told us about, but that we so seldom find today.

Conclusion

Much of what we Americans do in political campaigning is fairly benign. In the case of campaign finance, however, there are red flags all over the place. We have talked much about reforming our mechanism of financing campaigns, but so far we have done little more than minor tinkering. It is time to look the matter straight in the eye, and make the needed major changes. That change needs to come from outside the present system—since the system clearly will tend to perpetuate what works best for those in it. Ultimately the citizens will have to make it happen. The question is, do the citizens have the will to bring about needed change before we have gone irrevocably down the road to putting our democracy up for sale?

8

Political Campaigns and American Society

In the end, American culture determines what political campaigns are like, and what role they play in our society and in our lives. Culture is not a prison, forcing us to do things we would rather not do, or making us pay for sins of omission or commission. It is rather a framework within which we must act, and carry out the tasks of maintaining the social order. In this instance, culture determines how we carry out our electoral campaigns in order to identify and select public officials and government leaders. It is the way we as Americans have chosen to define and establish our democratic political system. Other cultures choose leaders differently; we put on a circus, and turn campaigns into a spectacle, a form of mass entertainment.

At its most basic level, our culture determines what politics means to us as citizens. "What politics means to us" is a shorthand way of placing politics and political life in the context of everything that happens in our society and in our lives. It means putting it into a list of priorities of what we as Americans think are of importance. "What politics means to us" also provides guidance as to how we go about performing basic governing housekeeping functions, so that we don't have to reinvent the wheel every so often; we just more or less do it the way we did it before, maybe with some modifications, but essentially following similar patterns. "What politics means to us" also defines how we face collective challenges and tasks, such as educating children, cleaning up the air and the water, and protecting ourselves from foreign adversaries.

The phrase "what politics means to us" can help us understand why we engage in the type of political campaigning that we do. If politics were something with which most Americans felt comfortable, and if it occupied a high position on our list of national priorities, it is likely that our campaigns would be a good deal different. We might, for example, demand that candidates address public questions in a serious way; we might even take seriously what they say.

But we don't. Americans are not, for the most part, comfortable when they are forced to put on their political hats and carry out political tasks. We do so out of a spirit of civic obligation established in us long ago by elementary-school teachers and parents; only rarely do we perform these tasks—following candidates, learning about issues, going to a city council meeting, writing a letter to a congressman, voting—out of feelings of joy or delight. Our predisposition for things political tends toward the suspicious, the distasteful, the negative. Even the sense of accomplishment or feeling of participating in a vast common enterprise—feelings that at least some people experience when they finish voting—are often tempered by the knowledge (or fear, anyway) that the wrong candidate will be elected.

There is the further problem that politics and political campaigns are but a small part of the many burdens and challenges Americans face every day. Jobs, bills, family problems, health, the care of aging parents, the raising of children—the list, in no particular order of priority, is endless. The campaign has somehow to break through all of this, and if not get to the top of the list at least move far enough up to be noticed. The most frustrating thing, for candidate, consultant, and political junkie alike, is to be asked after months of campaigning and the expenditure of large amounts of money and energy, "Oh, are you running for something? When's the election?" Obviously, at least for such a voter, the campaign has been an exercise in futility.

Seen in this light, it is easy to understand why the modern political campaign takes the form it does. If it seems full of hoopla and noise, composed of irrelevancies and character assassinations and innuendoes, replete with windbaggery and self-promotions and empty phrases, it's because we as Americans don't take naturally to it, as a duck does to water. We have to be cajoled, prodded, persuaded, entertained, before we will pay attention. If we regard it as distasteful, a waste of our time and an insult to our sensibilities, it is because efforts to worm into our collective and individual consciousness inevitably involve a search for the lowest common denominator. The highbrow approach does not work;[1] almost worse than being ignored is being regarded as condescending or a snob. Incumbent presidents may be expected to "act presidential" and not get down and dirty,[2] but they also need to generate some excitement in order to get their supporters motivated to vote. Campaign staffers spend virtually as much time dreaming up campaign gimmicks as they do scheduling events and planning media buys.

There is another problem, one we have left for the end of the book. Political campaigns are inherently adversarial. Ultimately there will be a victor and a vanquished. This does not mean that positive, clean campaigns, rare as they are, cannot be carried out, or that they must fail. It does mean, though, that sooner or later voters have to make choices. These decisions pit individuals and groups against one another; hard feelings, or worse, can result unless they decide to agree to disagree. For many people, the cost of participating in this adversarial process is too high. They may not feel the candidates are sufficiently worthy to want to make a choice, and they may not feel the stakes are sufficiently important, or the outcome makes any difference at all, so they refuse to participate. Others may recognize that they should choose, but cannot or do not bring themselves to do so. For others, who feel the obligation to go to the polls and decide, the process is still painful. They do not discuss "politics" or the campaign at home or the job—the choice, after all, is a private matter, and we do protect the secret ballot—and in fact they may duck political discussion altogether. The adversarial process is too strenuous; no wonder so many people ignore or overlook the campaign, regard it distastefully, and even decide not to vote. Why participate in something whose outcome is uncertain, leads to unknown consequences, and drives people apart as much as it brings them together?

Fortunately, not all Americans feel this way. Many—but probably not enough—brave the adversarial winds and do make a choice.[3] But the whole endeavor further undermines the value and priority Americans place on politics and campaigns. In a culture that values teamwork as much as rugged individualism, trade-offs have to be made. One of the easiest pieces of baggage to jettison is a willingness to attend to political campaigns and then go out and vote. This is yet another challenge facing the modern political campaign and candidate; it is a little bit like trying to swim up a waterfall, since the natural political inclinations of the citizens are, at least in this country, a torrent headed in the opposite direction.[4]

The Rules of the Game

Like everything else in politics, the modern political campaign has to follow certain rules. We use rules in order to regularize behaviors into acceptable patterns; rules determine what is legitimate activity from behaviors or actions that go beyond the pale. In the case of political campaigning, rules keep our actions from degenerating into mob action or civil war, something other countries have had to learn the hard way.

Perhaps most important, rules create certain expectations about what candidates must do, and how campaigns are to go forward. For example, virtually all states require that if candidates secure the endorsement of citizens, a statement of agreement or approval for the use of that endorsement, signed by the endorser, must be available for inspection; most media outlets will not accept endorsement ads without first inspecting these signed forms. There is no law that says a candidate has to use or even seek endorsements; but the existence of rules for their use creates both an incentive for candidates and an expectation for citizens that they will become a part of the campaign trappings, apparatus, and baggage.

It happens further that the rules of the game create certain rituals that campaigns must observe if they are to be regarded as serious, legitimate efforts by voters. Rituals, as anthropologists have noted for a long time, are an essential part of private and public life. They give meaning and order to the way we do things. For example, in this era of instantaneous electronic communication, when it is so easy (if expensive) to reach massive numbers of people with a carefully crafted positive or negative message, candidates (or their surrogates) often stand out on street corners waving signs at passing motorists. Why? Is there any evidence that a citizen will decide to vote, or change a vote from one candidate to another, because somebody thrusts a sign in front of the windshield, adding yet another hazard to rush-hour traffic? The most we can say is that such sign waving shows some level of enthusiasm for this or that candidate, and possibly it might reinforce in some voters' minds their previous decision of whether or not to vote and, if so, for whom. But there is no evidence that this kind of behavior actually affects the outcome of campaigns.

It can, however, be understood as ritual. Candidates and their supporters stand out on street corners with signs because the local tradition and culture decrees that they must. All of them could probably be doing something more politically useful. But not to observe the rituals of the campaign, however they are defined locally, is to invite disaster. People will think something is the matter: perhaps the candidate is not a serious one, or has less support than supposed. To underscore a point made earlier, the culture of campaigning, at least in its local manifestation, may not be a straitjacket, but observance of the rules is essential.

The rules and rituals of campaigning are both formal and informal. What is further important about them is that they have a discriminatory effect—they clearly favor certain types of candidates and certain types of activities over others. Sometimes this is trivial: candidates who use strange colors on their campaign materials, for example (watch out for purple; green can be poison unless it's a deep, rich shade; yellow or pink or rose sends all the wrong messages, while gold needs a complementary rich, dark, cool color to soften its impact), can hurt themselves. But sometimes the discriminatory effects can be serious, especially those that work against candidates with modest bank accounts.

This leads to an important thought. It has been a theme of this book that most of what we do in political campaigning doesn't do us any harm. But some of the rules and rituals surrounding the campaigns may actually do so. Especially is this true of formal rules codified as statutes. For example, it is not uncommon to require substantial qualifying fees before one becomes a bona fide candidate. While no one disputes that there are administrative costs to the state or local government associated with campaigns (printing ballots, for example, is not cheap), when fees are too high, some candidates cannot afford to pay them. Some people might argue that part of the job of the candidate is to raise funds to pay these fees; but even in local elections the fees can sometimes run into thousands of dollars, and constitute an additional burden to candidates already faced with bankrolling increasingly expensive campaigns. In recent years some states have allowed state and local candidates to get on the ballot by petition, bypassing the qualifying fee. There is some evidence, largely anecdotal but plausible, that the public—now surfeited by groups and candidates regularly thrusting petitions in their face—is less willing to sign every petition request that comes along. Besides, the political parties object to the petition process, since in some states party organizations collect a portion of the qualifying fee.

We also know that the formal rules of campaigning discriminate against third-party and minor-party candidates. Rules for getting on the ballot are essentially the product of what the two major parties want. While courts will not allow them to create a monopoly, petition requirements for getting on the ballot and minimum vote percentages to stay on it from one election to the next have in the past worked against the interests of third parties, and in the interest of allowing the major parties to keep the field pretty much to themselves.

Not all formal rules and statutes necessarily discriminate in this way, but their perpetuation as part of campaign ritual sometimes seems unrelated to any real function they play. For example, many states and local areas have codes of ethics to which candidates are expected to pledge; these might not be legally binding, but they constitute a set of canons that are supposed to keep campaigns high-minded and clean. Sometimes they are even accompanied by watchdog commissions or other organizations that are supposed to blow the whistle in the event of violations. Experience suggests, however, that little more than lip service goes to observing these codes; once mortar rounds start falling, candidates are quick to respond with some of their own. The enforcement of the codes usually amounts to little more than finger pointing, often well after the fact and always with little clout; the commissions have no real sanctions available to them to force compliance.

Even campaign financial reports, required at all levels of activity and generally highly publicized when filed, have a ritual status that transcends their effectiveness and use. Let it quickly be noted that proper accounting of campaign finances is essential to ensure that there is no more monetary abuse in campaigns than there already is; as noted in the last chapter, money in campaigns is the one element in the political mix of which we need to be very wary. Indeed, there probably needs to be more frequent, and more detailed, reporting of campaign finances than there already is.

In spite of the already strict laws, however, abuses do exist. No one should be deceived into thinking that campaign finance reports necessarily are comprehensive documents about the financial doings of campaigns. While morally reprehensible as well as illegal, it is also true that some campaigns have been known to keep two sets of books—the official ones, and the ones that actually pay for the campaign.[5]

This is not an attack on campaign finance laws, nor should there be any inference that such behavior can be tolerated; the contrary is true. It is to point out, however, that we engage in rituals to try to ensure the purity of our campaigns. They make us feel better. They make us think we do our campaigns in a way consonant with the spirit of democracy, with openness and full accountability. That the rituals fall short, or seem to have little functional purpose, and in some instances make things worse, hardly undercuts our need to continue them. Without these formalistic rituals, we might not be able to convince ourselves that we at least try to conduct campaigns in a way consonant with democratic norms, and differently from the way cave dwellers might have done it if they had had political campaigns.

Informal rituals are equally important in helping us understand and justify campaign behavior. American culture generally, and local political styles and preferences (subcultures, perhaps), define what is acceptable, permissible, required, and forbidden. The example of sign waving on street corners is but one instance of many local rituals that could be cited. Seldom are these codified.

They take many forms. Candidates, for example, almost always insist on making a formal announcement of their candidacy. Why bother? Usually it occurs months before the election, when scarcely anybody is paying attention to politics. Unless it is for a major office, the media generally offer little coverage; a few lines in a newspaper may be all the candidate gets, and often no television or radio announcement. The candidate could buy coverage, but that starts to get expensive. Perhaps to rally supporters? At the early stage of a campaign, those willing to come to a rally or announcement are already convinced; so the event does little more than serve to preach to the choir. Still, candidates insist on a formal unveiling of their campaign. In different areas the announcement might be done differently, but the purpose is the same.[6] All such announcements are part of the informal rules of the game, the rituals of the way we do our political campaigns.

The same could be said of position papers, debates, and forums. Does anybody actually read position papers, or take them seriously? Maybe a few political junkies and policy wonks, and perhaps the candidate's spouse or parent; hardly anyone else ever notices them, and if they do, they are treated exactly the same way other campaign

literature is treated: as eminently disposable. Political forums and debates? Perhaps for major offices like the presidency, or governor, people tune in; but we also know that even at this level the debates serve
more to reinforce decisions about candidates already made by voters,
and perhaps to push a few undecideds one way or the other. They
seldom actually change people's positions on the candidates. And at
the local level, it is not unusual to find that the number of candidates
appearing exceeds those in the audience; hardly anyone notices these
events, or takes the trouble to go out after supper to a cavernous,
essentially empty school or other auditorium and listen to the candidates make their pitch. Again, however, we are talking about rituals;
candidates fail to observe them at their own risk, and even if hardly
anybody is in the audience, the presence of an empty chair on the stage
does not bode well for the candidate's electoral success.

Campaign rituals, whether formal or informal, are then not to be
trifled with. For voters committed to political activity, for those who
actually like to follow candidates and campaigns, the rituals give a
sense of worth to the process, a feeling of participation in and appreci-
ation for the grand tradition of how we choose our officials and leaders. For indifferent or skeptical, even hostile, citizens, the rituals of
campaigns make them tolerable. Even if they don't like what they see
or hear, rituals at least help them to grasp that this is the way things are
done in campaigns; and just as certain rituals in religious or other
aspects of life may not always make sense, they help define who we
are as a political community, and there is a certain obligation to see
that they are maintained.

Why Bother?

Still, readers may not be satisfied. Granted, rituals are important, and
many of our secular (if not political) rituals are just silly. Why play
"The Star-Spangled Banner" at the start of baseball games? What does
it add to the game, especially since nobody can sing it anyway? Does it
inspire the players to greater feats of athletic prowess on the field? Or
is it just that we expect it, because ever since we were children we've
listened to it at the games, and they would not be the same without it?

The same argument can be made about political campaigns. Why
bother? If they are empty vessels, merely public rituals that do little to
inform the citizens, fail to inspire us to engage in political discourse or

carry out our civic responsibilities of studying issues and making informed decisions about candidates, and are expensive and often nasty
to boot, why not spare the trouble? Why not find some other way to
choose public officials and leaders, and not go through all of this?

The answer is that campaigns actually do serve purposes beyond
merely repeating what our grandfathers did, and reaffirming certain
public rites and rituals. For some people, of course, this is enough
justification; in our democracy, carrying on traditions in choosing our
leaders ensures continuity with the way we go about governing ourselves. This is one of the ways we define ourselves as a political
community and make our form of democracy unique. These considerations, while abstract and normative, are not trivial. The linkage with
the past is very important in democratic government. It allows us to
test present challenges and possibilities against those of citizens and
leaders who came before us. It is a way of discovering whether we
continue to reaffirm our commitment to our version of democracy, or
somehow have gotten away from it.

But there are more reasons to continue political campaigns than to join
a historical tradition. As Stephen Hess pointed out some years ago, political campaigns are useful for assessing the mettle of candidates, and seeing
if they are capable of withstanding the pressures and demands of holding
public office. He was talking about presidential campaigns, but his remarks assuredly apply to other political offices as well.[7]

Hess recognized that the requirements of a successful campaign are
not necessarily positively related to the capacity to govern. On the
other hand, campaigns place tremendous strains and pressures on individuals that are not dissimilar to those they will face in office. Can the
candidates handle them, or do they crack and show serious weaknesses?
Coupled with the length of time campaigns occupy, even reaching
marathon proportions for major offices,[8] they may well give us insight
into a candidate's true character and suitability to uphold the public
trust.

Red flags will immediately be waved by some readers. Campaigns,
they will note, are indeed searches for character flaws—as happened to
Bill Clinton in 1992 and 1996, and he was elected twice anyway, in
spite of them. But Hess had a different set of character traits in mind
than did those criticizing Clinton. He was concerned about traits that
are important in a public enterprise, not about what people do in private. In this sense, courage, resolution, good humor, an ability to focus

energy, vision, imagination, and a capacity to identify with fellow Americans, among others, become more important than what happens in candidates' private business. Clinton did not rank badly on most of these traits, and compared with Dole probably a good deal better. It should also be pointed out, of course, that virtually all presidents have had certain character flaws that were either overlooked or disregarded by the public as the president carried out the duties of office, and only in a few cases did they affect our assessment of them.[9]

Thus, there is a good deal of validity in the character-test-by-campaigning thesis proposed by Hess. The public, however, needs to remember which aspects of public character are relevant to the selection of candidates; private traits may not have much bearing. The problem, of course, is that nowadays the public does not always want to make public/private distinctions of character, and in fact the more private matters are revealed the greater the level of public titillation. Perhaps we need to reassess our own judgment and standards of what is acceptable, and what we can reasonably demand, in a candidate; but that is a topic for another time.

A third reason to continue campaigns is that, on an empirical basis, they seem to have an impact. Political scientists have been able to document that, over time, campaigns do have an effect on the way in which voters perceive candidates, issues, behaviors, and the like. It turns out, as might be expected, that the relationship between candidate activity in campaigns and voter learning is neither simple nor direct; an extra dollar's worth of campaigning does not necessarily result in a dollar's more votes.

Still, the data are clear enough. Consider the following. Political scientists have been able to create models of voting behavior that can predict the outcome of a presidential election in early September. If this is true, why should anybody bother to campaign? If we already know what is going to happen, what is the point of going through all the hoopla and expense?[10]

The answer is that the political scientists' models are statistical approximations. Some are more accurate than others; some are luckier than others. In virtually all campaigns there are ebbs and flows, changes in momentum, upswings and dips. Mistakes are made, revelations are revealed, October surprises are unveiled, undecided voters decide. The accuracy of predictive models is determined in part by when the election takes place relative to the movement of campaign activity and the public's view of what is happening. In 1968, at least some analysts thought that if the campaign had gone on for just a few more days, Hubert Humphrey would have won; in the last hours of the campaign there was a rapid shift of public opinion in his direction, but the election came too soon for it to help him. In 1996 the electoral numbers barely moved throughout the campaign—but even at the end, as it was clear Dole would lose, Clinton's numbers began to decline as Perot launched a final, negative blitz that resonated with the voters far more than did Dole's jeremiads.

Thus, we know that the public does respond to campaigns. They do influence what happens, and who wins; predestination is rarely associated with political campaigns. It is clearly in the candidates' interest, and the public's, to campaign, and to do so vigorously. It could very well make the difference between victory and defeat.

Finally, what if we did not have campaigns? We would have to find some other way to identify and choose our public officials. This could be done, perhaps even in a vaguely democratic way; military coups are not the only other option available to us for putting people in office. On the other hand, the type of campaigns we have, as noted before, help us identify our type of political community, and define our version of democracy. Eliminating campaigns would severely change those identifications and definitions; we would become a much different nation and society, and not necessarily a more democratic one.

All right, then, even if we can't get rid of campaigns, could we not change them, make them somehow "better"? Aside from there being no particular public agreement on what a better campaign would be, there is a real question about how we would bring about the transformation. True, we could tinker at the margins: make campaigning seasons shorter, require free access to media for candidates, demand more forums, impose campaign contribution and expenditure limits, and so forth. Probably none of these would ultimately have much impact on the way we go about campaigning; as said before, campaigns reflect our culture, our sense of what politics is and how the game of politics should be played. One simply does not pass laws or create rules that run counter to cultural norms; legislating decent or even acceptable standards of campaign behavior does not seem to work either, nor is it possible or desirable to write laws requiring either informed candidates or knowledgeable voters. Rather, if we want different campaigns, we need to change what we think about politics, and the role it plays in our collective and individual lives. In other words, we need to change our culture. That failing, we probably will retain what we have, pretty much, in the future.

In Harm's Way?

Are our political campaigns bad for us? Do they undermine our democracy? Are we in peril, or are we weakening our democratic institutions with the kind of campaigns we conduct, through which voters and nonvoters alike (as well as candidates) have to suffer?

By now, the answer to these questions should be reasonably clear. While campaigns are not always ones we are proud of, neither are we necessarily injuring ourselves or our governing institutions by the way we carry them out. For one thing, we've been campaigning in much the same way for nearly two hundred years; the technology changes, but the mudslinging and negativity seem to remain fairly constant. We have survived to this point, and there is no reason to think we cannot continue to do so.

Moreover, we are increasingly aware that the requirements of campaigns and the requirements of governance are very different. In a sense, this acts as an insurance policy, as the excesses of the campaign must be tempered by the cold, harsh reality of what government can actually do, afford, and accomplish. This in no way undermines the value of campaigns, as noted by Stephen Hess before. They do serve as a good test for candidates' capacity to work hard, handle stress, and balance a host of competing demands. It is to suggest, however, that the antics and behaviors of candidates as they seek to win may bear only a slight relationship to their demeanor, attitudes, and proposals once they are in office. If campaigns often take the form of circuses and other forms of mass entertainment, governing is a much more sober business, indeed.

The questions posed, however, have another component. That is, just because campaigns don't hurt us or undermine our system of democracy, should we therefore be proud of them? Do they not in fact degrade us? This is a very different set of considerations. All of us are familiar with campaigns that were insulting and degrading to all concerned, participants and citizens alike. Perhaps there are too many of them. But it is a very different thing to say, on the one hand, that some of our campaigns get pretty down and dirty, and another to say that therefore they hurt our democracy. The connection between the two is tenuous at best, given the historically demonstrable staying power, elasticity, and strength of our democratic political institutions at all levels of government. Campaigns may often be distasteful, even disgusting, but that does not mean they harm anything other than our sensibilities.

Finally, campaigns actually have their own functional logic and rationality. This statement may surprise some readers, especially those thinking about some of the zany things that often happen during political campaigns. But the statement applies to campaigns in the aggregate, not necessarily to any one in particular. Political rationality is not easy for many citizens to grasp, since it seems to violate the logic of the syllogism and other logical models taught to us from elementary school onward.

In this regard, addressing the political rationality of campaigns means asking, do they make sense in terms of what they are supposed to accomplish? Recall our definition of campaigns from the first chapter: they are activities designed to get voters to choose a candidate or an issue, or vote against someone or something. Given their limited purpose, and given the value system of American culture that places politics in a fairly low position, campaigns may in fact be highly rational. The negativity, the noise and hoopla, the zaniness may all contribute to voters' realization and understanding of what they have to do: carry out their civic obligations by making a choice about candidates and public questions at the voting booth. Many citizens might feel that our way of doing this is crazy and silly. But appeals to civic duty seem to work only for a limited segment of the population; while voter turnouts in this country are not what many would like to see, it is not at all clear that they would improve if our campaigns became more serious, more substantive, more cerebral. In this regard, the logic and rationality of our political campaigns may very well contribute to citizen awareness, knowledge, and participation in our political life.

The Postmodern Campaign

In recent years, observers of the American cultural scene like to talk about postmodernism, in everything from art to economics. What will the postmodern political campaign look like?

This is a hard question to answer, as it is not always clear what postmodernism really is. Often it refers to a reduction or leveling of standards, an unwillingness or inability to establish priorities, perhaps even deconstruction of a whole into a virtually structureless entity. Seen in this way, many (but not all) campaigns may have been postmodern for a long time: no standards seem too low, and structurally and organizationally they are often noted for being amorphous, with little sense of priority or message.

On the other hand, some trends seem clear. Electronic technology, especially the virtually instantaneous transfer of information, is likely to have a huge impact even in the smallest campaign. Interactive home pages already exist that allow candidates, campaigns, and voters to connect cheaply, almost instantly, and continuously. As costs fall and technology becomes even more sophisticated, candidate access to individual voters will become easier, faster, more frequent. It is already possible to conduct at least some campaign activities by television satellite hookups; undoubtedly these will increase as well. At some point, the concept of the virtual campaign, existing exclusively in cyberspace, may push aside the cumbersome technical requirements of the satellite hookup. Already in Japan virtual television images of singers and other icons of culture are as popular as real, live television celebrities; why not virtual candidates, as well?

There will be limits, of course. Unless there are major changes in American culture, we may continue to insist that candidates show themselves in person, at least occasionally, even as they perfect their home pages, e-mail systems, and virtual campaigns. The reason is that at some basic level, voters seem to want to have physical contact with their candidates. It is possible to conduct a campaign using television, mail, and other forms of media almost exclusively even now. Yet candidates find, as do voters, that there is no replacement for pressing the flesh, having an actual moment of contact when a voter and a candidate actually look each other in the eye. Thus, while baby kissing has gone out of fashion for candidates (why risk a possible charge of child abuse?), they continue to hold rallies, go to shift changes at the factory at odd hours, walk neighborhoods, even schedule town-hall meetings designed to allow interaction between candidate and citizens. It is not at all clear that, in a postmodern era, the basic personal ties and symbiosis between candidate and voter can be denied. Candidates may well conduct cyberspace campaigns, but they may also have to continue to show up in the flesh, at least at certain times and places, if they expect to make a serious appeal to voters.

The Modern Political Campaign

We hear talk, especially around election times, that Americans get what they deserve, at least as far as candidates and campaigns are concerned. If we don't demand the best, the critics say, why should we get the best? If we don't pay much attention to politics, if we take a devilish pleasure in paying more attention to a candidate's personal life than political agenda, if we regard campaigns as little more than a transitory form of mass entertainment, no wonder so many potential voters stay home, and those who do go to the polls tell us they hold their noses while filling out the ballot.

Do we deserve better? Probably we do; too many campaigns do us, and the candidates, little credit. Some are genuinely degrading to both. All of us would like to think we are better than that, and that we really do deserve something a little better, anyway. But not all campaigns follow this pattern. Some—not all, but enough to be noticed—really do inform voters and help them make intelligent decisions. It is not true that all of our political campaigns are insulting to us; some actually do us, and the candidates, proud.

In the end, campaigns are mirrors of Americans and our culture, at least that part of culture that defines the place and meaning of politics in our lives. Our campaigns may not always be what we deserve, but there is a strong possibility that they really are what we want. We want political campaigns to be lively, entertaining, exciting, because so much of governing—the end result of campaigns—is exactly the opposite. If we had a more positive view of politics and politicians and government, perhaps our campaigns would be different; we would not have to make the distinction between campaigns and governance. But we do not have a positive view, and we continue to make the distinction. It is a reasonable conclusion, then, that our campaigns are not only what we want, but in fact are reflections of who we are as an American political community.

Notes

Chapter 1. Thinking About Political Campaigns in America

1. This comment is based less on available empirical data than on the observations of more than twenty years of teaching political science at the university level. Even political science majors are cynical, often turned off by politics. At least this group is inclined to vote. Students with undeclared majors are much less inclined to participate even at this modest level of involvement. The percentages vary considerably by age, levels of education and employment, region of the country. See Harold W. Stanley and Richard G. Niemi, *Vital Statistics on American Politics* (Washington, D.C.: CQ Press, 1988), pp. 66–67.

2. Campaigns on referenda have become similar to, and as complex as, those for candidates. See, for example, Penelope Lemov, "Bond Votes: How to Win," *Governing* 3, no. 5 (February 1990), pp. 34–40.

3. There is a lengthy, complex, and fascinating literature in political science on voting behavior, specifically the roles "issues" and "duty" play in influencing how Americans vote. Angus Campbell et al., in *The American Voter* (New York: Wiley, 1960), argued that "rational" models of voting behavior explained relatively little. Their model of voting behavior has influenced much of the recent literature on American voters. However, this seminal work provoked a response from V.O. Key, who worked on a refutation and reinterpretation of voting behavior suggesting that "rational" considerations did drive voting behavior. V.O. Key, with Milton Cummings, *The Responsible Electorate: Rationality in Presidential Elections, 1936–1960* (Cambridge: Belknap Press, 1966). Two other important works suggesting that issues play a role in American voting behavior are Norman Nie, Sidney Verba, and John Petrocik, *The Changing American Voter* (Cambridge: Harvard University Press, 1976), and Morris P. Fiorina, *Retrospective Voting in American National Elections* (New Haven: Yale University Press, 1981).

4. See Barbara G. Salmore and Stephen A. Salmore, *Candidates, Parties, and Campaigns,* 2d ed. (Washington, D.C.: CQ Press, 1989).

5. Illustrative of this point is Alfred B. Clubok, John M. DeGrove, and Charles D. Farris, "The Manipulated Negro Vote: Some Preconditions and Consequences," *Journal of Politics* 26 (February 1964), pp. 112–29. "Boss" Ed Crump of Memphis was famous for bringing blacks across the Mississippi River from West Memphis—in Arkansas—and "voting them" to ensure he stayed in power.

6. An office seeker in Alachua County (Gainesville), Florida, once listed as part of his credentials that he had played football for the legendary coach Paul "Bear" Bryant at Alabama. When it was discovered that he had never even matriculated at the university, much less played football there, he was forced to withdraw from the race.

7. Salmore and Salmore, *Candidates, Parties, and Campaigns,* p. 159.

8. It has been known for a long time, for example, that the *Washington Post* refused to print articles about President Kennedy's liaisons with women even though they were well known in Washington, yet at least one recent pretender to the White House—Gary Hart—saw his campaign crumble because of printed revelations in the *Miami Herald* about his extramarital affairs. Even more recent revelations by NBC News and the print media about Senator Charles Robb of Virginia—once mentioned as a future Democratic presidential nominee—and his involvement with a former beauty queen derailed his political plans. On the other hand, continued emphasis on President Clinton's involvement with women other than his wife did not cause his defeat in either 1992 or 1996.

9. "Violence Goes Mainstream: Movies, Music, Books—Are There Any Limits Left?" *Newsweek,* April 1, 1991, pp. 46–52.

Chapter 2. Mudslinging: As American as Apple Pie

1. Quoted in Paul F. Boller, Jr., *Presidential Campaigns* (New York: Oxford University Press, 1984), p. 13.

2. Harry Carman, Harold Syrett, and Bernard Wishy, *A History of the American People,* 3d ed. (New York: Knopf, 1967), p. 303.

3. The reader is reminded that at this early date the electoral college voted differently than it does at present. Electors from each state actually voted twice: for a first and second choice for president. The person receiving the most votes became president; the one with the second highest total became vice president. Thus, "tickets" as we know them today did not exist then; the nominees from each party could actually vie with one another. The modern system inextricably linking party nominees for president and vice president as a ticket was established by the Twelfth Amendment, ratified in 1804.

4. Boller, *Presidential Campaigns,* p. 11; emphasis in original.

5. Ibid.

6. James MacGregor Burns, *The American Experiment* (New York: Knopf, 1982), p. 151; Boller, *Presidential Campaigns,* 11–12.

7. Boller, *Presidential Campaigns,* p. 12.

8. Eugene Roseboom, *A History of Presidential Elections* (New York: Mac-

millan, 1979), p. 45; John Durant and Alice K. Durant, *A Pictorial History of American Presidents* (New York: A.S. Barnes, 1964), p. 33.

9. The Twelfth Amendment specified that only the top three vote-getters in the electoral college could be considered by the House of Representatives.

10. Roseboom, *History of Presidential Elections,* p. 89.

11. Quoted in Boller, *Presidential Campaigns,* p. 42.

12. Burns, *American Experiment,* p. 322.

13. Boller, *Presidential Campaigns,* p. 44; Burns, *American Experiment,* p. 323.

14. Roger Butterfield, *The American Past* (New York: Simon and Schuster, 1957), p. 78.

15. Burns, *American Experiment,* p. 323.

16. Ibid., p. 420.

17. Carman, Syrett, and Wishy, *History of the American People,* p. 449.

18. Roseboom, *History of Presidential Elections,* p. 119.

19. Burns, *American Experiment,* p. 420.

20. Carman, Syrett, and Wishy, *History of the American People,* p. 449.

21. Quoted in Boller, *Presidential Campaigns,* p. 66.

22. Burns, *American Experiment,* p. 420; Roger A. Fischer, *Tippecanoe and Trinkets Too* (Urbana: University of Illinois Press, 1988), pp. 29–49. See also Keith Melder, *Hail to the Candidate* (Washington, D.C.: Smithsonian Institution Press, 1992).

23. Quoted in Burns, *American Experiment,* 421; other songs are quoted in Carman, Syrett, and Wishy, *History of the American People,* p. 449, and Boller, *Presidential Campaigns,* p. 67.

24. Quoted in Boller, *Presidential Campaigns,* p. 65.

25. Ibid., p. 70.

26. Quoted in Burns, *American Experiment,* p. 421.

27. Quoted in Boller, *Presidential Campaigns,* p. 71.

28. Burns, *American Experiment,* p. 421.

29. Butterfield, *American Past,* p. 104.

30. See Joe McGinness, *The Selling of the President* (New York: Penguin, 1988).

31. Durant and Durant, *Pictorial History,* p. 73.

32. Ibid., p. 183; Butterfield, *American Past,* p. 238.

33. Roseboom, *History of Presidential Elections,* p. 265.

34. Ibid., p. 269.

35. Butterfield, *American Past,* p. 239.

36. Quoted in Boller, *Presidential Campaigns,* p. 147.

37. Ibid., p. 148.

38. Roseboom, *History of Presidential Elections,* pp. 270–71; Boller, *Presidential Campaigns,* pp. 148–49.

39. Butterfield, *American Past,* p. 239.

40. Roseboom, *History of Presidential Elections,* p. 271.

41. Quoted in Boller, *Presidential Campaigns,* p. 149.

42. Ibid.

43. Quoted in Roseboom, *History of Presidential Elections,* p. 272; Boller, *Presidential Campaigns,* p. 149.

44. Butterfield, *American Past,* p. 241.

45. Quoted in Roseboom, *History of Presidential Elections,* p. 272.

46. Ibid., p. 474.

47. Butterfield, *American Past,* p. 274; Roseboom, *History of Presidential Elections,* pp. 304–5.

48. Quoted in Carman, Syrett, and Wishy, *History of the American People,* p. 259.

49. Ibid.

50. The same could be said of the Republican view of their last president, Benjamin Harrison. Henry Adams once noted that "one of them had no friends; the other only enemies." Quoted in Boller, *Presidential Campaigns,* p. 162.

51. The consequence of this for the South was to foster the advent of the one-party Democratic dominance of the region's politics until well into the second half of the twentieth century. See Richard K. Scher, *Politics in the New South,* 2d ed. (Armonk, N.Y.: M.E. Sharpe, 1997).

52. Roseboom, *History of Presidential Elections,* p. 313.

53. The descriptive terms and quotations are from Boller, *Presidential Campaigns,* p. 170.

54. Fischer, *Tippecanoe and Trinkets Too,* pp. 144–45. The Bryan forces used them as well. They subsequently became a staple of campaign incunabula and memorabilia.

55. Butterfield, *American Past,* p. 274.

56. Durant and Durant, *Pictorial History,* p. 199.

57. Butterfield, *American Past,* p. 274.

58. Quoted in Boller, *Presidential Campaigns,* p. 171.

59. Quoted in Carman, Syrett, and Wishy, *History of the American People,* p. 259.

Chapter 3. Distilling History: Lessons from Past Campaigns

1. The "liberal" epithet was used effectively in TV ads during the 1988 Florida U.S. Senate race by conservative Connie Mack against moderate congressman Buddy MacKay of Ocala. The announcer said "liberal" with a sneer. Mack won by thirty thousand votes in four million cast.

2. E.E. Schattschneider, *The Semisovereign People* (Hinsdale, Ill.: Dryden Press, 1975).

3. See, for example, Stephen A. Salmore and Barbara G. Salmore, *Candidates, Parties, and Campaigns*, 2d ed. (Washington, D.C.: CQ Press, 1989).

4. See Jack Germond and Jules Witcover, *Whose Broad Stripes and Bright Stars* (New York: Warner, 1989), on the 1988 campaign.

5. For an extended discussion of this point, see James MacGregor Burns, *The American Experiment* (New York: Knopf, 1982).

6. Readers will recall that 1840 was the first time that a presidential candidate—Harrison—actually made a number of campaign appearances. Later, Blaine traveled widely, as did Bryan. But extensive, widespread campaigning by presidential candidates did not really begin until well into the twentieth century.

7. Roger Butterfield, *The American Past* (New York: Simon and Schuster, 1957), p. 77.

8. Bureau of the Census, Part 2, Series R 163–171, "Postal Service Revenues and Expenditures, 1789–1970," and Series Y 335–338, "Summary of Federal Government Finances—Administrative Budget, 1789–1938," *Historical Statistics of the United States, Bicentennial Edition, Colonial Times to 1970,* Parts 1 and 2 (Washington, D.C.: Department of Commerce, Bureau of the Census, 1975)

9. See Series Y, *Historical Statistics.*

10. Based on 1967 = 100. Source: Series E 135–166, "Consumer Price Indexes, All Items, 1800–1970," Part 1, *Historical Statistics.*

11. Perot of course spent nowhere near this amount in 1992; in the 1996 campaign he received federal money for his campaign.

12. See Stephen Hess, *The Presidential Campaign,* 3d ed. (Washington, D.C.: Brookings, 1988).

13. Harold Stassen first ran for the Republican nomination in 1944, and was a regular candidate thereafter. He was never successful in his quest.

14. The modern analogue to Clay of course is Bob Dole, who also spent nearly twenty years seeking the office; in 1996, in his last effort to reach the White House, he fell far short of the mark.

15. Quoted in Paul Boller, *Presidential Campaigns* (New York: Oxford University Press, 1984), p. 71.

16. Ibid. Readers will note, in the first sentence, the comment about the wasted two years, a view that has modern counterparts.

17. Ibid., p. 72.

Chapter 4.   Candidates and the Modern Political Campaign

1. Theodore Zeldin, *The French* (London: Collins, 1983).

2. In 1952 television ads were used extensively for the first time. One of the first of the major ads was a Republican one on behalf of Eisenhower; but it was animated, not live. It was literally a cartoon ad.

3. This is a large topic, noted by many scholars. For two major statements, see Emmet John Hughes, *The Living Presidency* (New York: Coward, McGann, and Geohegan, 1973), and especially Michael A. Genovese, *The Presidential Dilemma* (New York: HarperCollins, 1995); Genovese's book contains an extensive bibliography.

4. See, for example, Thad Beyle, "Governors: The Middlemen and Women in Our Political System," in *Politics in the American States,* ed. Virginia Gray and Herbert Jacob, 6th ed. (Washington, D.C.: CQ Press, 1996), pp. 207–52; Thad L. Beyle, "Being Governor," in *The State of the States,* ed. Carl E. Van Horn, 3d ed. (Washington, D.C.: CQ Press, 1996), pp. 77–107; and Richard K. Scher, *Politics in the New South,* 2d ed. (Armonk, N.Y.: M.E. Sharpe, 1997), chapters 9 and 10.

5. Alan Ehrenhalt, *The United States of Ambition* (New York: Times Books, 1991), p. 106

6. Ibid.

7. See Garry Wills, "What Makes a Good Leader?" *Atlantic Monthly* 273 (April 1994), pp. 63–80, for an enlightening discussion of the symbiotic relationship between leaders and followers.

8. Ehrenhalt, *United States of Ambition,* chapter 1, and p. 206.

9. Ibid., p. 165.

10. See Stephen C. Craig, *The Malevolent Leaders* (Boulder: Westview, 1993); and Stephen C. Craig, ed., *Broken Contract?* (Boulder: Westview, 1996).

11. Ehrenhalt, *United States of Ambition,* chapter 1.

12. Nearly fifty years ago V.O. Key noted this element present in some aspects of southern politics, especially in Florida, where there was no organizational base of support either—although there was a common commitment to keeping blacks and poor whites out of the system. V.O. Key, *Southern Politics* (New York: Knopf, 1949).

13. Ehrenhalt does not use this term, but it is clear he is close to it. See Edward Banfield and James Q. Wilson, *City Politics* (Cambridge: Harvard University Press, 1965).

14. Scher, *Politics in the New South.*

15. Ehrenhalt, *United States of Ambition,* p. 165.

16. *Gainesville Sun,* October 22, 1996, p. 1; Richard L. Berke, "Poll: Attack Hurt Dole's Image," *New York Times,* October 22, 1996; "Aggressive Turn by Dole Appears to Be Backfiring (Berke, p. 1).

17. There is no agreed-upon definition of community or its attributes in scholarly or journalistic literature. The view developed in this chapter is wholly that of the author. There is a large literature devoted to community; helpful recent pieces include John W. Gardner, *Building Community* (prepared for the Leadership Studies Program of Independent Sector, 1991); John W. Gardner, *On Leadership* (New York: Free Press, 1990); David Mathews, *Politics and People* (Urbana and Chicago: University of Illinois Press, 1994); "Civic Declaration: A Call for a New Citizenship," a project of the American Civic Forum (Kettering Foundation, December 9, 1994). This chapter specifically rejects the communitarian vision of community offered in *The Spirit of Community,* by Amitai Etzioni (New York: Touchstone, 1993). Writings by the eminent sociologist John Shelton Reed are also helpful in defining community; Reed argues in several places that "community" can be found (1) to the extent that members of a particular group identify themselves as belonging to a recognizable universe that shares certain common goals and characteristics, and (2) are identified by outsiders as belonging to (or, at least, identifying with) that group. Thus, in Reed's formulation, to denote a community both members and outsiders must be able to "draw a boundary" around it. However, this boundary need not be physical; one can be a member of a community without necessarily living in close proximity (Reed, for example, points out that it is possible to be a "southerner" even outside of the South). See his works *The Enduring South* (Lexington, Mass.: Lexington Books, 1972), *One South* (Baton Rouge: Louisiana State University Press, 1982), and *Southerners* (Chapel Hill: University of North Carolina Press, 1983).

Chapter 5.   Issues in the Modern Campaign: Where's the Meat?

1. Richard Berke, "For Both Camps in Final Debate, Hopes, Risks and a Few Surprises," *New York Times,* October 18, 1996, p. 1, and the Internet edition of that date, http://www.nytimes.com/.

2. James Bennett, "Dole Plans Big Shift to California Effort," *New York Times,* October 24, 1996, and the Internet edition of that date, http://www.nytimes.com/.

3. Alan Ehrenhalt, "The Voters Sober Up," *New York Times,* October 20, 1996, Sec. 4, 15, op.-ed. page, and the Internet edition of that date, http://www.nytimes.com/.

4. See Richard K. Scher, *Politics in the New South,* 2d ed. (Armonk, N.Y.: M.E. Sharpe, 1997).

5. See Stephen C. Craig, *The Malevolent Leaders* (Boulder: Westview, 1993), and Stephen C. Craig, ed., *Broken Contract?* (Boulder: Westview, 1996).

6. Ibid.

Chapter 6. Media and the Modern Political Campaign

1. It has often been noted that, if a candidate concluding a campaign speech falls off the dais or platform, the media will report the accident more extensively than the content of the presentation.

2. This is a vast topic. Several accessible references that can take the reader further include Shanto Iyengar and Donald R. Kinder, *News That Matters* (Chicago: University of Chicago Press, 1987); Kathleen Hall Jamieson, *The Interplay of Influence* (Belmont, Calif.: Wadsworth, 1992); Kathleen Hall Jamieson, *Dirty Politics* (New York: Oxford University Press, 1992); Judith S. Trent and Robert V. Friedenburg, *Political Campaign Communication,* 3d ed. (Westport, Conn.: Praeger, 1995); Kenneth L. Hacker, ed., *Candidate Images in Presidential Elections* (Westport, Conn.: Praeger, 1995); and Kathleen Hall Jamieson, ed., *The Media and Politics,* special ed., (Thousand Oaks, Calif.: Sage, 1996). Readers should be aware that this is a mere sample of the available literature addressing this crucial point.

3. It is interesting to speculate on how the information about campaigns carried over the Internet will be perceived in the future. In the 1996 election, there was a good deal of material available, ranging from hard news sources (including text from newspapers such as the *New York Times* and *Washington Post* down to regional and local papers) to propagandistic home pages prepared by candidates and political parties from the presidential level down to local races. We know little, at the moment, about how this information was used or understood. We do know that the audience for political information coming over the Internet is still relatively small, in part owing to limited technical availability, but it is highly likely that the audience will be much larger in 1998, and still greater in 2000, when more desktop and portable computers, and possibly television sets, will have access to the Internet.

4. See Richard G. Niemi and Herbert F. Weisberg, *Controversies in Voting Behavior,* 3d ed. (Washington, D.C.: CQ Press, 1993).

5. There are of course too many examples where the press is not free but in fact is either the willing partner or captive of government or a ruling elite; the point here is not to discuss this empirical reality but to focus attention on the alleged existence of giant conspiratorial mechanisms keeping us all submissive and unquestioning.

6. The Internet may represent a hybrid, involving some of each. We shall discuss this nascent media mechanism only briefly, while recognizing its future importance. Perhaps a future edition of this or some other book can give it the treatment it will undoubtedly deserve.

7. Photo ops are common during presidential and some important statewide

campaigns; they rarely are used in local campaigns except in large metropolitan areas, mainly because most television stations and newspapers lack the resources—personnel, time, and money—to cover every political event that occurs.

8. It is a commonplace to point out that in the case of many, perhaps most, newspapers there is a concerted and valid effort made to keep the news pages separate from the editorial or opinion pages. The *Wall Street Journal* may well be the nation's best example of how this separation is consistently observed, but other examples could be cited as well. But it is also well recognized that sometimes the wall is breached, and not only in small newspapers owned or published by powerful and opinionated individuals.

9. In the following paragraphs we are excluding from the discussion small, shoestring newspapers; house organs of interest groups or other organizations that subsidize their own publications; newsletters; and other such examples of the print media. Similarly, we also omit television and radio stations that are part of larger conglomerates and serve as a mouthpiece for those conglomerates: broadcast units owned and operated by a church, for example. The argument presented here is virtually exclusively focused on news organizations operated as business enterprises, whose function is essentially that of a business operation, namely, to supply a product for a price.

10. Many, but not all, talk-show hosts probably should be omitted from this group. The emphasis on this form of radio and television "journalism" is more likely to be weighted toward sensationalism and conflict generation than toward thoughtful presentation of facts and evidence.

11. We have not discussed the complaints of reporters and editors about candidates and campaigns, but they are legion. "Boring," "arrogant," "superficial," "ill informed," "unresponsive," "out of it," are but some of the terms members of the media apply, off the record, to candidates and campaigns they have to cover.

12. Critics of this point will note that "pack journalism" tends to do exactly this—namely, to funnel materials (factual and otherwise) from candidates and campaigns directly into their news stories. The existence of pack journalism is often disputed, but there are instances in which reporters, often faced with severe deadlines and other constraints, rely more heavily than they might wish on those materials in order to file their stories. The point being made here is not whether pack journalism continues to exist, or even if it ever did. Even if it did and does, our point here is that journalists want and expect to do their own fact finding; that they sometimes fail to achieve these goals does not undercut the argument. See, for example, Timothy Crouse, *The Boys on the Bus* (New York: Ballantine, 1973).

13. The classic examples in America, of course, are Ambrose Bierce and H.L. Mencken, but there are more recent ones as well.

14. In the nineteenth century, of course, newspapers were far more overtly partisan, including on the news pages, than they are today. In the modern world of professional journalism, such practices would be unacceptable.

15. Journalists appear more likely to report about the clothes, hair, and makeup of women candidates than of men. I am indebted to Professor Lynn

Leverty, Department of Political Science, University of Florida, for making this observation and showing me documentation to support the point.

16. This discussion should not be viewed in the same way as the old philosophical dispute over whether the tree falling in a forest makes a sound or not. In the present instance, we are not raising metaphysical issues over what constitutes reality. Rather, we are outlining the difficulty journalists face in relaying to the public what they think is real.

17. Again, publications or electronic stations of highly partisan or narrowly conceived issue groups may exhibit these tendencies; our concern here is with the general media aimed at a mass public.

18. The sources included in note 2, above, will help readers wishing to locate more information on this point.

19. "Drive times" includes the morning and evening rush hours, when people tend to be in their cars and more or less paying attention to the radio. At other times, they may have the radio on, but generally pay little attention. It is little more than background noise, as far as political advertising is concerned, during other parts of the day.

20. Research has repeatedly shown that it is not the amount of money spent in a campaign that strongly affects the outcome, but the financial gap between candidates. We shall return to this point in the next chapter.

21. Readers are referred to some excellent collections and compendia of campaign advertisements readily available; one of the best is "Classics of Campaign Advertising," produced by the editors at *Campaigns and Elections* magazine, June 1986.

22. We ignore the possibility and more-than-occasional reality that the message the candidate wants, and the campaign produces, is wrongheaded, silly, or dysfunctional.

23. In the 1996 race for sheriff of Alachua County in Florida, a challenger to the popular incumbent alleged in several thirty-second spots late in the campaign that the incumbent had been arrested three times, including once while serving in office. The facts were that when the sheriff was nineteen, he had received a traffic citation in St. Petersburg and another for hunting out of season. In his second year in office, he (along with other prominent public officials and private citizens) was cited for hunting on an allegedly baited field. None of the incidents constituted an arrest either by legal definitions or any stretch of the imagination. The challenger was forced to withdraw the TV spot because it generated such negative reaction. The day before the election, the challenger placed a large ad in the local paper claiming that it had endorsed him; in fact, the paper enthusiastically endorsed the incumbent for the general election, but indeed had endorsed the challenger in the Democratic primary. Nothing in the challenger's ad indicated that the earlier endorsement was limited to the primary. The publisher and editorial-page editor of the paper were so incensed about the challenger's ad that on election day they wrote an editorial reaffirming their support of the incumbent and rejecting the challenger's message and ethics. The incumbent, a Republican, won with 57 percent of the vote, getting the second highest vote total of all candidates in an overwhelmingly Democratic county. Clearly the voters made a distinction

in viewing thirty-second spots and fast-back ads between negative ads resonate and are credible and those that simply offer lies and nonsense.

Chapter 7. Money and the Modern Political Campaign

1. For a thoughtful, if conventional, attack on the role money plays in campaigns, see Michael Duffy and Nancy Gibbs, "The Money Mess," *Time,* November 11, 1996, pp. 32–36.
2. It is worth noting the biblical injunction, "The love of money is the root of all evil." I Timothy 6:10.
3. See, for example, Herbert Alexander, *Financing Politics,* 4th ed. (Washington, D.C.: CQ Press, 1992). Alexander also has an extensive list of other publications dealing with the financing of political campaigns. See also the wealth of data supplied by the Federal Elections Commission; much of it is available on the Internet at http://www.fec.gov/.
4. Duffy and Gibbs, "The Money Mess," p. 33. FEC data, "Financing the 1996 Presidential Campaign." The Internet address for the FEC is http://www.fec.gov/; the specific document cited here can be found at http://www.fec.gov/pres96/presgen1.htm .
5. Readers are reminded that in 1988 there was no incumbent running for president, so both parties had spirited primaries. FEC data, "Financing the 1996 Presidential Campaign."
6. Ibid.
7. Ibid.
8. Both parties' conventions received federal grants of slightly more than $12 million. In addition, local host committees raised considerable funds to defray costs to the city holding the convention. The 1996 conventions also saw substantial corporate donations, as businesses vied to have their products displayed, sold, or available at convention sites. FEC data, "Financing the 1996 Presidential Campaign."
9. Ibid.
10. Ibid.
11. Readers might recall that in 1988, the infamous Willie Horton ad, considered by some observers to be the most negative and hard-hitting in that year's presidential campaign, was not paid for by either the Bush campaign committee or the Republican Party. Theoretically soft money cannot be used on behalf of individual candidates, but as a practical matter it often is. See Duffy and Gibbs, "The Money Mess," p. 33.
12. Duffy and Gibbs, "The Money Mess," p. 33.
13. FEC, "Congressional Spending for '96 Elections Reaches $469 Million." This Internet document, dated November 1, 1996, can be found at http://www.fec.gov/press/can12.htm. All of the data in the following paragraphs come from this document.
14. In 1994, the Republican nominee for senator in California, Michael Huffington, was thought to have spent about $28 million of his own funds on his losing campaign. All told, that Senate campaign cost more than $40 million. B. Drummond Ayres, "Ad Nauseous: Campaigns Takeover California TV," *New*

York Times, October 14, 1994, p. 1; Todd S. Purdum, "G.O.P. Senate Contender Asserts D'Amoto Is Undercutting Her Bid," *New York Times,* October 18, 1996, p. 1; B. Drummond Ayres, "Californians Pass Measure on Aliens: Courts Bar It," *New York Times,* November 10, 1994, Section B, p. 7.

15. FEC, "1995–96 PAC Contributions Increase $17 Million over 1993–94." This is an Internet document which is dated September 27, 1996, and can be found at http://www.fec.gov/press/pac18tx.htm .

16. The committee formed to promote gambling was called Proposal for Limited Casinos. It raised and spent in excess of $16.5 million. David Rancourt, director of the Florida State Division of Elections, Department of State, Tallahassee, e-mail communication to the author, December 16, 1996.

17. These are estimates based on FEC data from primaries, general-election federal grants, money raised for legal and accounting services, and reported funds spent by the parties on the presidential campaign. The figures do not include money spent by other organizations on behalf of the candidates or soft-money figures. Thus, the $423 million is a conservatively estimated baseline figure only.

18. Data are from 1992. The sources are *Supermarket News,* April 12, 1993, pp. 24, 32; May 10, 1993, p. 134; June 28, 1993, p. 17; *Advertising Age* Special Issue, "Advertising Fact Book," January 4, 1993.

19. The data cited indicate that we spent very close to $2 billion on yogurt products alone in 1992; throwing in toaster pastries ($440 million) exceeds our spending on campaigns by a wide margin.

20. Put differently, the per capita cost of elections is relatively low. Assuming that approximately $425 million was spent on the presidential campaign (start to finish, including primaries), the cost per voter was about $4.65 (based on a total of 91,372,385 votes cast in the election for the three major candidates; omitted are the totals for minor-party candidates). The figures for presidential campaign spending and presidential voting are used because if we were to use the total expenditure for all campaigns in 1996 (about $2 billion), it would seriously distort the figures upward, since any given voter is likely to have voted in multiple elections. It is also not possible to determine how many "repeat" votes were cast, which if eliminated would also push the cost per vote up. Thus a cleaner figure can be obtained by focusing solely on presidential expenditures and number of voters.

21. There were of course exceptions in 1994, when the political mood of the country shifted rapidly away from the Democrats and toward Republicans beginning in midsummer. GOP challengers for U.S. House and even Senate seats found fund-raising somewhat easier than they would usually have expected.

22. The author attended the 1992 Republican presidential convention in Houston. What was of interest there was less the renomination of the Bush-Quayle ticket than the vigorous efforts by potential nominees for 1996 to test the waters, meet with state delegations, schedule meetings with established party fund-raisers, and the like. It was not unusual to find these individuals and their entourages literally running through the convention site, and various hotel lobbies housing delegations, as they scurried from one campaign activity to the next—all with an eye toward four years down the road.

23. In the medium-sized city of Gainesville, Florida, a campaign for city commission in the late 1970s and early 1980s cost a few thousand dollars at most.

Then one candidate began using television; immediately, everyone did, and the cost of running increased to well over $10,000, and in some cases more than double that, largely because of TV.

24. The author has had occasion to consult with candidates in the Dominican Republic. On any number of occasions he was trotted out in front of a rally, or brought to important meetings and forums, as an example of the seriousness and quality of the campaign. The fact that he was a university professor added additional luster to this public relations gambit.

25. Readers are reminded that the names of people making donations to campaigns must be reported and are public information. Some potential donors become skittish at this, especially if names of donors are published in the local newspaper.

26. On ambassadorships for sale, see Duffy and Gibbs, "The Money Mess," pp. 33–34.

27. On December 13, 1996, the *Gainesville Sun* under a large-type headline, "Fund-raiser's Firm Gets Big Grant," ran a story about a Commerce Department grant going to a campaign donor's company in spite of warnings from government auditors against it.

28. But even this statement has become subject to qualification. Duffy and Gibbs, "The Money Mess," p. 33. The November 11, 1996, article quotes a prominent Washington lobbyist complaining that even large donations don't have the impact they used to: "We've given $100,000 a year to the Democratic Party for a long time. We used to be a big player. But now we don't exist" (p. 33). Assuming this is true—and similar complaints have been heard in state capitals— a bidding war may be developing over how much money it costs to become "a player."

29. Money is not always needed to become a player: expertise, prestige, notoriety, fame, friendship, organizational affiliation, belonging to the "old boy" (and increasingly, "old girl") network can accomplish the same purpose. In December 1996 the Florida Senate was rocked by the disclosure that a senator chairing a major committee dealing with telephone and other utility regulation was having an affair with a lobbyist from a telephone company. Such activity, even though it is generally widely condemned, does occur, and of course serves to undermine public confidence in governmental institutions.

30. The scope of the discussion in the preceding paragraphs has expanded well beyond political campaigns. In fact, the matter of money in campaigns goes beyond this important issue to an increasingly intractable problem in American political life, namely the way money determines who are the real players, who merely the spear carriers, who's at the table and who is not, and what topics are on the table as governmental decisions are made.

31. See for example, Joanne Marie Green, "Dynamics of Open Seat Elections for the United States House of Representatives," Ph.D. dissertation, Department of Political Science, University of Florida, 1994. Green cites a large literature supporting this point.

32. FEC data, "1995–1996 Financial Activity of Senate and House General Election Campaigns," Internet address http://www.fec.gov/finance/cansum12.htm

33. *Gainesville Sun,* Sunday, December 8, 1996, Section B, p. 1.

34. There is a famous story, perhaps apocryphal, about the late representative Claude Pepper of Miami. In one of his last campaigns, Pepper seemed distracted and uninterested, causing some concern among his consultants and supporters since the Republicans had put up a viable candidate. They could not get him to attend to campaign business, even though money was pouring in. Finally, in mid-September, Pepper called a meeting of his campaign advisers, told them all to collect their fees, have some bumper stickers and signs printed and distributed, and send back the rest of the money. He won in a landslide, as usual.

35. Florida has recently begun to provide PAC financial reports on-line; the address is http://election.dos.state.fl.us/comm/comindex.shtml.

36. Sometimes candidates at the state and local levels try to make political capital out of their decision, usually publicly trumpeted, not to accept PAC money. It is not unusual to find, however, that at least some of these candidates accept corporate or union money, sometimes both. When this occurs, it is difficult to grasp the justification or rationale for not accepting PAC money.

37. It is true that PACs must publicly account for their campaign contributions. This is the only mechanism that even partially holds them in check. But it is also true that this mechanism exists primarily after the fact; while reports are due throughout the campaign season, a PAC that does much of its work toward the end of a campaign may not be noticed until the election is over and its influence already felt.

38. Duffy and Gibbs, "The Money Mess," p. 33.

39. In 1992, the same organization prepared some ads aimed at the presidential campaign, which were regarded by those who saw them as equally inflammatory as the Horton one. The Bush campaign, however, repudiated the offer and disassociated itself from this effort. In 1988, however, the Bush campaign never repudiated the Horton ad.

40. This was the theme of one of Kevin Phillips's election postmortems heard occasionally on National Public Radio's news program *Morning Edition*. Phillips made these remarks on Monday, December 9, 1996.

41. In Florida, legislators cannot legally raise money while the legislature is in session. All this does, of course, is force fund-raising efforts to periods prior to or following the sixty-day sessions. The amounts of money incumbent legislators have been able to raise seems not to have been adversely affected by this rule.

42. Legislatures in particular might be helped, as parties with real strength and authority behind them would actually have to face honestly and seriously questions of governance. Much gridlock in government simply results from too many private interests clashing so that questions of public governance get lost. Private interests could still be articulated in legislative chambers, but the looming presence of powerful parties would not allow them to dominate as they have in recent decades.

43. Forbes ran as a Republican; apparently he never gave any serious consideration to running as an independent, although there were observers who thought he might have done better following this route in order to get away from the crowded Republican primary field. One of the reasons Forbes was thought to have run was that he could not find a legal way to fund a presidential bid by Jack Kemp.

Chapter 8. Political Campaigns and American Society

1. This does not mean that candidates of dignity or substance cannot conduct effective or winning campaigns. In a recent campaign in Alachua County (Gainesville), Florida, a very popular public official, knowledgeable and charming in public but shy and self-effacing in private, rode in a parade accompanied by supporters dressed in dog costumes dancing and prancing about in a silly way. When asked about it later, the candidate said he felt totally embarrassed, even foolish, but he also knew that people would pay more attention to his candidacy if he rode in the parade in this manner than if he just tried to make a speech about his next four-year agenda.

2. This appeared to be the major strategy of President Bill Clinton in his reelection campaign against Bob Dole. The latter engaged in a good deal of character assassination and mudslinging, the former virtually none, at least until the campaign's very end.

3. Voter turnout in the 1996 presidential election was reportedly the lowest since the 1920s. In 1992 it had risen somewhat over previous years, but 1996 apparently constituted a return to the downward trend in voter turnout. Evidently the campaign failed to generate much excitement in the electorate; either that or, more likely, the voters were not in a restive or disquieted mood.

4. The metaphors are not as far-fetched as they might seem. It is a commonplace to talk about "bandwagons" and "landslides" for campaigns. These are comparatively rare. For most candidates and campaigns, the struggle is all uphill, very hard and expensive; there are also far more losers than winners, making the psychological battle inside the candidate's head at least as hard as the physical campaign itself.

5. If adopted, the proposal floated in the previous chapter on campaign finance will overcome some, but not all, of the abuses that exist.

6. The author has personally attended numerous campaign opening announcements, from fish fries to catered white wine and hors d'oeuvre events, from giant rallies to quiet statements on the city hall steps.

7. See Stephen Hess, *The Presidential Campaign,* 3d ed. (Washington, D.C.: Brookings, 1988).

8. The term even enters book titles. See Jules Witcover, *Marathon* (New York: New American Library, 1978).

9. Both FDR and Dwight Eisenhower were thought to have been involved with women other than their wives during their White House years, but neither's reputation has suffered much because of this behavior. Kennedy's liaisons have become the stuff of legend. Nixon, whose moral fiber was always in question, was discovered to be worse than originally thought; he also had a foul mouth of monstrous proportions. The arrogance of Johnson was well known during his administration. Kennedy's, Johnson's, and Nixon's reputations have suffered as the public became more and more aware of these private flaws that become manifest during their service in the White House.

10. See the essays in *American Politics Quarterly,* a special issue, vol. 24 (October 1996), for an elaboration of this point.

Index

Presidential elections *(continued)*
of 1980, 101, 106
of 1984, 90–91
of 1988, 11, 14, 58–59, 91, 161, 162
of 1992, 76, 108, 194n.22
of 1996, 12, 76, 84, 179
advertising in, 134–135
campaign spending in, 142–143
character issue in, 92, 94, 96, 134, 197n.2
issues in, 91–92, 94, 95, 96, 97, 98, 106, 107, 109
media coverage of, 112, 130
voter turnout in, 197n.3
Procter and Gamble, 149
Public Broadcasting System (PBS), 117, 119, 137
Public Ledger, 39, 66
Public opinion
of campaigns, 3–6, 66
of candidates, 72–73, 75–78, 135
issues and, 94–98, 102–103
leading, 103–108
media influence on, 112–115
polling, 107–108, 153–154
See also Voting behavior

R

Radio. *See* Media
Reagan, Ronald, 59, 76
issues and, 90, 93, 95, 100, 101, 105, 106
media coverage of, 131
Reed, John Shelton, 87, 189n.17
Republicans, *vs* Federalists, 29–32
Riordan, Richard, 81–82
Robb, Charles, 185n.8
Robertson, Pat, 91

Roosevelt, Franklin Delano, 52, 75, 104, 197n.9
Roosevelt, Teddy, 41
Ros-Lehtinen, Ileana, 12

S

Schattschneider, E.E., 57
Sectionalism, voting behavior and, 8
Single-issue voters, 11
Sloganeering
in nineteenth-century campaigns, 37, 42, 51–52
political identity and, 99
Soft money, 161–162, 166
Stassen, Harold, 65
State and local campaign finance, 144–145, 158, 173–174
Stevenson, Adlai, 22

T

Taft, Robert, 75
Tammany Hall, 41
"Tariff of Abominations" of 1828, 33
Taylor, Morry, 142
Television. *See* Media
Third parties, 168, 174
Thirty-second spots, 135–137, 192–193n.23
"Tippecanoe, and Tyler too," 37, 51, 57
Truman, Harry S., 52, 74, 75
Tyler, John, 36, 39

U

United States of Ambition, The (Ehrenhalt), 78

About the Author

Richard K. Scher (Ph.D., Columbia, 1972) is professor of political science at the University of Florida, Gainesville, where he won the Teacher of the Year Award in 1992–93. He is coauthor of *Florida's Gubernatorial Politics in the Twentieth Century* and principal author of *Voting Rights and Democracy: The Law and Politics of Districting.* His book *Politics in the New South: Republicanism, Race, and Leadership in the Twentieth Century,* was published in a second edition by M. E. Sharpe in 1997. Dr. Scher is an active political consultant and a frequent commentator on political affairs.